REAL WORLD

micro

SEVENTH EDITION

edited by

Randy Albelda, Marc Breslow,

Ellen Frank, Abby Scher, and

the Dollars & Sense Collective

REAL WORLD MICRO, SEVENTH EDITION

ISBN: 1-878585-37-1

Published by:
Dollars and Sense
Economic Affairs Bureau, Inc.
One Summer Street
Somerville, MA 02143
617-628-8411

Real World Micro is edited by the *Dollars & Sense* Collective — publishers of *Dollars & Sense* magazine and *Real World Macro, Real World International, Current Economic Issues,* and *Real World Banking.*

The 1997 Collective: Randy Albelda, Skip Barry, Phineas Baxandall, Marc Breslow, Brian Burgoon, Randal Divinski, Laurie Dougherty, Ellen Frank, Amy Gluckman, Erkut Gomulu, Brenda Lautsch, David Levy, John Miller, Laura Orlando, Abby Scher, Bryan Snyder, Chris Tilly, Ramón Vela.

Cover Art and Design: Nick Thorkelson
Cover Photo: Jim West, Impact Visuals
Production: Jonathan Case, Randal Divinski

Printed by:
Saltus Press
24 Jolma Road
Worcester, MA 01604

TABLE OF CONTENTS

(Continued on next page)

CHAPTER 6: LABOR MARKETS

CHAPTER 7: DISCRIMINATION, POVERTY & WELFARE

CHAPTER 8: THE ENVIRONMENT

CHAPTER 9: THE GLOBAL ECONOMY

INTRODUCTION

Conventional microeconomic theory assumes that the market system, with minimal regulation, provides the best of all possible worlds. Consumers acquire exactly what they want (within their budgets) and firms produce the most socially desirable goods while making a profit. The articles in this book challenge such assumptions, demonstrating that markets are not producing ideal results for the majority of people in the world today.

The seventh edition of *Real World Micro* contains 43 articles that have appeared in *Dollars & Sense*, a bi-monthly economic affairs magazine. Together, they present an alternative vision of how markets work — a vision based on real markets and real people.

Chapter 1 explores privatization and deregulation, two major economic trends throughout the world today. Edward Herman gives an overview of the practice and consequences of privatizing government enterprises and services. We examine the current push to deregulate the electric utility industry, and the ongoing changes in how health care insurance is provided. Finally, we look at how democracy has become a market, for sale to the highest bidder.

The second chapter, "The Problem With Markets," looks at the imperfect functioning of markets as they respond to supply and demand. Traditional theory disposes of hard questions in this area by assuming that markets naturally maximize social welfare. The articles in this chapter analyze why this is frequently inaccurate, through case studies of child care, rental housing, "fringe" banks, and tobacco taxes.

Much of the conventional microeconomics curriculum is devoted to consumers, who account for the bulk of spending in the economy. Consumers are typically assumed to have complete and perfect information about both their own economic resources and the products they buy. In contrast, Chapter 3 demonstrates how consumers' choices are constrained by their resources or manipulated by external forces, most notably advertising.

Microeconomics treats firms as profit-maximizing enterprises. This is one assumption the editors of *Dollars & Sense* don't challenge. However, unlike most texts, the articles in chapters 4 and 5 of *Real World Micro* argue that profit maximization can be dangerous to an employee's health — and to the overall health of the economy. In Chapter 4, we examine firms and competition, showing how different management structures, from traditional top-down management to worker participation programs to co-ops, yield contrasting results for workers. In Chapter 5, the articles show how different market structures — monopoly, oligopoly, and competition — affect consumers and workers in such industries as supermarkets, trucking, and the media.

Chapter 6 covers labor markets, which differ sharply from markets for pizzas, haircuts, or airplanes. Unlike other factors of production, labor is a human input. These articles explore the human dimensions of labor markets, examining the low-wage labor market, unions, downsizing, temporary workers, "workfare," the minimum wage, and the debate over the labor market consequences of immigration.

Chapters 7 and 8 confront pressing issues facing society today: discrimination, poverty, and inequality; and the health of the environment. Chapter 7 uncovers the extent and origins of poverty and inequality in the United States, and documents the inadequacy of government responses. The articles also address racism and sex discrimination in the labor and mortgage markets.

Chapter 8 examines current controversies in worldwide efforts to reduce pollution and preserve natural resources. "Does Preserving the Earth Threaten Jobs?" debunks claims that environmental protection will cause large-scale job losses. The other articles look at mangrove forest destruction due to shrimp farming in Thailand, recycling, and "environmental justice" for low-income communities.

The final chapter examines the global economy, with the first article providing a basic critique of free trade and investment. Three concluding articles address the effects of the North American Free Trade Agreement both outside and inside U.S. borders.

As you'll see, *Real World Micro* is a lively and provocative supplement to your standard microeconomics textbook. We hope you enjoy it.

— The Editors of *Dollars & Sense* magazine

CHAPTER 1

Markets Everywhere: Privatization and Deregulation

March/April 1997

PRIVATIZATION

DOWNSIZING GOVERNMENT FOR PRINCIPLE AND PROFIT

BY EDWARD S. HERMAN

The U.S. government is encouraging private HMOs to service much of the Medicare system, and the debate rages over whether Social Security should be shifted to private management. Privatization of such public functions is one of the mantras of the New World Order. Economic, political and media elites assume that privatization provides undeniable benefits and moves us toward a good society.

But while it sometimes reduces costs, privatization is often less efficient than public enterprise, and frequently is socially harmful, taking a disproportionate toll on women and minorities. Privatization also weakens democracy by bypassing unions and shifting power away from governments and nonprofit organizations, which can respond to democratic political processes. Instead, power moves to corporations that serve only the interests of their owners and financiers.

Privatization means the shift of activities from the government and nonprofit sectors to the market. It may take the form of the sale of public (or nonprofit) sector assets to private companies or the contracting out of services previously supplied by public employees.

Privatization is not new. In France before the Revolution of 1789, the King farmed out government tax collecting to individuals in a system notorious for corruption. Along with contracting out the provision of supplies for the French armed forces, private tax collecting was the basis of many great fortunes. Ending this system was one of the French Revolution's accomplishments.

Throughout the nineteenth century, the U.S. government engaged in massive privatization through the sale of millions of acres of public land (a domain greatly extended by the Louisiana and Alaska purchases and the seizure of Mexican territory). Many tycoons derived their fortunes from shrewd and sometimes fraudulent public land acquisitions. Abuses in the use and disposal of public property have continued throughout the twentieth century, manifested in both periodic scandals (such as Teapot Dome) and the subsidized use of public property, which continues today through, for example, underpriced sales of national forest timber, bargain-rate use of mineral lands, and commercial broadcasters' free use of valuable air rights.

Western European and Third World governments have commonly owned airlines, railroads, telecommunications and electric power systems, and sometimes banks, petroleum refining and other industrial enterprises. But in the United States government has been largely excluded from activities of interest to private business, and its periodic entry into these fields has been limited and often stripped away. The government did take over many private sector activities during both World Wars I and II, but it speedily privatized them after the wars.

Since 1932, Congress, under the prodding of business, has made periodic surveys of government activities that compete with the private sector, with a view toward minimizing government competition. Ronald Reagan's Office of Management and Budget formalized the pressure on government agencies to minimize in-house production, ordering government managers to consider contracting out all functions, including data processing, janitorial services and vehicle maintenance.

Despite this long-standing bias against public enterprise in the United States, with the rise of monopoly power in railroads, electric power, and telephones during the late 19th and early 20th centuries the government created a regulatory apparatus. It grew with urbanization and the

6   Real World Micro, Seventh Edition

need for water supply and waste disposal, and the coming of the automobile and road building. The public sector grew further with the social democratization that accompanied the Great Depression and World War II, including the growth of organized labor and a new governmental health and welfare apparatus.

Privatizers from the early 1970s onward have been selling off government property — mainly water and waste water facilities, parking garages, roads, airports, public lands and buildings, and mortgage portfolios. But privatization in the United States has focused mainly on the contracting out of government services, including the operation of government-owned facilities.

State and local governments carry out most public economic activity, and contracting out at these levels has soared over the past decade. The Mercer Group, an Atlanta consulting firm, estimates that between 1987 and 1995 the number of municipalities contracting-out services increased as follows: janitorial from 52% to 70%, street maintenance 19% to 38%, solid waste collection 30% to 50%, and data processing operations 16% to 31%.

This new wave of contracting-out ignores historical lessons. A great deal of current government provision of services originated in the failures of contracting during the late nineteenth century and into the 1920s, under political systems that were often corrupt. Ending such arrangements and turning them over to public agencies was a major accomplishment of the 1920s and later.

ROOTS OF THE NEW PRIVATIZATION WAVE

The privatization wave over the past twenty years is rooted in increased corporate power. This growth, based partly on greater capital mobility, has led to renewed aggressiveness by business, political successes (including the elections of Ronald Reagan, British Prime Minister Margaret Thatcher, and neoliberals widely), and a parallel weakening of labor.

Enhanced corporate power has also contributed to the triumph of neoliberal ideology. Central beliefs of this ideology include the efficiency of the private market, the inefficiency of government, and the dual menaces of inflation and budget deficits. With neoliberalism in place, helped by corporate domination of think-tank funding and the mass media, along with great influence within the ivory tower, scaling back government was an obvious policy thrust.

Part of the design of neoliberal politicians and intellectuals has been to weaken the state as a power center that might serve ordinary citizens and challenge the rule of the market. The success of these efforts is evident in both Britain and the United States, where formerly liberal parties now denounce big government, genuflect to market-based solutions, and contribute to eroding the welfare state.

Governments' budgetary problems gave further impetus to privatization. As the *Wall Street Journal* pointed out in 1995, referring to talk of selling the federal oil reserves, "Both Congress and the White House want to change budget-accounting rules so they can count money raised by selling assets toward reducing the deficit — even if such sales would reduce government income... in future years." At the state and local level, "cash-strapped cities, such as Wilmington, Delaware, want the upfront cash they can get by selling the local sewage-treatment plant, or look to private ownership as a way to finance improvements of existing facilities."

The new global economic order itself has contributed greatly to these financial difficulties. Capital has fled from urban cores, leaving them in fiscal straits, and corporations have bargained aggressively with governments to extract concessions as conditions for their keeping jobs in place (or to induce them to move). All governments have had to limit business taxes and spending on social benefits in order to provide a "favorable investment climate," leaving them under financial stress. Intel Corporation, for example, bargained so effectively in 1995 with Rio Ranchos, a small New Mexico town eager to be the site of an Intel plant, that the town was forced to sharply cut its school budget.

Another force for privatization has been the growing power of financial markets, which reward and penalize governments as they meet or fall short of market policy standards. Financial market players want low inflation and balanced budgets. They are keen on privatization because it yields short term revenues and is a mark of commitment to neoliberalism.

Privatization has also been pressed by innumerable entrepreneurs eager to buy up government property and provide services previously supplied internally. Partly in anticipation of privatization opportunities, many of them had obtained political leverage by funding the electoral campaigns of politicians now in office.

EFFICIENCY GAINS OR WAGE REDUCTIONS?

Although the privatizers claim that their objective is to increase efficiency, this is contradicted by their indiscriminate actions and their frequent disposal of public enterprises noted for efficiency. There is also evidence that they are often responding to financial and political pressure. Furthermore, many bids for government property and contract service base their savings largely on shifting from union to non-union and contingent labor.

Take, for example, contracting of the cleaning service for state buildings in Buffalo, New York in 1992. While initially claiming that the low contractor offer was based on efficiency improvements, state officials eventually admitted to the *Buffalo News* that the savings would come from the use of "more part-time workers at lower salaries and with fewer benefits." Study after study has shown that contractors offer lower wages and limited if any health and pension benefits. But gains from lower wages and benefits are not true "efficiency" improvements, which imply a reduction in the use of resources such as labor and materials. They are actually income transfers from wage earners to employers (profits) and to government managers and taxpayers.

Even the nominal savings in privatization may be illusory or short-lived. A common phenomenon in contracting out was made famous in the weapons contracting formula "buy in, get well later." The contractor bids low, knowing that he can obtain cost adjustments after the government gets locked in to the contract and would find it difficult to cancel and locate another source, or do the job in-house.

The most famous case was Lockheed's bid to produce the C-5A giant transport plane in the 1960s, which led to a huge cost overrun that doubled the price before a single plane was produced. Lockheed's contract had an automatic cost-based price escalation clause that was soon dubbed the "golden handshake."

Even fixed-price contracts could be raised through "improvements" offered by the contractor or demanded by the Pentagon — a process known as "gold-plating." One result of this abusive contracting system was that for decades the major contractors had profit rates on their Pentagon business roughly twice those in their commercial operations.

WHO WATCHES THE CONTRACTORS?

There is a contradiction in conservative enthusiasm for contracting, glossed over by their assumption of vigorous contractor competition. Conservatives consider governments corruptible and incapable of efficient operation. But contracting-out demands exceptional knowledge and honesty on the part of politicians and government bureaucrats: they must negotiate contracts that defend the public interest, and they must monitor them carefully. If they are incompetent and/or crooked, contracting-out can be disastrous in terms of cost and performance.

Contracting-out causes competition to assume the form of skillful use of political influence, public relations, and even bribery. In addition, profits can be enhanced by carving loopholes in contracts, keeping monitoring weak and capturing regulators. It is true that with in-house government production political influence can also be damaging, but the lines of responsibility are clear. With contracting-out these lines are more obscure. This can yield the worst of both worlds (government and private enterprise), with limited efficiency incentives, high levels of politicization, and unclear responsibilities.

Many years ago the U.S. government did weapons research and produced many of its weapons in government arsenals. This was gradually phased out in favor of farming out research and production to private sellers. But without in-house production and research capabilities the government's bargaining position was reduced. It no longer had the option of producing for itself, and lacked the expertise to be a knowledgeable buyer, and so could be taken advantage of more easily. This point applies to other public functions — without a skilled body of managers and technicians the government is a ready victim in contract negotiations with knowledgeable private parties.

Contracting out is at an initial cost disadvantage compared to in-house production. It requires the additional expense of writing and evaluating contracts and then monitoring performance over their lives — the latter entailing a permanent bureaucratic apparatus on top of that deployed by the contractor. If that apparatus is skimped on, politicized, or corrupt, the road is open to massive cost escalation. Contracting out is often not able to overcome the disabilities of monitoring costs and potential corruption.

There is some truth to charges of inefficiency in public enterprises and nonprofit service activities. Many of these have become over-bureaucratized, over-staffed and politicized. Free market proponents speak of "state failure" to counter claims of "market failure" by the private sector. But many state and nonprofit enterprises and services have done well, and when they have done poorly it is often the result of conservative macroeconomic policy and crippling state intervention. When macro-policy is designed to keep a large reserve army of unemployed labor, labor strenuously resists staff cuts and public agencies find it harder to trim staff.

Underfunding, political appointments, and capture of regulatory agencies by corporate interests frequently undermine the functioning of government entities. Such damaging interventions are often deliberate, as in the case of the Reagan-era budget cuts and political appointments to the Environmental Protection Agency and the Corporation for Public Broadcasting, both designed to demoralize and weaken the organizations. In these cases and others the damage inflicted reflects corporate efforts to undermine public bodies through the political process.

PRIVATIZATION AND COMPETITION

Conservatives assume that government sells or contracts out its operations under competitive conditions, and that such competition then and later will restrain exploitation of the contracting authority and the public. This is sometimes correct, but often is not. There are frequently only a few local bidders for contracts, and they sometimes collude, divide markets and rig prices. One contractor testifying in a national antitrust action noted that "as far back as I can remember" Northern Virginia contractors met annually to carve up contracts that the Virginia highway department was expected to allocate during the year. Numerous suits have been brought and won against Waste Management Inc., Browning Ferris and SCA Services for collusion and price fixing in the trash disposal industries.

In major contracting-out businesses there has been steady growth of national operators, like Waste Management and Browning Ferris in waste disposal and ARA in food services. These large operators are able to undercut local firms, some or all of whom disappear, making it possible for the large firms to "get well" later. More generally, once contracts are won, systems installed, relationships cultivated, and rivals driven from the market, the power of the contractor is strengthened and it becomes costly for a public agency to shift the service elsewhere.

In contrast, changing from private to public ownership can *increase* competition. When the Tennessee Valley Authority (TVA) was organized in the 1930s, for example, it broke up the cartel-like high pricing policy of the private electric utilities in the Tennessee Valley, and private companies hated the TVA because it increased competition. As many U.S. and global markets have few sellers (oligopolies), and as private oligopolists often collude, publicly owned firms can disturb cosy private market arrangements.

CORRUPTION

Corruption is built in to the privatization process. Bidding on contracts is not carried out in perfect markets, and in real world markets, with only a few sellers, they almost always seek political influence as a rational business strategy. In a process dubbed the "revolving door," it is now standard procedure for companies seeking contracts to hire former politicians and managers of public agencies to lobby on their behalf.

The *New York Times* noted recently that one reason federal Justice Department and prison officials have warmed up to privatizing prisons, despite their experience that privately run prisons costs more, is that private industry's ranks "now include many former colleagues as senior and other law enforcement officials have taken positions at private corrections companies, Washington's latest revolving door profession."

Corruption operates at many levels: contributing to political election campaigns, cultivating politicians and other public officials, hiring them or their friends, relatives and staff, and straightforward bribery.

LESS SERVICE FOR YOUR MONEY

Another secret to the profitability of privatization is reductions in service. Contractors reap their "efficiency" savings by hiring cheaper and less well-trained labor, with higher turnover rates, and by cutting the quantity, quality and scope of service. There may be fewer service personnel or fewer trash collections or lavatory cleanings. Older, more polluting school buses

may be used, and bus and train stops at out-of-the-way places may be terminated. Or charges may be imposed on services formerly provided free, thereby pricing poor customers out of the market.

Contracting out of hospital management and purchases of nonprofit hospitals by large HMO systems are classic cases of service reductions. These contractors and HMOs have strong incentives to exclude unhealthy customers and scale down usage for the remainder. To this end they systematically impose barriers to usage, through toughened standards for referrals to specialists, perverse incentives to doctors on their payrolls, and cuts in staff quantity and quality. To some extent these changes offset occasional lavish usage under cost-plus systems, but contracted and HMO systems have established a direct conflict between the interests of patients and medical servers. They also entail large bureaucratic expenses for evaluation, review and collection, plus incentives to exclude the poor.

The largest hospital system, Columbia/HCA Healthcare, is currently the owner of 350 hospitals in 38 states, and continues to gobble up public hospitals left and right. Its CEO, Richard Scott, says that "Healthcare is a business like anything else," and "Is any fast-food restaurant obligated to feed everyone who shows up?" His company has a 20% gross profit target, and he has been meeting that goal, partly by lower costs for large scale purchase of medical equipment and supplies, but more importantly by union avoidance, "reengineering" nursing personnel (increasing their workloads, substituting non-nurses), and "cream skimming" (taking billable patients, dumping non-billables on other hospitals).

The Department of Health Security in Indiana recently fined Columbia/HCA for understaffing, and doctors and nurses at the Good Samaritan hospitals in San Jose, California, have complained bitterly at the medical damage wrought by the "economies" installed following Columbia/HCA's takeover in 1996. Lee County, Florida officials calculated that in 1994 the public hospital there provided $13 million in "charity/uncompensated care," whereas Columbia/HCA's three hospitals in the county provided $1 million in such unprofitable service.

THE BENEFITS OF BEING PUBLIC

Public corporations, nonprofits, and in-house government activities can bring benefits to communities that are neglected by market-oriented businesses. They are more open to unions and provide more secure jobs than private companies. The security and benefits of such jobs are of great value to workers, but the market gives them no weight. The stability of government spending and jobs also helps mitigate recessions, since governments need not cut their spending when consumer demand and private investment fall.

In transportation there are enormous social costs associated with the growth of auto travel — pollution, congestion, and urban sprawl. Public transportation in the form of trains and buses is a vital means of reducing those huge costs. But in a privatizing world, trains and buses are not given credit for limiting auto travel, and so are not seen as deserving of public subsidies. Instead, once privatized, transit riders are expected to pay the full cost of transit in their fares. Inevitably, this leads to lower ridership, driving up the social costs from auto use.

Another illustration of the damage from privatization is the preference given private over public broadcasting. Public stations can focus on "public service" programming, including information that helps to promote democratic citizenship. In contrast, private broadcasting marginalizes public affairs in favor of entertainment, under bottom line pressures and in response to advertiser preferences. Private broadcasters also resort heavily to audience-drawing sex and violence, which have anti-social consequences.

ACCOUNTABILITY

Privatization reduces accountability. Governments can be voted out, but private owners are insulated from the opinions of ordinary citizens and contractors are protected by legal agreements. In fact, governments frequently try to fob off difficult problems onto contractors, but this often makes for confusion, because, while allocating tasks to third parties, the government often cannot escape its own responsibilities.

This is most obvious when the government assigns to private parties jobs that require the application of sovereign powers of government. In the case of prisons, now rapidly being privatized, where the prisoners are held by force and are subject to possible parole or penalties for misbehavior, to what extent can private contractors dispense such sovereign actions? Don't they have a conflict of interest in dealing with parole and extended sentences when their economic interest calls for higher prison occupancy? Isn't there a danger that the drive for profits will lead to hiring unqualified and inadequately trained personnel and the mistreatment of prisoners?

As Princeton political scientist John DiIlio wrote in 1987, "The history of private sector involvement in corrections is unrelievedly bleak, a well-documented tale of inmate abuse and political corruption." A dramatic illustration of this tendency made front page news in 1995, when a riot by immigrant detainees in an Immigration and Naturalization Service (INS) prison operated by Esmor Corporation led to "a scathing report detailing an atmosphere of abuse and penny pinching in the jail for illegal immigrants and asylum seekers. Poorly paid, ill-trained guards physically and verbally abused detainees, shackling them with leg irons, roughing them up with no reason in the middle of the night." Esmor had obtained a contract with the INS despite having no experience, by hiring the campaign manager of a New York politician to lobby for their interests.

Because of the public nature of the functions of running prisons, the American Bar Association resolved in 1986 that privatization of prisons should be halted "un-

til the complex constitutional, statutory, and contractual issues are satisfactorily developed and resolved." These issues have certainly not been resolved, but privatization is moving ahead full speed, because of inflated perceptions of possible budget savings, the political revolving door, and the emergence of a new "prison-industrial complex."

PRIVATIZATION VERSUS DEMOCRACY

Margaret Thatcher, Augusto Pinochet and others have deliberately used privatization as a means of weakening popular forces and consolidating the power of capital. The West's support of Boris Yeltsin's privatization program, hugely corrupt and beggaring the population, is also designed to make the transformation to capitalism irreversible. These leaders, and the IMF, recognize privatization's political dimension. Governments can be mobilized to serve ordinary citizens — so that shrinking their functions, making them more dependent on the private sector, reducing public-sector unions, and strengthening capital diminishes the democratic threat. Privatization in the United States has been part of this global corporate and right-wing effort to undermine the democratic gains of the past half century. ∎

Resources: "Poverty Profiteers Privatize Welfare," Mark Dunlea, *Covert Action Quarterly*, Winter 1996-97; "The Pitfalls of Private Penitentiaries," Jeff Gerth and Stephen Labaton, *New York Times*, 11/11/95; "The Patient as Profit Center: Hospital Inc. Comes to Town," Carl Ginsberg, *The Nation*, 11/18/96; *The Emperor's New Clothes: Transit Privatization and Public Policy*, Eliot Sclar *et al.*, Economic Policy Institute, 1989.

January/February 1997

COMPETITION COMES TO ELECTRICITY

INDUSTRY GAINS, PEOPLE AND THE ENVIRONMENT LOSE

BY ROGER COLTON

"People will die." That's why Bobbi Bennett, an energy specialist at the National Training and Information Center (NTIC) in Chicago, opposes competition in the electric utility industry. "Many people simply can't afford to pay their bills," Bennett says. "Some of them will die if their protection is left up to a competitive utility."

It was nighttime and Philadelphia Electric had turned off the electricity to Gloria Blackwell's home. The kids were playing by candlelight in a back bedroom. Their eyes flickered shut but the candle didn't flicker out. The result? A seven year old child dead and a five year old scarred for life with third degree burns over 35% of his body.

"We don't like to shut people off," the utility's spokesperson was quoted as saying, "but if they're not going to pay, we can't keep giving them free electricity."

This scenario is likely to play out in increasing numbers as utilities "get tough" in their collection efforts. These efforts are necessary to be more competitive, the utilities say. In one case, Southern California Edison chose to treble its service disconnections, to one-half million customers in 1995 alone.

The lights blinked once... twice, and then went out. Suddenly, consumers were looking at computers that were not computing, lights that were not lighting, and refrigerators that were not refrigerating. At one point in July 1996, two million consumers in eleven western states and Canada were without power. Only six weeks later, two million customers of Pacific Gas and Electric Company lost power in California.

What happened? As electric utilities serving the region geared up (and scaled down) to meet competition, routine maintenance, such as tree trimming around power lines, was reduced in the name of cost-cutting. Then a storm battered the West coast, trees fell on the power lines, and the lights went out.

These threats to public safety and to reliable electric service, along with pending threats to air quality, are examples of what the current movement toward competition and deregulation of the electric industry may mean. Today, electric companies are state-sanctioned monopolies. They have "exclusive service territories" — geographic areas in which other companies are not allowed to compete. The utilities generate the electricity, transmit the power from their plants to local switching stations, and distribute the power to homes and businesses. In exchange for government protection against competition, electric utilities are subject to state regulation over the reasonableness of their rates and the quality of their service.

In the past, utilities could prevent industrial and commercial businesses from obtaining inexpensive power from non-utility generators, because the utilities had monopoly control over the transmission lines. But federal regulations now require that utilities provide fair access to such lines for all generators, not merely the utility's own plants. So while utilities will retain a monopoly over local distribution, they will have to compete with non-utility generators to produce the cheapest electricity. This threatens the financial stability of many electric utilities, especially those with billions of dollars in stranded costs from expensive nuclear plants.

THE FALL OF THE LAST GREAT MONOPOLY

The gain will be greater consumer choice, argues Central Illinois Lighting Company (CILCO) spokesperson Calvin Butler. Butler recently told a national gathering of consumer advocates in Chicago that "No one tells you where to shop for groceries. Why should they tell you where to shop for electricity?"

The power to choose will save money, according to CILCO. "In a state like Illinois — where [the vast majority] of residential electric consumers [are] supplied by investor-owned utilities [and] pay 20% to 25% more than the national average — the lack of consumer choice is costly to everybody." Other benefits, CILCO claims, will include better service as well as new and expanded services.

Nonsense, says University of St. Thomas (Minnesota) professor Steve Hoffman. The fuss is about the exercise of power, both political and economic. Today's threats to switch to competitive suppliers of electricity are simply the next generation of big industry's threats to move to new locations in order to get lower rates. Because alternative generators now have the legal right to transmit electricity over the local utility's lines, companies need not move their plants in order to switch suppliers.

The recent conflict between Raytheon, a major defense contractor, and Massachusetts Electric Company is one example of how corporations exercised power even under the old system. In response to threats by Raytheon to leave Massachusetts, the local electric company offered rate discounts of 20% and more for five years, with lower discounts being offered in subsequent years. Even then, Raytheon refused the discount in 1995, arguing that the deeper discount should last longer.

Ultimately, a discount was agreed to and approved in January 1996. Raytheon would say only that its deal with Mass. Electric would yield "significant savings" on its $20-million-plus annual electric bill. The state Department of Public Utilities ordered that the precise terms of the discount be kept confidential. The secrecy was necessary, the Department said, because the rates were "competitively sensitive." Several dozen similar deals on both gas and electric rates for large industries had been approved at the time of the Raytheon agreement, with more pending.

In contrast to these actions toward big business, Hoffman says, electric industry competition will almost surely leave the small and less powerful in the dark. These consumers are simply not big enough and economically attractive enough to gain the interest of electric industry competitors. Instead of receiving the promised benefits they will instead receive the harms of increased disconnections, reduced service quality, and higher rates.

With typical residential bills for Mass. Electric Company at just over $700 a year, for example, it would take

nearly 30,000 customers having 30,000 meters read each month, resulting in 30,000 monthly bills and the accompanying credit and collection activity, to generate the same revenue as Raytheon's pre-discount bill of $20+ million. The utilities are likely to make up the lost revenue by increasing prices to residential and small-business customers.

For example, in Michigan, one of the states which has experimented with electric competition, during 1995 Consumers Power Company raised electricity rates for its 1.4 million residential users by 8.2% ($42 on a typical annual bill), while lowering rates for the state's 9,000 industrial users by an average of 4.2%. Like Raytheon in Massachusetts, the largest and most powerful Michigan industrial consumers such as General Motors and Dow Corning got rate cuts of up to 20%.

Two developments have led to the push for deregulation of the electric industry. First, competition in the industry will help the big and powerful in society obtain lower energy bills. Many utilities have built more generating capacity than their customers now need, and often they rely heavily on outrageously expensive nuclear power plants. As a result, they have electric rates far higher than their potential competitors, often termed non-utility generators, or "NUGs." Such competitors can run new or existing power plants, usually fired by natural gas, at costs much lower than the average costs of a utility that is saddled with its historical mistakes.

These mistakes — excess capacity and nuclear plants — constitute as much as $200 billion in "stranded costs." Large commercial and industrial users of electricity want to escape from paying for these costs through their electric rates, and have found two methods for doing so. One is bargaining with the utility to provide discounted rates, as in the Raytheon case. The second is competition — having the freedom to buy their power from non-utility generators (or utilities in other states) who have lower costs.

Second, technological changes in the generation of electricity, allowing relatively small plants to operate more cheaply, helped to provide large users with an alternative to the utilities. In the telecommunications industry, the advent of microwave and satellite transmission allowed companies to compete with then-monopoly supplier of telecommunications services AT&T. Similarly, technological improvements have allowed smaller companies to build and operate power plants, making it unnecessary to treat utilities as a "natural monopoly."

The poor, the payment-troubled, and other customers who the electric industry considers less than desirable will suffer from a deregulated free market. Hoffman notes that experience in other deregulated competitive industries shows that the poor and hard-to-serve are disadvantaged by business actions taken to help meet competition. In 1982, for example, Congress largely deregulated the inter-city bus industry. Within ten years, the number of rural locations receiving regular route inter-city bus service had shrunk by more than 50%. A 1992 study by the U.S. General Accounting Office concluded that "the riders who

DEATH AND DESTRUCTION

Increasing the operation of old coal-fired power plants will directly lead to increased deaths. According to the ME3 report, "simply put, the more often a plant runs, the more pollution it will emit." ME3 then cites estimates that 64,000 people may die prematurely from heart and lung disease each year due to emissions of particulates.

Those deaths are likely to be concentrated among people of color and lower income groups. The political power of such customers is usually far less than that of large industries and more affluent residents. As a result, when electricity generators make facility siting decisions, they will search for low-income neighborhoods to locate their plants in.

have been losing service are those least able to afford and least likely to have access to alternative modes of transportation."

DOES COMPETITION BRING NIRVANA?

Even in industries that have never been regulated, competition often imposes higher prices and reduced services on those customers least able to protect themselves, including the poor. Competitive grocery stores in low-income urban neighborhoods, for example, charge prices up to 20% higher than in suburban areas because of claimed higher costs. Appliance and furniture prices in inner-city neighborhoods run 50% higher. Institutions financing mortgages for mobile homes charge far more in interest than for loans on more conventional housing, based on claimed higher default rates.

Competitive industries provide fewer services to poor people as well. One study in Los Angeles found 19 branch banks in South Central Los Angeles, a predominantly poor black community having a population of 587,000 people. In contrast, the study found 21 branch banks in nearby Gardena, a middle class white community of only 49,800 persons. A separate study in Washington, DC found that residents in predominantly white neighborhoods have three times as many branches available, per person, as do residents of predominantly African American neighborhoods.

Similarly, consumer advocate Bobbi Bennett asserts that even if competition "works" in the electric industry, it will not address concerns that are important to society but yield no profits. These include the ability of low-income customers to afford power, and protection of the environment. Such concerns, often termed "externalities," are not of direct interest to businesses, since the businesses neither pay the cost nor receive the benefit of seeing the social goal achieved.

Some vital goods and services, such as electricity or water, should be available at affordable rates to all who seek them, regardless of ability to pay. But since the damage from a lack of universal service is imposed on society, not on the company, a competitive electric utility has little incentive to ensure affordable power. In addition to affordability a competitive market does not ensure that electric utilities will have fair procedures in the denial or termination of service.

Is there any way to make a deregulated electric industry palatable for small users? Some would say yes, if mechanisms are developed to combine small users into large buying blocks that can bargain with power producers. Such aggregation methods might include allowing communities to bargain on behalf of everyone who lives within their boundaries. Large membership organizations such as the American Association of Retired Persons (AARP) and the American Automobile Association (AAA) have set a precedent for this by negotiating discounts on life and auto insurance for their members. Others say that small users simply cannot be aggregated into large enough blocks to convince competitive electric companies to pay sufficient attention to their needs.

DIRTY AIR AND TOXIC NEIGHBORHOODS

Environmental damages are also externalities, so that a competitive firm will not voluntarily try to minimize them. Statutes or regulations can mandate the clean-up of pollution, since the regulated utility now has to pay for them. But a competitive, unregulated environment leads firms to more strongly resist cost increases, and to ignore environmental issues.

A report done for the National Association of Regulatory Utility Commissioners (NARUC) agrees, concluding that "industry restructuring will likely result in competitive pressures to increase the operation of currently underutilitized coal facilities with relatively high air pollution emissions, and to extend the operation lives of these facilities."

Competitive electric utilities that achieve increased sales are likely to rely on old, inexpensive, highly polluting coal-fired power plants. As a result, the public, especially urban dwellers, will be stuck with damaging increases in air emissions as a result of utility sales to new markets.

A report by Minnesotans for an Energy Efficient Economy (ME3) finds that Minnesota's largest utility has four coal plants in the Minneapolis/St. Paul metro area that could increase their output. According to that report: "The plants have several common characteristics, the most important being that they are all aging, coal-burning generators operating in densely-populated areas." In addition, because old plants do not need to meet the pollution control standards of new plants, emissions from the metropolitan plants "are extraordinarily high compared to current standards governing new power plants," ME3 concludes.

Past reliance on improving energy efficiency, instead of building new plants, as a way to control this environmental damage is not likely to continue in a competitive electric industry. According to one industry analyst, Robert Smock of the publication *Electric Light & Power*, "survivors of ruthless competition will not be doing much to reduce electricity sales. They'll be doing their best to sell more of their product." The numbers bear this out. A survey of 50 utilities found that planners expected a 2% growth rate in energy efficiency programs between 1995 and 1998. This is far less than the 17% annual growth rate from 1990 to 1995.

Coke or Pepsi? MCI or AT&T? K-Mart or Walmart? Ford or Chevy? Consumer choice. Substantial bill savings. This is the mantra of competition advocates in the electric industry. But consumer advocates say the real choice is whether to protect the interests of the big and powerful, or those of the small and dispossessed. The electric industry should not be just another business, but rather an industry responsible for serving the public interest. The choice is whether to create an industry whose decisionmaking is governed only by the profit motive, or to maintain regulations that ensure universally affordable electricity and protection of the environment. ∎

Resources: Coal Plants in the Neighborhood: Stopping Increased Air Pollution from the NSP Merger, Kevin Bengston, Michael Noble and J. Drake Hamilton, Minnesotans for an Energy Efficient Economy (St. Paul, Minnesota) 1996; *Competition in the Electric Industry: Assessing Impacts on Residential, Commercial and Low-Income Customers*, Roger Colton, National Conference of State Legislatures (Denver, Colorado), 1996.

March 1996

THE SICK HEALTH CARE SYSTEM

ARE CORPORATE HMOs THE CURE?

BY EDIE RASELL

Although the level of cost was 13% lower in HMOs than in fee-for-service plans ($3,663 compared to $4,229) this is not necessarily because HMOs provide care more efficiently, as I will describe below.

Since HMOs, on average, cost less than traditional plans, as beneficiaries shift to HMOs, there often is a one-time savings. But evidence shows that in subsequent years, costs continue their uphill climb, unchecked.

While policymakers have abandoned the idea of comprehensive health care reform, the private health care system has been undergoing revolutionary change. The industrial revolution has come to the health care sector. The practice of medicine is being transformed from a cottage industry of many independent crafts-men and -women, to an industry where health care is provided by corporations employing thousands of people. The goal of the "corporatization" of health care, just as in the early days of the industrial evolution, is to facilitate control of workers (doctors and other providers) by managers, and capture profits for the owners of the corporation.

Health Maintenance Organizations (HMOs) will not solve the problems of the US health care system — high costs, millions of people without access to health care, and large disparities in outcomes and treatment between the rich and the poor. But HMOs are a useful diversion for people who refuse to acknowledge that only fundamental reforms can address the problems of both the public and private health care sectors. Costs, uninsurance and lack of access to care, and disparities in outcomes will continue despite the growth of HMOs. They can be eased only through a universal health care system, financed by a "single payer" (a government agency) — something like an improved Medicare system for all.

PROBLEMS PERSIST AND WORSEN COSTS

National health expenditures continue to rise rapidly, much faster than overall growth in the economy. Peak rates of growth were prior to 1985, but between 1992 and 1993, the most recent years for which we have data, spending rose 7.8% — an unacceptably high rate. Some analysts even worry that once talk (or the "threat") of comprehensive reform has faded, spending growth rates could rise even higher.

Even for employer-sponsored health insurance (insurance received on the job), where the media have reported stories of successful decreases in growth rates, the numbers are not encouraging. In 1994, in both traditional fee-for-service type plans and HMOs, costs per employee rose 10%.

INSURANCE COVERAGE AND ACCESS TO CARE

The number of uninsured continues to grow. Between 1989 and 1993, the number of below-65-year-olds without health insurance grew from 34.4 million to 40.9 million, an increase of 6.5 million. This rise would have been even larger had not Medicaid coverage of the poor also increased by 10 million people in this period. Nonetheless, in 1993 one-third of the nonelderly poor — 12 million people — remained uninsured.

The growth in the number of uninsured is largely driven by an ongoing decline in employer-sponsored coverage. Between 1989 and 1993, 16 million more people below age 65, of whom 7 million were children, found themselves without employer-sponsored coverage. In 1993, employer-sponsored health insurance — the backbone of the system for people under age 65 — covered just 61% of all people under age 65, down from 66% in 1989.

Over half of the uninsured are full-time, full-year workers or live in families with such workers. An additional one-third of the uninsured are workers or family members of workers who are employed part-time. Only the elderly who are covered by Medicare have health care security (and the recent proposals to "save" Medicare would have weakened this security).

QUALITY OF CARE

Despite high spending, health outcomes are worse in the United States than in many other countries. This is due both to the structure of our health care system — lack of access to care and disparities in treatment — and to the extreme income inequality and prevalence of poverty in the United States.

Life expectancy at age 40 (the average number of years of life remaining for 40 year-olds) is lower in the United States than in six other countries. Infant mortality (the likelihood of death in the first year of life) is higher here than in 14 other nations. Infant mortality is nearly two and one-half times higher for blacks than whites and this difference is growing. Death rates are higher among people with lower incomes and less education compared to those with higher incomes and more education, and these disparities are widening, not shrinking.

The likelihood of being alive five years after being diagnosed with cancer is 30% to 40% greater for whites than blacks, and this disparity is growing. These racial differences have little to do with genetic differences, but are primarily related instead to socioeconomic status and access to health care. In addition, research shows that within the health care system, treatment may differ according to race or class even among people with the same type of health insurance.

CORPORATE HMOS

Many policymakers and employers are looking to HMOs to solve our health care problems — but they are likely to be disappointed. The fastest-growing HMOs today are very different from traditional HMOs that were widely admired in the past. The first Health Maintenance Organizations began in the 1930s and 1940s. These HMOs promised, for an annual fee, to provide enrollees with all necessary health care. They were typically not-for-profit institutions run by governing boards which included patient representatives to speak in the interest of those who would be most affected by the decisions made.

Unlike many fee-for-service plans, preventive care was covered and encouraged. It was thought that if the HMO kept its enrollees healthy, it would be able to contain costs and more successfully attract additional members. Since all necessary care was covered, patients and doctors did not have to worry about whether a medically-desirable treatment was covered or affordable and could instead focus on optimum health care. These HMOs usually owned their own offices and hospitals, and their medical staffs worked only for the HMO. Doctors were often salaried; unlike in fee-for-service care, there were no financial incentives for doctors to over treat in order to raise their incomes.

Unfortunately, today's fastest-growing HMOs are far removed from this tradition. These HMOs are for-profit corporations that contract with a loose network of doctors, usually practicing in their own offices, who have agreed to treat HMO enrollees in return for specified reimbursements. Providers often sign up with multiple HMOs. They may be paid a fee for service (i.e., receive a fee for each service performed) or, alternatively, they may receive a lump sum, set in advance, for each HMO patient that they agree to treat for a 12-month period.

In addition to agreeing on a base rate of payment, for more than half of all doctors signed up with HMOs, some portion of their reimbursement depend on the number and cost of referrals they make for services they cannot provide themselves. Under these arrangements, a doctor with a higher than specified referral rate to specialists will face a financial penalty (see the box).

Many HMOs also require doctors to sign "gag clauses." For example, US Healthcare, one of the largest

HMOs in the country, requires doctors to sign a contract that enjoins them against making "any communication which undermines or could undermine the confidence of enrollees, potential enrollees, their employers, their unions, or the public in US Healthcare or the quality of US Healthcare coverage."

On the surface, HMOs can appear to be less costly than other types of plans. There are several reasons for this, but it is not necessarily because they deliver care more efficiently. First, healthier people tend to choose HMOs while sicker people, if they have the option, tend to remain in fee-for-service plans so they can keep the doctor they may have had for many years.

Second, HMOs commonly negotiate discounts with hospitals and doctors. This reduces costs for HMOs, but can lead to additional costs being shifted to fee-for-service plans as providers try to maintain their incomes by raising fees that have not been negotiated downward. Third, HMOs provide fewer services. Since we know that too many unnecessary services are provided, this could be beneficial for patients and save money also. However, it may be that necessary as well as unnecessary services are being denied.

When HMOs move into a region and begin to market themselves to employers and sign up doctors, a majority of employers may switch to the HMO within just a few years. This occurs because HMOs are often cheaper than fee-for-service plans. But if many employers contract with HMOs, this means that doctors, too, must sign up or they will have few patients. Moreover, if doctors are dropped by their local HMOs, they can lose their capability to make a living. This gives HMOs enormous power over providers. Arguably, financial incentives to restrict access to care, gag clauses, and HMOs' excessive power over providers' ability to practice medicine create an environment in which patients may not receive needed care.

In recent years, these new corporate HMOs have been very profitable, as described in one *Wall Street Journal* headline: "Money Machines: HMOs Pile Up Billions In Cash." During 1994, four of the largest HMOs netted over $1 billion and "nine of the biggest publicly traded HMOs are sitting on $9.5 billion in cash."

This occurs, at least in part, because so little of HMOs' revenues are actually spent on health care — as little as 70 to 75 cents of each dollar in fees received. During the early

DESPITE HIGH SPENDING, HEALTH OUTCOMES ARE WORSE IN THE UNITED STATES THAN IN MANY OTHER COUNTRIES.

1990s there was also phenomenal growth in the value of HMOs' stock. Since these high-flying days, profit rates have somewhat moderated, but HMOs remain one of the nation's most lucrative industries.

WILL HMOS SOLVE OUR PROBLEMS?

Many people who obtain their health care from HMOs are very satisfied; others are not. Quality and attentiveness to patients' concerns vary widely. Many of the new for-profit corporate HMOs lack most of the attractive features found in the traditional type of HMO. Financial incentives have returned, but now they serve to encourage undertreatment. Providers and patients worry whether particular services will be covered or whether providers can even inform patients of their options.

Given these concerns, consumers need to question whether HMOs will solve, or even ameliorate, the problems of high health care costs, high numbers of uninsured, limited access and disparities in outcomes.

• Costs: HMOs' potential to contain costs, even with the draconian measures they employ, is still uncertain. And once a few HMOs in any region enroll the majority of patients, this bodes poorly for cost containment — oligopolies rarely engage in strong price competition. Even if HMOs do manage to rein in spending, will the cost in terms of reductions in quality be too great?

• Access: Despite the growth in HMOs, the erosion in employer-provided coverage will continue. This decline is driven by the growth in health costs (which will continue with HMOs), desire for high corporate profit rates (currently at 25-year highs), and the weakening of corporate commitments to be responsible members of the community. Moreover, as hospitals and other health care providers deliver ever-larger shares of their services to patients covered with rates negotiated by HMOs, there is less excess revenue to pay the costs of treating the uninsured. We can anticipate that the rising number of uninsured will have greater difficulty finding providers who are willing to deliver care for which they are unlikely to be reimbursed.

• Quality and Disparities in Care: HMOs probably do reduce unnecessary services. But satisfaction with this positive outcome must be tempered with a concern that necessary services are also being denied. Moreover, will doctors' primary responsibility — to provide health care in the best interests of their patients — be compromised through gag clauses and financial conflicts of interest?

The greatest threat to quality comes from HMOs that enroll only or primarily Medicaid patients, a growing practice. There is evidence that race and class affect treatment decisions even in our current system of care where rich and poor, white and nonwhite, for the most part receive care side by side, often through the same providers. The potential for disparities in treatment skyrockets when only people with low incomes, many of whom may be minorities, are treated in any particular system.

WHAT SHOULD BE DONE?

Americans need universal health care coverage, financed by a single payer — something like an improved Medicare program expanded to cover the entire population. Universal coverage is unlikely to be achieved with an employer-based system unless employers are required to provide coverage. But even if such a mandate were imposed, we would still have a crippled system. People change jobs frequently (eight job changes during one's working life is now being suggested as the norm), unemployment rates are high, and there is growing use of part-time and contingent workers. These trends mean that if access to health care is tied to employment, frequent changes in coverage and lack of continuous care, if not outright periods of uninsurance, will take place.

Health insurance must be separated from employment. Enrollment of everyone, as a right, in Medicare would break the already tenuous link between insurance and employment, and provide universal, continuous coverage for everyone.

We need cost containment and a reduction in the growth rate of spending. Medicare has been a pioneer in cost containment. In seven of the last ten years, the growth of per person costs in Medicare has been below the rate in the private sector. More cost containment must be achieved. In the past, to remain compatible with the realities in the private sector, Medicare's cost containment options wre limited. When cost containment can be applied to the system as a whole, it can be much more effective.

Medicare also has low administrative costs. The U.S. General Accounting Office has estimated that if a system like Medicare were to replace our piecemeal network of over 1200 private insurance companies, some $100 billion in administrative overhead would be saved in 1995 alone.

Given the dangers of segmenting population subgroups into different systems of care, we need one health care

---

TOP-SECRET CONTRACTS

One HMO's "incentive" contract with a physician, who agreed to care for 925 of the HMO's enrollees, contains these provisions:

Hospital Stays — If the doctor's patients collectively stay fewer than 178 days in the hospital per year, the doctor receives a bonus of $2,063 per month. If the patients collectively spend more than 363 days per year, the doctor receives no extra bonus.

Referral to Specialists — If specialist costs per patient average less than $14.49 per month, the doctor gets a monthly bonus of $1,323. If the costs exceed $30.49 a month, the bonus falls to zero.

delivery system in which everyone can participate. Medicare provides such a system. Once everyone has equal access to high quality care, we can turn our attention to the other factors — such as poverty and unemployment — that create disparate health outcomes.

The current infatuation with HMOs is potentially dangerous. Politicians, providers, and insurance companies who do not want to contemplate comprehensive health care reforms hide behind the illusion that HMOs will solve the problems of the health care system. Meanwhile, the number of uninsured continues to grow, costs continue to rise, and disparities in outcomes continue to widen. Comprehensive health care reform must return to the top of the political agenda. This time around, a simple solution — Medicare for all — should be the goal. ■

Resources: National Center for Health Statistics, *Health, United States, 1994,* Hyattsville, MD, Public Health Service, 1995.

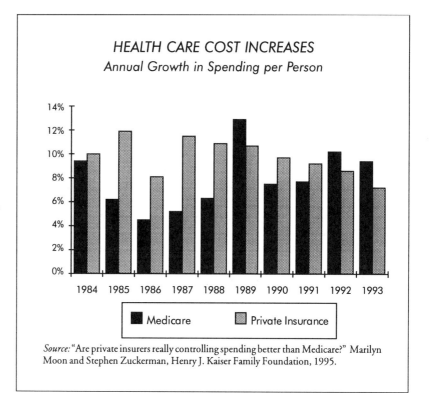

HEALTH CARE COST INCREASES
Annual Growth in Spending per Person

Source: "Are private insurers really controlling spending better than Medicare?" Marilyn Moon and Stephen Zuckerman, Henry J. Kaiser Family Foundation, 1995.

July/August 1996

GOVERNMENT OF, BY, AND FOR THE WEALTHY

It's not easy to directly tie campaign contributions from special interests to votes by members of Congress on their behalf. Since buying votes is illegal, there is never a written record showing that a Senator or Representative made their choice on the basis of money.

But several progressive organizations, including Common Cause and the Center for Responsive Politics, have specialized in "following the money" — showing that large contributions to public officials have coincided with votes and other actions to help the contributing industries. The officials often respond that this is guilt by association, and that in reality they have always supported the policies in question, so that contributors are simply supporting like-minded politicians.

Judge for yourself. The evidence, while "circumstantial" for those of us accustomed to watching TV crime dramas, should be enough to convict our political system of serving the interests of the wealthy. Whether the subject is health care reform, environmental regulation, farm subsidies, weapons production or trade policy, it is difficult to even get a hearing in Washington without spreading around a lot of dough.

SELLING THE ENVIRONMENT

Despite the takeover of Congress by anti-government, anti-regulation Republicans in 1994, opinion polls have shown overwhelmingly public support for continued strong efforts to protect the environment. But this power of public opinion is counterbalanced by the greater access of anti-environment forces to money. During the three years from 1992 to 1994, while pro-environment advocates gave $2 million in national political contributions, corporations and PACs opposed to environmental regulation gave $24 million, twelve times as much.

One anti-regulation effort, Project Relief, is a coalition of PACs representing 350 corporations, according to a report by Mark Schapiro in *Environmental Action*. The Project, whose members include such outstanding citizens as Adolph Coors Company, the Chemical Manufacturers Association, Chevron, General Electric, and the National Chamber of Commerce, contributed an average of $21,000 to each of the 21 members of the House Regulatory Task Force.

A key goal of Project Relief is obtaining legislation that would require the EPA to conduct an extensive cost-benefit analysis before it could impose any new environmental regulation. Such a provision was in the original Senate version of the fiscal 1996 federal appropriations bill, but was held up by Democratic opposition. Yet among the Democrats, Sen. Charles Robb (D-Va.) has been an industry ally in trying to obtain the legislation.

Mark Schapiro reports that between January 1993 and June 1995 Robb received $28,000 from another industry front group, the Alliance for Reasonable Regulation. Contributors included Amoco Oil, Hoechst Celanese Chemical, Consolidated Natural Gas, and Abbott Pharmaceuticals. Robb also got $71,000 from members of Project Relief, including Chevron and General Electric.

Another industry goal is gutting the Clean Water Act, passed in 1970 as one of the nation's premier pieces of environmental regulation. One "reform" being pushed by industry is redefining the term "wetland" so that more than two thirds of existing wetlands would no longer be regulated by the EPA. Another would only allow the feds to require polluters to use the "best available technology" for clean up when it can be shown "to maximize net social benefits," not in all circumstances, as is currently required. This would again force the EPA to conduct a cost-benefit study before imposing any regulation, greatly hampering the agency.

Between 1989 and 1994, 267 PACs opposed to current provisions of the Clean Water Act contributed a total of $57 million to Congressional candidates, according to a study by the U.S. Public Interest Research Group (PIRG). Giving freely were the PACs of most major corporate polluters, including Exxon, Du Pont and Dow Chemical. Those Congresspeople voting in favor of the industry-sponsored changes received about twice as much money on average as those who voted against the revisions, PIRG found.

— *Marc Breslow*

PORK FARMERS

If you want to find pork, in campaign contributions and in the federal budget, look no further than the U.S. Department of Agriculture's (USDA) farm support program. But wait, in April President Clinton signed a reform bill hailed as a pork-buster because it begins to dismantle the USDA's subsidy payments to farmers.

Just last year, large parts of the farm lobby were trying to block such changes. What happened? Big farmers came out on top, and those farm sectors that provide the most PAC money — sugar, dairy and peanuts — found their programs changed the least. Their programs also cost the government the least since they operate by manipulating supply — passing along the cost to consumers in the form of higher prices — rather than by providing direct subsidies to farmers when prices are low.

The farm sectors that contributed the least in PAC money — those receiving the direct USDA subsidies for rice, corn, cotton, wheat and other grains — found their program the most changed. Their PACs only contributed $457,000 to congressional candidates in 1993-94, while the sugar PACs contributed $1.8 million, according to the Center for Responsive Politics. Moreover, those opposing direct subsidies to grain producers had their own lobby — a coalition of businesses and trade associations, largely from food processing industries, whose PACs contributed $3.4 million to congressional candidates for the 1994 elections. Altogether, the agricultural sector spent heavily on PAC contributions, ranking third among all business contributors.

But it is not just that the small PAC spenders got screwed in the reform plan while the big spenders stayed on easy street. One skeptic is C. Ford Runge, an agricultural economist who co-authored a book championing massive reform. Runge says the grain farmers receiving the direct subsidies — and the lowest spenders in PAC money — jumped on the reform bandwagon once it looked like they would get grants even when commodity prices are high. In other words, they were bribed with even more pork in the short run. Under the old Depression-era system, the USDA only paid out subsidies — about $11 billion annually — when prices were low. Under the new "Freedom to Farm" program, the USDA will send farmers flat payments for the next seven years and give them the freedom to grow whatever they want. Farmers can even grow nothing and still receive payments. The payments drop gradually each year, and by the last year, the assumption is, the Depression-era programs will be repealed entirely. While wheat and corn lost their federal price subsidies completely, the subsidies will still kick in for cotton and rice if the market falls, and the price support system for sugar and peanut farmers is largely unchanged (see below).

Under the old system, the biggest farms took home most of the federal bacon; 29% of the subsidized farmers received 80% of the benefits. It will only get worse under the new system. Instead of being capped at $20,000 per farmer and paid only when prices were low, as some reformers proposed, flat payments can reach as much as $80,000 even when prices are high. Even worse, some of the one-third of American farmers who are tenants may be cast from the fields as their landlords scramble to keep the new cash grants for themselves.

— *Abby Scher*

SUGAR HIGH

We shouldn't be surprised that the revolutionary farm reform legislation passed by Congress in March did not revolutionize Big Sugar. Big Sugar's cushy relationship with both Democrats and Republicans is longstanding.

It allows them to pollute the Everglades and engage in environmentally devastating agricultural methods. It protects the big benefits they receive from USDA price supports and makes sure that trade barriers against Caribbean and other foreign sugar stay high. Its influence reaches into the White House, so that Clinton's negotiator held up the North American Free Trade Agreement until it was certain U.S. sugar would be protected.

Why do Congresspeople feel safe supporting the system? One reason is consumers pay the cost of the program in pennies at the supermarket, not in direct government handouts to agribusiness.

But while Big Sugar's $1.8 million PAC contributions in 1993-94 make wealthy sugar families even wealthier, not all parts of the industry benefit equally. Sugar cane and corn syrup production is highly concentrated in large operators, unlike the Midwestern farmers who cultivate sugar beets. The benefits they receive from government price supports have been highly concentrated as well. Forty-two percent of the benefits from higher sugar prices go to just 1% of sugar producers and four Florida companies received more than $20 million apiece due to price supports, says the Center for Responsive Politics.

For the corn industry, four companies — including Archer-Daniels-Midland and A.E. Staley Manufacturing Company — receive 87% of the $548 million in federal payments. Giving $41,500 for the 1994 reelection campaign of Rep. E. "Kika" de la Garza (D-TX) when he was chairman of the House Agricultural Committee seems like a small price to pay for such dividends.

Candy and ice cream manufacturers are fighting back, furiously spreading their own PAC money around to try to dismantle the sugar program, but it has not been working. Despite contributing $1.4 million to Senators over a six year period, some of those Senators still voted in favor of the sugar program this spring.

Even the $200 million land fund environmentalists wrung out of the agricultural bill to restore wetlands from the devastation of sugar runoff is not safe. Some politicians want to spend some of the money on established restoration projects, not new ones.

— *Abby Scher*

BANANA REPUBLICANS

The United Fruit Company, established in 1899, is notorious for dominating banana-growing in Central America, and for helping to install dictators who were sympathetic to its operations. Now known as Chiquita Brands, its chairman and largest stockholder is Cincinnati billionaire Carl Lindner. As of 1992 Chiquita sold almost half of its bananas in Europe, but in 1993 the European Union (EU) imposed quotas and tariffs that limited the company's ability to profit from banana sales.

Not one to give in easily, Lindner found a solution. During the 1993-94 election cycle Lindner, his company American Financial Corporation, its subsidiaries, and its executives made $955,000 in "soft money" political contributions (funds given to political parties, rather than individual candidates), according to the citizens' lobby Common Cause.

As the second-largest generator of soft money donations during this period, Lindner was remarkably even-handed, giving $525,000 to the Democrats and $430,000 to the Republicans. While both the parties and Lindner would surely deny that there was any quid pro quo for this money, Chiquita quickly got major assistance from leading Democratic and Republican politicians — although it grows no bananas in the United States.

On August 12, 1994 twelve Senators, including John Glenn (R-Ohio) and Robert Dole (R-Kan.), petitioned U.S. Trade Representative Mickey Kantor "for a formal investigation into the EU banana-import policy," reported the *Cincinnati Enquirer*. One month later, U.S. trade officials opened an investigation into the EU's policies, under a trade-law provision known as Section 301. Lindner also called for sanctions against Costa Rica and Colombia, which had accepted the EU's restrictions.

On November 17, according to the *Enquirer*, House Majority Leader Newt Gingrich (R-Ga.), Dole, and House Minority Leader Richard Gephardt (D-Mo.) all signed a letter to the Clinton Administration to open "immediate retaliation hearings against the European Union 'proportionate to the enormous U.S. harm already caused by the EU banana policy.'" In January, Kantor's office decided that the banana quotas were discriminatory, and suggested that a proper U.S. response could include trade sanctions against European exports.

During the national budget debate in 1995, Dole attached a provision aiding Chiquita to budget legislation and told other Senators that "bananas are a top priority," according to a report on the Public Broadcasting Service (PBS) show *Frontline*. And in January 1996, in a move that no doubt pleased Lindner, the White House declared that Colombia and Costa Rica were in violation of the trade laws (although Clinton declined to impose sanctions against them).

— *Marc Breslow*

HEALTH CARE REFORM?

Bill Clinton made health care reform a primary theme of his 1992 presidential campaign, and the drafting of reform proposals was a major initiative of his administration's first year. But despite its importance for the American people, reform was stymied in Congress. Instead of government measures that would control costs and ensure universal health coverage, we only have the Medicaid and Medicare reformers pushing managed care.

Special interests — namely physicians and the health insurance industry — have been the primary obstacle to real reform. Between 1985 and 1995 these two groups contributed $49 million to congressional campaigns and political party "soft money" accounts, according to Common Cause. The largest contributors included the American Medical Association ($13.7 million), Blue Cross & Blue Shield, Prudential Insurance, and Aetna Life & Casualty. During this decade doctors and insurers split their money evenly between Democrats and Republicans, although when the GOP gained control of Congress in November 1994 contributors quickly shifted the money toward their party.

While reform of private health insurance has stalled, by far the largest source of health care financing is Medicare, which the GOP aims to slash by $270 billion over the next seven years. Although this presents dangers for senior citizens, Congressional proposals would ensure that the pain for doctors and insurers is minimized.

The 1996 budget reconciliation bill would allow Medicare recipients to choose from among several health care options: the current fee-for-service program, a managed care plan, or a medical savings account (MSA). "By opening private health plans to the 37 million current Medicare recipients, the Medicare overhaul creates vast new markets for the health insurance industry," asserts Common Cause. The *Washington Post* reported that insurance companies could triple their share of the senior citizen health care market.

In addition, the GOP revised its Medicare proposal to include several provisions desired by physicians, including:

- lifting current regulations that prevent Medicare providers from charging more than 15% above cost levels approved by the federal government.

- permitting doctors to refer their patients to a laboratory or other facility in which the doctor has a financial stake.

- creating a new Medicare fee structure that would ensure that payments to physicians do not decline over the next seven years.

According to Common Cause, the AMA endorsed the Republican Medicare plan in October 1995, immediately after winning these concessions from House Speaker Newt Gingrich. "AMA officials said Gingrich had agreed to changes that would avoid 'billions' in fee reductions for doctors," reported the *Post*.

— *Marc Breslow*

ENDLESS BOMBER

The B-2 Bomber will fly forever. Nothing can stop it, not even a rebellion at the Pentagon. The Air Force says buying any more of the Cold War-era bombers would hurt defense, and using their rebellion as cover, President Clinton in February said he would not request any more B-2s in his 1997 budget.

What the generals, or Bill Clinton, said in February may not matter once the President's budget proposal gets inside Congress's budget-making machinery. Politicians as diverse as Rep. Ron Dellums (D-Calif.) and Sen. John McCain (R-Az.) have been trying to cut back the program for years without success. Last year, Congress slipped an extra $493 million into the 1996 budget to feed the bomber, out of a total of $7 billion that it larded onto the Pentagon's $257 billion budget request. Clinton says he's going to use some of the money to upgrade an old test plane instead of build a new one, but there are still 20 bombers yet to be built. PAC money is one of the reasons.

The B-2, the so-called "stealth" bomber, used to be protected because no one knew how much the program cost. Until 1988, it received $20 billion in funding through the Pentagon's secret "black budget." Now the bomber's leading defense contractor, Northrup Grumman, has to work a little harder to maintain its cash cow. It was one of the top corporate contributors to federal candidates in 1993-94 and, along with five subcontractors, contributed $2.2 million to candidates for the 1994 elections, according to the Center for Responsive Politics.

But there are signs its hold is weakening. Some senators who received B-2 PAC money voted against it in the Senate Armed Services Committee last year. And Northrup Grumman's campaign contributions are reportedly double what they were at this time last year.

The bomber's Washington friends are working hard too. Bob Dole said nice things about the B-2 while campaigning in the California primary. And though you'd think the boondoggle is on its way out since a strategic planning board is evaluating whether the plane is "cost effective," B-2 ally Sen. Sam Nunn (D-GA) is trying to pack the board with his allies. ∎

— *Abby Scher*

CHAPTER 2
The Problem with Markets

ARTICLE 5

April 1992, revised March 1996

SPIRALING DOWN
THE FALL OF REAL WAGES

Do you feel like you have less money in your pocket than 5, 10, 20 years ago? Yes? Well, you aren't alone. Since reaching their peak in 1973, real wages have fallen a dramatic 21%. In fact, wages are no better than they were in 1958, over 35 years ago.

Future paychecks may not improve either. If the 1990s recovery looks anything like the 1980s, wages will not boost most Americans' standard of living. Even when the economy has grown, workers' paychecks have not grown with it.

Real wages are measured by average gross weekly earnings, corrected for inflation. They include the money paid to production and non-supervisory workers in the private sector, approximately four-fifths of all those employed. (Excluded from this measure are agricultural and public-sector employees.) Real wage figures do not include the earnings of professional workers and managers, usually called salaried personnel.

The graph below depicts the changes in workers' purchasing power by comparing real wages from 1955 to 1995. Prior to 1973, economic growth and improving real wages moved together. From 1955 to 1973, the heart of the post-World War II boom, real wages rose almost every year. They didn't rise in 1958, the only sharp recession of the early post-war years.

After 1973, real wages plummeted beginning with the stagflation recession of 1974-75, that not only put the kibosh on workers' wages but also brought higher prices too.

A rather long but sluggish expansion during the late 1970s restored some of the purchasing power workers had lost to stagflation. But by 1978, a growing economy no longer improved workers' wages.

On the heels of that sluggish expansion came the double-dip recession from 1979 to 1982, the worst contraction since the Great Depression. Double-digit official unemployment rates and anti-worker corporate and public policy robbed workers of their bargaining power, and real wages fell sharply to only 85% of their 1973 peak.

When the recession ended, for the first time since World War II the slide in real wages did not end as well. By the end of the 1980s expansion, workers' wages had slid to less than they had been in 1982. How did this happen? When the economy grew quickly during 1983 and 1984, real wages improved. But as growth slowed, wages declined in all but one of the subsequent years of the Reagan-Bush administrations.

What this graph doesn't show is how falling real wages squeeze families. Americans have coped by working more hours and taking on second jobs. More family members are working. In part to keep family incomes from plummeting, women have joined the work force in increasing numbers. Compared with 20 years ago, women work considerably more hours per week and more weeks per year. Even the exit of women from the labor force during childbearing years has dropped off sharply. Women bear fewer children and return to paid work when their children are still young to keep the extra paycheck coming.

The history of wages over the last 30 years bodes ill for the 1990s. Families that can't boost their income with the help of a second or third wage-earner are likely to fall further behind. ∎

Sources: Economic Report of the President 1996, Table B-43; Council of Economic Advisors and Joint Economic Committee, Economic Indicators.

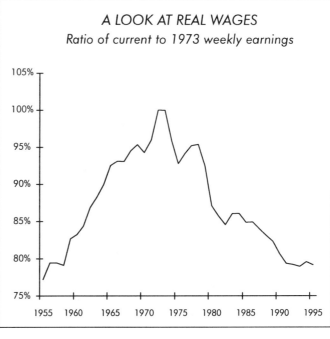

A LOOK AT REAL WAGES
Ratio of current to 1973 weekly earnings

September/October 1995

THE CHILD CARE INDUSTRY

WORTHY WORK, WORTHLESS WAGES

BY ROSEMARIE VARDELL AND MARCY WHITEBOOK

Subsidies for the poor — meals for children, heating oil for the elderly and shelter for the homeless — are lined up on the Congressional chopping block. The less visible subsidies provided to the well-to-do, however, have been spared the ax. And there is yet another subsidy that conservatives have little inclination to trim. It is the subsidy provided by over three million, mostly female, child care workers who receive wages that are far below what their education, skill, and experience should command.

These wages harm the personal lives of teachers and providers, and challenge their ability to continue the satisfying and important work of educating and caring for young children. Some examples:

"My own children and family do not have the income needed for our expenses because I have subsidized the care of other people's children for so long" (teacher, Naperville, Illinois).

"I quit working with children and families three years ago. I started my own family and found I could not support my family on child care wages. Now, I teach adults for three times the money but I find it less satisfying and much less challenging" (former child care teacher, Brighton, Michigan).

"Although I have a Master's Degree in Early Childhood Education and twenty years of teaching experience and I love what I do, I am seriously considering leaving the field so that my own children can attend college" (teacher, Austin, Texas).

The teachers who care for pre-school age children are part of the working poor. Their meager wages provide a subsidy to citizens across the economic spectrum — but only in the short term. The long-term consequences of our underfunded, haphazard child care "system" are alarmingly mediocre child care arrangements that harm children's development.

The most important characteristics that distinguish poor, mediocre, and good-quality centers are teacher wages, education and specialized training. The National Child Care Staffing Study documented that low wages create high turnover of child care staff. Child care centers paying the highest wages attracted better-trained and better-educated teachers, who created more appropriate and responsive environments for children. While children in these programs thrive, those attending centers with high staff turnover suffer in their language and social development. A child care coordinator from Idaho reports, "We see and hear the effects of the 41% staff turnover on children. They suffer anxiety and frustration that results in discipline and learning problems and low self-esteem."

WOMEN'S WORK

Given the documented developmental benefits for children of high-quality child care, and the relationship between this quality and the wages of teachers, why, as a nation, do we risk children's well-being by paying teachers near poverty level wages? In part, the answer lies in the legacy of child-rearing as women's work, and a historic tradition that sees the education of young children as a parental responsibility rather than as a public good and therefore a public responsibility.

The care and education of young children has historically been performed in the home by mothers, aunts, grandmothers, slaves or servants. This responsibility has been solidly located in the sphere of women and in the sphere of unpaid, or poorly paid labor defined as family life rather than "work." This legacy of nurturance as an unpaid responsibility of women overshadows the need to treat the care of children as skilled work demanding adequate compensation.

The result is that child care center teachers, 97% of whom are female, earn an average of $12,100 a year. Less than a third receive health insurance coverage through their child care center, and approximately 25% work second jobs. Regulated family child care providers, who work in their own homes, earn a meager $8,000 a year after expenses.

"Just this week I had to move out of my apartment because I can't afford an apartment and a car. I work in child care full time, plus 20-25 hours a week in retail." (teacher, Newton, Massachusetts)

"As a recent widow and after 15 years of working in child care, I find I cannot afford to live on my own. I have no retirement and am paid only $8.10 an hour. I feel I have made many sacrifices to do this work." (teacher, Bowie, Maryland)

The low wages of child care workers feed high turnover. Approximately one-third of the teaching work force leave their jobs each year, causing children to ask, "Who'll be my teacher tomorrow?"

WHO'S RESPONSIBLE?

The often heard phrase "children are our future" is one of many slogans suggesting that, as a nation, we value the well-being of children. In reality, we have developed a public policy of minimal responsibility toward young children and have left families to assume the burden of this charge privately. The increase in middle- and upper-class mothers in the labor force has made the issue only slightly more visible. U.S. society refuses to take collective responsibility for the care and education of young children.

In its absence is a rapidly growing child care industry lacking consistent or adequate public support — a patchwork of child care in which the "cost" of the service is closely tied to what parents are able or willing to pay. The result is a persistent and unfair linkage between what parents pay and what caregivers earn, captured succinctly in the verse, "Parents can't afford to pay, so teachers can't afford to stay."

Most young families cannot afford the real cost of good child care, which is estimated at $8,000 to $10,000 a year per child. This cost is far beyond the 10% to 15% of family income that is reasonable for child care expenses. Financial help is available only for a small portion of very low income families, and in small amounts through a tax credit received mainly by high income families. Most middle- and working-class families, and many poor families, get no assistance at all. As a result, the "cost" has been "adjusted" downward by paying teachers and providers unlivable wages that do not reflect their education, skill and responsibility.

Failure to break the link between teachers' wages and parents' ability to pay represents a fundamental refusal to regard young children's care and education as a public responsibility similar to that of educating school-age children. This unwillingness carries a price: children who do not enter school ready to learn, expensive remedial education services, and ultimately adults who lack emotional well-being and skills for the job market. For every dollar that we invest in good child care programs for children, we will save seven dollars of public funds down the road.

Adequate financing by government and by the employers of parents would make it possible to maintain a stable, qualified workforce and to keep parents' costs affordable. Breaking the link between teachers' salaries and parents' ability to pay is the principle shaping efforts to improve child care wages, while helping all parents gain access to high quality care.

POLICIES TO ENHANCE COMPENSATION

Leadership in the effort to enhance early childhood staff compensation and program quality has shifted between state and federal levels during the past decade. In response to pressure from unionized child care teachers and other advocates,

NORTH CAROLINA'S INNOVATIONS

North Carolina's T.E.A.C.H. (Teacher Education and Compensation Helps) project is an "umbrella" of scholarship programs that link early childhood training with improved compensation. Now in its fourth year of state funding, $1 million is available this year. The program partners state dollars with private money from child care programs, business, and foundations.

TEACH includes: a two course credential program whose participants receive a wage bonus; training options in which community college credits are tied to raises; a mentor teacher program in which experienced teachers receive raises in exchange for mentoring student teachers; and a four year degree scholarship and compensation program. Over 2,000 child care workers and administrators have participated in TEACH. In the program's first year, participating teachers gained salary increases ranging from 6% to 10%. Turnover among the group was 5%, a dramatic decrease from the state's average rate of 44%.

The Child Care Wage$ Project in Orange County, NC was developed to retain child care staff by supplementing salaries of workers. They can receive an extra $200 to $1,000 per year, depending on their current level of education. Recipients receive supplements after each continuous six month period of working in the same child care program. After just one year of the program, turnover dropped dramatically from 36% of the eligible participants to 14%. Said one family child care provider, "The scholarship program provided me with the financial incentive to further my education... and to provide the best possible home child care."

Massachusetts and New York made major strides in upgrading salary levels in the mid-to-late 1980's. At the turn of the decade, the federal government stepped forward with bold initiatives for military and Head Start programs.

Additionally, advocates successfully focused attention on federal child care legislation, resulting in the passage of the Child Care and Development Block Grant (CCDBG). It permits states to spend a small portion of their total allocation on quality improvement efforts, including increasing compensation for teachers and providers. This provision spawned a number of initiatives, several of which have been augmented with other state and private funds. The CCDBG also permits higher reimbursement rates for services than do other sources of federal funds.

BREAKING THE LINK BETWEEN TEACHERS' SALARIES AND PARENTS' ABILITY TO PAY IS THE KEY TO IMPROVING CHILD CARE WAGES.

The federal government, however, maintains a contradictory stance in relation to issues of child care quality and provider compensation. With regard to programs for which it maintains ultimate responsibility and governance, such as military child care and Head Start, the government recognizes that improved pay and training is the cornerstone of effective, high quality services for children. But when it comes to federal child care dollars distributed to the states through low-income funding streams, with the exception of the small CCDBG program, teacher and provider salary needs are ignored. In fact, federal guidelines limit the reimbursement rates for services provided by these funds, and these low rates contribute to the depressed wages of child care staff.

In contrast, the military recognized that better quality child care was integrally linked to its success as an employer. It could not afford to have soldiers miss work, or be distracted on the job due to inadequate or unstable child care arrangements. The Caregiver Personnel Pay Plan, included in the 1989 Military Child Care Act, links training to increased compensation. The result has been a dramatic decrease in staff turnover from over 60% a year to under 10% coupled with a striking improvement in staff training and program quality.

A primary goal of the program is to make early childhood staff salaries competitive with comparable professions within the military, and to break the link between staff compensation and parent fees. Center staff wages now average around $10 an hour, and efforts are underway to improve family child care provider reimbursement. Parent fees are subsidized by the military to cover the difference between what parents can afford to pay and what the service now costs.

Since the passage of the Head Start Expansion and Quality Improvement Act in 1990 and its re-authorization in 1994, $70 million has been allocated to increase salaries for the 100,000 Head Start personnel across the country. A quality set aside established in the 1990 legislation directed programs to spend a portion of their funds on salaries and/or benefits as well as training. While somewhat less comprehensive than the military initiative, particularly given the decentralized administration of Head Start programs, improvements in salaries and training have been sanctioned by law.

Limited CCDBG quality funds have been used creatively by some states, although improved compensation remains a low priority in many. Wisconsin developed a grants program as a way to infuse money into centers and homes without affecting parents' fees. In the program's first year, 155 centers and 69 family day care homes received $1.5 million. More than double that number have received grants of two types in subsequent years. Quality Improvement Grants help programs meet and maintain Wisconsin's High Quality Standards, which include competency-based credentials or degrees for all staff, improved compensation, and lower turnover. Staff Retention Grants are available for programs which already meet the High Quality Standards, and are primarily used for compensation and training.

Several states have developed mentoring programs for teachers and providers. California's Early Childhood Mentor Teacher Program, which operates at 28 community colleges throughout the state, is the largest in operation. Using approximately $650,000 per year, it offers experienced teachers advanced training to enable them to help train novice teachers. The mentors get a stipend of up to $3,000 per year for their work with new teachers who, in turn, receive college credit. This program has attracted a pool of highly qualified, veteran teachers who are unusually stable in their jobs. A number of states have also initiated scholarships, loan programs and direct salary supplements with a mix of CCDBG and other public and private funds (see sidebar).

Although limited in amount, the CCDBG quality initiative provided the impetus for experimentation with programs to address the staffing crisis in child care, and these have strengthened the resolve of many teachers and providers to remain in the field. Many advocates and policy makers involved in these efforts recognize, however, that resolution of the crisis rests with a major overhaul of the current "system" of child care delivery and financing. It would cost the nation $15 billion a year to raise the wages of the three million child care workers by $5,000 each per year — thereby expanding the services to families in need, and improving the lives of teachers and providers. This is far less than the $35 billion cost of the $500 per family tax credit currently proposed in the Congress.

But the dominant voices in current political debates discourage maintaining current levels of commitment to child care. Nor do they favor exploring the greater investments needed to realize child care's potential for helping children to enter school ready to learn, providing millions of stimulating jobs, and enabling parents to work without worrying about their children. The CCDBG quality provision, for example, may not survive current efforts to re-design and limit federal child care funding. And current efforts to restrict welfare by forcing mothers into the paid workforce will not necessarily guarantee affordable child care for their children.

The current political climate challenges teachers and providers and other advocates to juggle several strategies. These include fighting to maintain funding that permits experimentation with reforms providing immediate relief to some child care staff and providers; development of detailed visions that can help to re-focus the child care debate; and public education and constituency building among child care consumers.

THE WORTHY WAGE CAMPAIGN

Despite historical and social barriers, a grassroots movement of child care workers has begun examining the social attitudes that are at the core of their low wages, educating the public, and organizing for change. Begun in 1990, the Worthy Wage Campaign has grown to include hundreds of members in 44 states.

Historically, many child care teachers and providers believed their low wages were inevitable and expressed their discontent only by leaving the jobs they loved. Less than 5% of the workforce is unionized and most of these were organized in the 1970s and 80s.

Because teachers and providers are isolated in small centers and homes across the country, opportunities to come together and examine their own experiences in the context of larger social issues are limited. But by making connections at professional meetings, small groups organized and teachers have begun to analyze their experience as women whose work is caring for and educating children. They have begun to understand their low wages not as personal problems but as an undervaluing of their work, and as due to the lack of a national commitment to providing necessary resources. Out of this process has evolved an exploration of strategies to remedy the situation.

Members of the Worthy Wage Campaign understand that changing their wages and the child care system requires connection, education, action and resistance. Through organized activities such as the Leadership Empowerment Action Project (LEAP), members connect with other teachers and providers, challenge the expectations of occupational self-sacrifice as unjust and unnecessary, and develop their leadership and advocacy skills.

> A GRASSROOTS MOVEMENT OF CHILD CARE WORKERS HAS BEGUN EXAMINING THE SOCIAL ATTITUDES THAT ARE AT THE CORE OF THEIR LOW WAGES, EDUCATING THE PUBLIC, AND ORGANIZING FOR CHANGE.

Through an annual Worthy Wage Day and other educational events, they teach community members and parents about the skills required to perform their jobs, and the impact of low wages on their ability to provide the best care for children. Through public demonstrations, program closures, and other creative events their voices are increasingly heard in the public debate about child care.

The urgency and the spirit of these efforts is supported by the National Center for the Early Childhood Work Force (NCECW), formerly the Child Care Employee Project, which itself began as a teacher organization. NCECW documents conditions, evaluates strategies that work, gathers information on organizing models, and strives to influence policy makers and program developers.

One Wisconsin family child care provider describes what the Worthy Wage Campaign has meant to her and her work:

"I persevere in this field for one single reason: the Worthy Wage movement. It reminds me why I chose this field. I still believe that because of my education and skills, I can influence the lives of the next generation. I can be part of creating a community where individuals care for and about each other and are valued simply for who they are. A community where gender, race, physical abilities and economic status do not define one's potential — a community where life is fair. But it is difficult to do that when my larger community is not fair to me and when my wages are only enough to barely survive. I cannot imagine being part of this profession and *not* being involved in the Worthy Wage Campaign."

The silence has now been broken. Central to whether the Campaign succeeds will be its ability to motivate not only child care workers, but also parents and other caregivers. Those involved in the Campaign, and others deeply concerned about our nation's children and their caregivers, recognize the uphill nature of the road ahead. At issue is the value placed on work performed primarily by women, and on children as vital to our national well-being. ■

Resources: National Child Care Staffing Study, National Center for the Early Childhood Work Force, 1988. The Worthy Wage Campaign and NCECW can be contacted at: 733 15th St. NW, Suite 1037, Washington, DC, (202) 737-7700; *Policy Initiatives to Enhance Child Care Compensation in the Early Childhood Career Lattice*, National Association for the Education of Young Children, 1994.

RENTS OUT OF REACH

Just out of a shelter for homeless families, Harriet and her two young children live in an unsubsidized two-bedroom apartment in Chicago. Her entire monthly income consists of a welfare allotment of $377, plus $129 in Food Stamps and whatever cash local community groups give her. Her largest expense is the rent, $525 a month. Obviously, the numbers don't add up.

Harriet is among the two out of every three low-income renters across the United States who receive no housing assistance. Without such help Harriet and other low-income renters are continually faced with difficult choices between food, utilities, clothing and the rent, not to mention the ever-present threat of eviction. With numbers like Harriet's, it is only a matter of time before she rejoins the more than one million people, 40% of them children, who are homeless on any given night in the United States.

THE SCOPE OF THE CRISIS

Contrary to popular belief, housing unaffordability extends to every geographic region. It affects both working and nonworking households, and all racial and ethnic groups. As wages and government assistance continue to

UNAFFORDABLE RENTS IN CHICAGO

Family Size	Income Sources	Monthly Income	Affordable Rent (30% of income)	Fair Market Rent (FMR)
3 persons	AFDC, food stamps	$510	$153	$704 (2 BRs)
1 person	minimum wage ($5.15/hr)	$825	$250	$591 (1 BR)

decline and housing costs rise, it is harder for people living in poverty to find affordable housing — defined by the Department of Housing and Urban Development (HUD) as total housing costs amounting to less than 30% of a household's income.

Nationwide in 1970 there was a surplus of 900,000 low-rent units (7.4 million units for 6.5 million poor renters). But by 1993 there was a shortage of 4.7 million low-rent homes (6.5 million units for 11.2 million low-income renters). This shortage reflects what low-income people

already know: that rent consumes more and more of their income. At present, three-fifths of low-income households spend at least 50% of their income on housing.

The crisis is due both to falling incomes and rising housing costs. The percentage of people living in poverty increased from 11.6% in 1977 to 15.1% in 1993, partially reflecting declining real values of the minimum wage and welfare cash assistance. Meanwhile, the affordable housing stock has fallen due to decreasing government housing assistance, rising rents, high-end new construction, condominium conversion, neighborhood gentrification and demolition of deteriorating units.

THE FAILING FEDERAL COMMITMENT

The current housing crisis dawned in the early 1970s, as the private market failed to provide sufficient low-cost units. In 1973 there were 5.1 million unsubsidized private units available at low rents, but by 1993 the number of private low-cost units had shrunk to less than 3.0 million nationwide.

At first, Congress increased funding for housing assistance. From 1977 to 1980 HUD provided funds for 290,000 additional low-income units per year. But after 1980 assistance fell at an alarming rate, to a mere 15,000 additional units in 1995. Still, the proportion of low-cost units dependent on federal aid grew from 20% in the early 1970s to 49% by the 1990s.

More households living in poverty, combined with less affordable housing, means that low-income households may have to spend years on waiting lists for subsidized apartments. And only those that meet federal guidelines get priority on the waiting list. If they are not paying more than 50% of their income toward housing costs, living in severe substandard housing or subject to involuntary displacement, they are not likely to ever obtain housing assistance.

THE MINIMUM WAGE VERSUS THE RENT

A large fraction of all low- and moderate-income households cannot afford adequate housing. Using the guideline that affordable rent should be no more than 30% of total income, one-third of all renter households cannot afford a one-bedroom unit, and almost half of all renters cannot pay for a two-bedroom apartment. 47% of renter households in Louisiana, 62% in New York, 47% in Florida and 48% in Oregon do not pay affordable rents.

The inadequate minimum wage contributes to the problem. Neither the current hourly minimum wage of $4.25 or the soon-to-be implemented minimum wage of $5.15 are sufficient to pay affordable rents. In 45 states the minimum wage would have to be doubled, and tripled in many metropolitan areas, to pay the rent. If Harriet took a job at or near minimum wage in Chicago, her current rent would be 46% of her monthly income. She would have to earn $10 an hour to pay, at an affordable level, her $525 rent.

For those trying to survive on AFDC (welfare), the situation is of course worse. Harriet's monthly AFDC check of $377 amounted to only 72% of her current rent, and 58% of Chicago's "Fair Market Rent" (FMR) for a two-bedroom apartment (the FMR is a figure set by the Department of Housing and Urban Development). For states that provide lower AFDC payments the comparison is yet more dire. In Alabama, for example, the $164 maximum monthly grant is only 38% of the state's FMR.

Moreover, the recent federal government decision to severely curtail welfare benefits, combined with cuts in other programs such as Food Stamps, will reduce the overall resources available to the poor. Further clouding the future, for the first time since 1974 Congress allocated zero funding in both 1995 and 1996 budgets for new Section 8 certificates. These government subsidies allow low-income renters to pay 30% of their income to rent private units carrying market-rate rents.

Until there is a political commitment in this country to provide safe, affordable and permanent housing for all, short-range policies will be only band-aids. More and more families like Harriet's will be living on the perpetual edge of homelessness. ■ — *Skip Barry*

Resources: Out of Reach: Can America Pay the Rent?, 1996, National Low-Income Housing Coalition, Washington, DC; *In Short Supply: The Growing Affordable Housing Gap*, 1995, Center on Budget and Policy Priorities, Washington, DC.

June 1993

BUTTING HEADS OVER THE TOBACCO TAX

PRICE HIKES DISCOURAGE DEMAND FOR CIGARETTES

BY LIBERTY ALDRICH

The tobacco industry has a problem: 435,000 of its most loyal customers die every year. Fortunately for the industry, the one million young people who light up for the first time each year more than compensate for this consumer drain. Our government has utterly failed to curtail this deadly cycle.

There is, however, a way out: increasing tobacco taxes will cause a drop in consumption of cigarettes, promoting health and providing revenue to help cover the real costs of smoking. These benefits will more than offset any disproportionate impact that the taxes will have on low-income communities — turning money spent on cigarettes into money spent on good health for everyone.

While the link between smoking and disease stands out as the starkest reason to discourage it through taxation, the strain that it places on our economy should not be shrugged off. Studies have found that the price of cigarettes reflects only a portion of the social cost of tobacco consumption. The remainder is "external" to the price, and consequently imposed on non-smoking society.

This external cost is analogous to the pollution a factory emits into its environment: if the factory is not forced to pay for the harm it causes, then it will not take that into account when it decides how much to produce. Likewise, our society does not force smokers to pay for — and thus consider — the full cost of their decision to smoke. The point is not to make smokers pay for their sins; it is to send them a message, via a price tag, about the real consequences of their habit.

Medical costs are the most frequently cited, and perhaps most easily quantifiable, external costs of smoking. Thomas A. Hodgson, Chief Economist at the National Center for Health Statistics, conducted the most recent study comparing the medical expenditures of smokers to nonsmokers over their life cycles. Even without considering factors other than strictly medical costs, Hodgson got dramatic results: his most conservative estimate indicates that the population of smokers over the age of 25 in 1985 will incur $436 billion in medical costs in *excess* of those of non-smokers, despite the smoker's early death.

Calculations of smoking's cost to society are necessarily very complex and economists have gotten various results totaling up the bill. Proponents of tobacco tax increases frequently cite a 1985 Office of Technology Assessment (OTA) study which concluded that each pack of cigarettes costs $2.17 in external health care and lost productivity costs. A team of economists led by Willard G. Manning of the University of Michigan criticized the OTA study in the *Journal of the American Medical Association*. Arguing that the OTA study was flawed by its failure to reflect the financial benefits that accrue to society when smokers die before they can collect all of their pension and social security benefits, Manning concluded that current levels of tobacco taxation cover smoking's costs.

The very idea that low prices can lead to deaths that are economically beneficial calls into question the economist's project. It is impossible for cheap tobacco to be a benefit to anyone except in the most theoretical economist's head.

On close inspection, the analysis of externalities splinters into question after question. One arises from the assumption that a "rational" actor decides which product he or she values most and proceeds to purchase that product: how can we assume that internalizing costs will send a clear message to a consumer when he or she may be acting according to the dictates of physical and mental addiction, which may not dovetail with his or her notion of the product's value? Another underlies any attempt to analyze externalities: is it sufficient to simply internalize the cost of smoking into the price of a pack of cigarettes and call it a wash?

Studies may not provide the answer here. Calculating external costs can help us to render the economy more sensitive to health concerns, but it has serious limitations. The "internal" factors of death and disease — not externalities — must ultimately compel us to adopt a tax on tobacco.

HOW IT WORKS

A surprising number of smokers do overcome their addiction and make the economically rational decision: they quit when the price goes up. This decrease in consumption is the strongest argument for any tax on tobacco.

The chart reveals precisely how closely changes in price and consumption mirror each other. The American Lung Association has concluded that a 10% increase in cost leads to a 4% reduction in consumption. Increased price works especially well to reduce consumption among groups for whom price is an object — primarily the young and the economically disadvantaged. Teenagers have been shown to respond to fluctuations in price at three times the rate of adults.

There is data galore on this responsiveness. Several states have passed substantial tobacco taxes in the last several years. In 1988, voters ratified California's Proposition 99, which increased tobacco taxes by 25 cents a pack. Cigarette smoking subsequently dropped 17% between 1989 and 1991, about twice the national average. Canada's decision to sharply increase tobacco taxes in the 1980s — from 46 cents in 1980 to $3.27 in 1991 — has had dramatic results: teen-smoking has been reduced by two-thirds. Any argument against tobacco taxes must confront the human implications of these statistics.

THE REAL IMPACT

Many specious arguments have been made in opposition to an increase in the tobacco tax — that it will spawn a "prohibitionesque" black market (virtually everywhere else, cigarettes are much more expensive than in the U.S., so there would be little supply for such a market), and that it will put millions out of work (a sound conversion strategy could solve this problem). But one criticism demands serious attention: that a tobacco tax is regressive. Like other consumption taxes, the tobacco tax would require low-income groups to pay proportionally more than rich people. However, flatfooted rejection of the tax on the grounds that it is regressive puts theory before reality, and turns a blind eye to the specifics of the tobacco situation.

Economists analyzing this question have by and large neglected to consider the overall impact of the tobacco tax, including reduced consumption and the accompanying health and economic benefits to low-income communities. Tobacco taxes save lives — a monumental benefit that distinguishes them from other taxes on consumer goods. In one attempt to fill out the picture, Joy Townsend concluded that, because low-income populations quit at a higher rate in response to price increases, tobacco taxes were actually progressive in the United Kingdom. A similar study has not yet been conducted in the United States.

The tremendous financial and political power of the U.S. tobacco industry has enabled it to stave off taxes to a remarkable degree. As a percentage of pack price, the tobacco tax has dropped dramatically in the past forty years. According to the Tobacco Institute, taxes made up over 50% of the pack price in the late 1960s, and only slightly more than 25% in 1991. This failure to maintain the same percentage of taxes has left the industry plenty of room to raise cigarette prices at almost three times the rate of inflation. The profits reaped by tobacco companies through the sale of cigarettes are virtually unparalleled by profits on any other non-durable products. Philip Morris' recent decision to cut Marlboro's price by 40 cents per pack drew attention to just how much profit it was making — 56 cents on each pack, or almost $5 billion a year.

The poor already suffer an unfair share of smoking's costs in this country because of the tobacco industry's clever "regressive" marketing techniques. Advertising directed at impoverished communities of color has recently ignited organized protests in those communities, but historically, it has met with little resistance and achieved its ends efficiently: 29% of blacks andThe and 31% of Native Americans smoke, as compared to 26% of whites. The industry's favorite targets have little access to health information and care, but would quit in response to price increases. Finely printed messages on cigarette packs may pass unheeded, but a $5 price tag will not. Moreover, the government could earmark the revenue from a tobacco tax to pay for more direct, comprehensive health information for everyone.

Tobacco taxes provide a unique opportunity to tie revenues to programs that directly benefit low-income areas, thereby eliminating any regressive impact that is not already offset by reduced consumption. In California and Massachusetts, voter referenda tied tobacco tax revenue to a variety of such programs, including medical care for the poor.

Progressives oppose regressive taxation because it favors those who have over those who don't — but tobacco taxes benefit everyone. While they should not be considered a substitute for instituting a more equitable income tax code, neither should they be considered inimical to the goal of all progressive change: a fair distribution of society's resources. Health, too, is a resource, and one that our government can do a great deal more to spread around. ■

TOBACCO TAXES HURT LOW-INCOME SMOKERS

BY JOHN STAMM

Bill Clinton has a problem. Throughout his campaign he pushed the health-care crisis button often and hard, and now must deliver on promises of lower costs and universal access. But promises-to-keep don't come cheap: the tab for Clinton's reforms could run as high as $80 billion. And where's a president going to raise cash like that these days? By moving to a single-payer health care system and saving Americans the $200 billion wasted every year by private insurance companies? By raising income taxes on the wealthy to pre-Reagan levels? Or by taxing blue-collar, poor, and less-educated Americans? For Clinton, and many in Washington, the choice is door number three.

The motives behind a "monster" $2 or $3 per pack cigarette tax hike provide clues to its dangers. Does a newfound concern for people killing themselves with tobacco lie at the root of it? Are there new merits to the oft-repeated calls for justice, for smokers to assume the costs they now impose on the rest of society? Or is there simply a new need for cash?

Taxing smokers is easy. Consumption taxes, which usually show up as pennies here and there, are the easiest taxes to slip by voters. And "sin" taxes, alcohol and tobacco excises, are the easiest consumption taxes to sell. No one, except the corporations exploiting them, likes sinners. And smoking, done only by a shrinking minority of addicts, is easier still to tax than alcohol.

There are clearly more equitable ways to raise money. There are also better ways to discourage consumption. Even with well-intentioned efforts to return revenues to the communities they come from, a tobacco tax will inevitably demand most from those who can least afford it.

HOW MEAN IS THIS MONSTER?

Since Surgeon General Luther Terry released the first official warnings in 1964, smoking in the United States has — until this year — been steadily declining. But surveys have consistently shown this decline to be smaller and slower among less-educated Americans.

Studies done for the Center for Disease Control detail these trends. While smoking decreased across all groups between 1974 and 1984, the percentage of college graduates who smoked declined almost five times faster than that of the rest of society. By 1985 18% of college graduates smoked, versus 34%

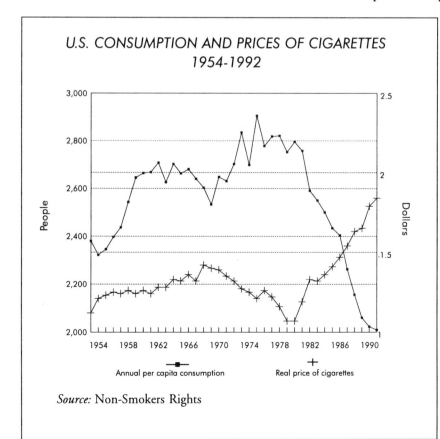

U.S. CONSUMPTION AND PRICES OF CIGARETTES 1954-1992

People / Dollars

- ■ Annual per capita consumption
- + Real price of cigarettes

Source: Non-Smokers Rights

of those who didn't graduate from high school. Most (60%) college graduates who had ever smoked had quit. Only 40% of high school graduates or dropouts had kicked the habit.

Using this data to project American smoking trends to the year 2000, researchers found the education gap widening. They predicted that more than 30% of Americans who do not continue their education past high school will be smoking in the next century, while less than 10% of college graduates will still be lighting up. This three-to-one ratio led the authors to conclude that "smoking in the U.S. is increasingly becoming a behavior primarily of the less educated and the socioeconomically disadvantaged."

Because more people who have less money to pay for the habit are smoking, you would be hard pressed to design a tax that hits our poorest families harder. Numbers published by the Congressional Budget Office show that, on average, families in the lowest-earning fifth spend, as a percentage of income, nearly 8 times more on cigarettes than the wealthiest fifth.

Any monster-sized tax that hit Americans in these proportions would be vicious. To estimate just how vicious, Citizens for Tax Justice (CTJ) started with the figure President Clinton has painted on trial balloons — $35 billion for health care reform. They found that the wealthiest 1% of families would be asked to contribute 0.1% of their income to the cause, while, on average, the middle fifth of wage-earners would cough up 1.1% of their income. For the lowest-earning fifth, CTJ's estimates are staggering: 3.2% of their income would be taken to help fund health care reform. With more than $3 being taken out of every $100 our poorest citizens earn, progressives had better hope this measure fails to raise money.

The poor have already endured years of state excise hikes. Unable to run deficits and faced with voter hostility toward income and property taxes, state and local governments in budget crises have increasingly relied on sales taxes, sin taxes, and fees. Between 1985 and 1990, there were 22 separate increases in state sales taxes and 62 separate increases in state cigarette excises. These increases have piled further demands on the poor just as their real incomes have fallen. On average nationwide, lower and middle income families pay three to four times more of their income on sales and excise taxes than the wealthy, while the poorest 20% spend seven times as much on such taxes as the richest 25%.

Health care is already at the center of these tax hikes, as states point to mushrooming Medicaid budgets as the number one cause of fiscal crisis. The poor, therefore, will pay twice for the health care crisis if Clinton's monster comes a-knocking.

THE SINNERS SHALL PAY

Both Clintons have cited the costs smokers impose on the rest of society as a reason for the monster hit. In February, the President opposed several ideas for new health care taxes, saying "I'm not ready to admit that I think that the people who have paid the bill for health care in the 1980s should turn around and pay more right now." But, when asked about sin taxes and their effects on lower- and middle-class Americans, Clinton thought differently. "Why? Because I think that we are spending a ton of money in private insurance and in government taxpaying to deal with the health care problems occasioned by bad health habits, and particularly smoking."

This concern for what smokers do to the rest of society, not just to themselves, has emerged recently as federal decision-makers' favorite reason to tax smokers. But estimates of these costs — particularly those cited by Clinton and other politicians — fail to separate costs smokers impose on others from the damage they cause themselves. Many studies, such as the oft-cited Office of Technology Assessment 1985 analysis, which estimated annual costs as high as $65 billion, add together both social and personal costs.

But another extensive study, done by Willard G. Manning and a group of economists for the University of Michigan in 1989, focused only on the costs to the rest of "us" — the expenses Clinton means by "a ton of money." Adding up the costs of medical bills, fire damage, and lost output due to sickness, the Rand study found that smokers already pay these costs in the current state and federal excises. Key to this finding is the rather grim truth that, by dying young and quickly, smokers give society their most productive years and leave behind unreceived pension and social security payments.

The distinction between social and personal costs is key to judging Clinton's stand on sin taxes. To sell the tax to the general public, he has emphasized the need to get sinners back for what they're doing to the rest of us. If that's justice, it's already done.

POLICY NOT PUNISHMENT

Some have argued that funnelling revenues back into low-income communities would offset the regressivity of the tobacco tax. Legislative maneuvering could easily derail efforts to do that, but even if they were successful the tax would still follow the past decade's tax path of least resistance and dig deeper into the pockets of our least-educated and least-compensated citizens. There is no erasing its initial regressive impact.

Better arguments in favor of the tax focus on consumption: the potential for curbing smoking is any tobacco tax's greatest asset. But it's possible to value its power to save lives and still ask how many, who will pay the price, and whether we have alternatives.

First of all, it's difficult to predict precise effects on consumption. Smaller excise hikes have reduced the number of smokers by a wide range of 4-7% for every 10% rise in price. If Clinton were to double the price of cigarettes, we could see anywhere from 4 to 7 out of every 10 smokers quit or not start as a result — and anywhere from 3 to 6 smokers left paying the hefty tab.

These projected reductions are small compared to the enormous success public officials and antismoking activists have already realized with methods that do not punish: thirty years of government warnings, advertising restrictions, anti-smoking advertising and education, and restrictions on smoking in public spaces. A 1989 report published in the *American Journal of Public Health* concluded that "in the absence of the anti-smoking campaign, adult per capita cigarette consumption in 1987 would have been an estimated 79-89% higher." The continued damage smoking causes shouldn't obscure the success of these efforts. With this campaign, we have been better able to reduce the damage caused by nicotine than that of any other drug — or any other self-destructive habit — in our society.

Education — not coercion — is the best solution to our smoking ills. We must continue, and intensify, the thirty years of education we have begun. Progressives should not allow punishment to prevail. The politically quiet, captive, and economically disadvantaged victims of the smoking habit should not become Bill Clinton's scapegoats or his cash cows. ■

Resources: Federal Taxation of Tobacco, Alcoholic Beverages, and Motor Fuels, Congressional Budget Office, August 1990; "Trends in Cigarette Smoking in the United States: Projections to the Year 2000" and "Educational Differences are Increasing," John P. Pierce, *Journal of the American Medical Association,* January 6, 1989; "The Taxes of Sin," Willard Manning, *JAMA,* March 17, 1989.

ARTICLE 9   *July/August 1997*

FRINGE BANKS EXPLOIT THE POOR

BY MICHAEL HUDSON

Bennett Roberts, 74, never had it easy. He was brought up on a modest farm in Virginia's Blue Ridge Mountains, and worked for a paving company, an orchard and a quarry. He says he was hoping for a quiet retirement in 1979 when he plunked down his savings and bought himself a little house in a lower-income neighborhood in Charlottesville, Va., a university town two hours south of Washington. But by last year — more than a decade and a half later — he found himself $44,000 in hock on his home.

How this happened is described in a lawsuit filed by the Charlottesville-Albermarle Legal Aid Society. A company named Associates Financial Services talked Roberts into signing a series of 11 mortgages — loans liberally laced with upfront finance charges and closing costs totalling more than $20,000. With each refinancing, his debt grew like a cartoon snowball rolling down a ski slope. On the final refinancing, he pocketed $1,043 in new money but was charged $4,593 in prepaid fees and costs. The mortgages' rates of interest — which reached as high as 18.99% — didn't help matters either.

Roberts, who has lung disease, signs his name with an "X" or in a shaky printed hand. He says the loan officer never read the documents to him; Roberts trusted him. "I just pictured him to be an excellent friend. I found out what kind he was."

The payments got so high Roberts feared he'd lose his home. He tried to find a private attorney who would help him file bankruptcy. No luck. Finally he showed up at the Legal Aid Society with a plastic garbage bag stuffed with loan papers. The lawyers there calculated he was shelling out 73% of his retirement income to cover the monthly house note. They sued Associates, alleging fraud and "undue influence." Last summer Associates — which happens to be a subsidiary of Ford Motor Company — agreed to a confidential settlement that saved Roberts' home for him. The lender denied any wrongdoing, but during negotiations a spokesman said the company sought a settlement because "it's something that we need to do — just to do the right thing."

Bennett Roberts' story is not uncommon. You can go just about anyplace in the country, small town or big, mountain hollow or inner-city neighborhood, and hear the same sort of tale.

These stories are symptoms of economic apartheid in the world's wealthiest nation, a sign that America has two systems of financial services: one for the well-off and middle class, and one for the poor and near poor, black and white, who are struggling to get by from week to week.

These are consumers who for the most part are shut out or ignored by banks and credit-card companies — or who shut themselves out because they feel intimidated or distrustful. Where they go instead is to a growing number of companies that are happy to have their business — pawnshops, easy-credit used-car dealers, "rent-to-own" furniture and appliance dealers, consumer-finance companies, and old-fashioned "tin men" who peddle home repairs.

Most Americans have relationships with banks, but a growing number do not. And they pay a high price for it: as much as 20% interest on mortgages, 240% on pawnshop loans, 36% on finance-company loans, 100% to 300% to buy televisions on the installment plan from rent-to-own stores, and 2,000% — that's no typo — to get a quick "payday loan" from a check-cashing outlet.

The poor have always paid more. But the big change today is that the businesses that operate in the fringe economy are more and more funded or owned by some of the nation's largest corporations. They include NationsBank, BankAmerica, Citicorp, American Express, Western Union, and, until recently, ITT and New England's largest bank, Fleet Financial Group.

Not everyone who does business with the poor is a greedy exploiter. Few would argue that lenders shouldn't be able to charge higher rates to cover what are clearly the higher risks and costs of doing business with customers who have shaky credit histories or unstable incomes. But it's clear that the poor frequently pay many times more than what it takes to recoup the legitimate costs of providing them financial services. They are frequent targets of fraud and high-pressure sales tactics.

Here are a few examples of the big-name companies that apparently engaged in fraud and other illegal activities in the fringe market:

• Associates Financial Services, the same Ford subsidiary that ripped off Bennett Roberts, agreed to pay nearly $3.4 million to settle a private lawsuit and an Arizona attorney general's investigation involving about 8,000 borrowers. The company was accused of illegally manipulating borrowers into buying high-priced insurance with their loans.

• Another Ford subsidiary, First Family Financial Services, agreed to pay an estimated $3.5 million to about 2,500 customers to settle allegations that it had paid kickbacks to mortgage brokers to encourage them to steer borrowers into higher-cost loans.

• ITT Corp. got out of the high-rate loan business after it was forced to pay more than $80 million to settle lawsuits and state investigations accusing it of fraud, insurance sales abuses and other violations involving hundreds of thousands of customers.

• Fleet Financial Group sold off its high-cost mortgage subsidiary after being forced to pay more than $280 million in settlements of lawsuits alleging predatory pricing and sales practices. In Georgia alone, the allegations involved up to 20,000 borrowers.

Despite the lawsuits, big companies moved into the "fringe economy" at a dizzying pace because they knew there was money to be made. One study of high-cost finance companies in Virginia found that their return on assets — a standard measure of profitability — was more than double that earned by state-chartered banks. Associates First Capital Corp., which operates Ford's downscale lending units, has more than 1,400 loan offices nationwide. In 1995, it earned pre-tax profits of just under $1.2 billion. By most estimates, the market for high-cost financial services to downscale consumers now tops $300 billion a year (see sidebar).

The nation's highest paid corporate chief executive is Larry Coss, CEO of Green Tree Financial Co. in St. Paul, Minn., a company that specializes in making higher-risk loans on mobile homes. He was paid $65.6 million in 1995 and $102 million in 1996. Green Tree's stock is among the best-performing on the New York Stock Exchange; its value has increased at a startling annual rate of 53% over the past five years.

THE POVERTY INDUSTRY

America's "poverty industry" began its dramatic rise little more than 15 years ago. It has become an increasing presence on America's street corners — and on Wall Street's trading floors:

• Since the early 1980s, the number of pawnshops across the nation has doubled to more than 10,000 and more are owned by Wall Street. By 1991, pawnshops were making about 42 million loans a year, totaling perhaps $3.3 billion.

• The number of check-cashing outlets has more than tripled since the late 1980s to an estimated 5,500. Conservative estimates are that these institutions cashed 128 million checks (totaling $38 billion) in 1990, taking in an estimated $700 million in fees. The nation's leading publicly traded chain of check cashers, ACE Cash Express, has expanded to more than 680 outlets with an infusion of capital from American Express.

• The number of rent-to-own stores has grown from 2,000 to 7,500 since the early 1980s. The industry's trade association estimates that rent-to-own is now a $4 billion a year market. The industry's leading chain, Rent-A-Center, is owned by Thorn EMI, a British conglomerate that also owns EMI Records.

• The market for auto loans to "high-risk" borrowers has become crowded with Wall Street companies. Stock analysts estimate it is now a $70 billion a year market.

• Analysts estimate that the market for high-rate mortgages to consumers with low incomes or flawed credit records may soon exceed $120 billion a year. Subsidiaries of NationsBank and Ford Motor Co. are leaders in this market.

• Consumer-finance loans — smaller, higher interest loans not secured by real estate — exceed $100 billion a year. NationsBank and Ford are major players here also.

Why is the financial "poverty industry" growing so quickly? There are several reasons. Increasing poverty and continued immigration since the early 1980s has helped increase the market for downscale financial services. More middle-income people are falling on hard times, hurt by "downsizing," escalating medical costs, and the growth in household debt (which resulted in a record 1.1 million personal bankruptcies in 1996). At the same time, the savings and loan feeding frenzy shuttered many once community-minded institutions that made meat-and-potatoes home and car loans. Meanwhile, merger-happy banks are driving lower-income customers away by closing neighborhood branches and hiking their fees to nose-bleed levels.

For their part, fringe financial institutions like Green Tree have taken advantage of both weakened consumer-protection laws and an infusion of Wall Street growth money — cash that has helped them use increasingly sophisticated marketing techniques to lure in customers. They're people like Tonya Cross, a mother of four in Roanoke, Va. She spent thousands of dollars trying to buy appliances on time from rent-to-own stores that charge three to four times more than retailers like Sears. She knew it was costly. But she told me that rent-to-own dealers' "easy weekly payment plans" were the only alternative for people like herself with bad credit and small incomes. Invariably, she'd pay a few hundred dollars in rental payments, then fall behind and lose the merchandise before she could take over ownership. But she kept trying: "The reality of it — you can't afford it any other way. If you want it, you're gonna have to get it from somewhere."

Often the advertising messages beamed at the poor follow along these lines: "You can have it now!" "You can have it all!" and "Make your dreams come true!" I was driving on Interstate 465 around Indianapolis a few years ago when I spotted a billboard advertising "Instant Auto Loans" with "No Credit Checks." In big letters over the top it said: "We Believe In You."

Low-income and minority consumers are often driven to these types of businesses by the racial and class discrimination that still flourishes in our economy. Despite years of neighborhood activism, newspaper exposes and legislation, banks are still more likely to reject loan applications from blacks than whites. This is true even when their incomes and credit histories are similar, according to a 1992 study by the Federal Reserve Bank of Boston.

All the discrimination in the marketplace can do further harm to the damaged sense of self-worth that many poor or minority citizens may carry. We live in a society where politicians and the news media are constantly putting them down, using them as scapegoats for most of the nation's problems.

Some entrepreneurs have used this "self-esteem" problem as a marketing strategy. Pawnshops and easy-credit appliance stores have long had bad reputations. People have the image of dingy, dim places with surly storekeep-

---

LOAN SHARKS IGNORED

Just how effectively are usury laws enforced? I took a look at the pawn industry in Virginia recently to find out whether it was following the state's legal limits — 5% a month for loans over $100, which works out to an annual percentage rate of 60%.

I checked 31 pawnshops around the state and found just four that seemed to consistently follow the law. Of the rest, 18 appeared to be charging around twice the legal rate; nine appeared to be charging three to four times the legal rate, with annual percentage rates as high as 240%.

At that top rate, a $150 loan that isn't paid off for one year would cost $360 in interest. The typical credit-card customer would pay between $25 and $30 to borrow that much for the same period. Some card holders might pay as little as $10.

---

ers, protected by wire cages or steel bars over the counter. But this is changing. In the early 1980s, a Texas pawnbroker named Jack Daugherty had a brilliant idea. What if someone were to clean up the pawn industry, make pawnshops look fresh and bright like a Sears and make sure the clerks were neat and courteous? In short, what if people didn't feel like they had to *slink* into a pawn shop?

He tried it, and it worked. Now Daugherty has a chain of more than 380 pawnshops across the United States. He calls his company Cash America, and it's traded on the New York Stock Exchange.

The Wall Street Journal has called this sort of marketing plan "merchandising respect." The rent-to-own stores that have replaced easy-credit furniture and TV stores have also worked hard to project a color-coordinated, well-scrubbed image. One chain, Rent-A-Center, has more than 1,000 stores nationwide. It says it's trying to clean up the repossession and collection abuses and other questionable tactics in the rent-to-own business.

The one thing that hasn't changed is the prices customers pay. Cash America charges an average interest rate of around 200% on its pawn loans. At Rent-A-Center and other rent-to-own stores, customers typically pay $1,000 or $1,200 in rental payments to buy a $300 TV. Many will pay a few hundred dollars, and then fall behind and lose their merchandise — and every cent they've paid. By the rent-to-own industry's own statistics, customers have only about a one-in-five to one-in-four chance of ending up with ownership of the merchandise.

Can something be done to fight back against businesses that profit from the misfortune of the nation's poorest and least-educated citizens? Part of the problem is that many people think that they don't have a choice, or that fighting back won't do any good. I've interviewed a distressing number of people who'd been taken in by shady home-repair contractors working hand-in-hand with big national loan companies. These homeowners are often ashamed. At first, many minimize what has happened to them. But often as they talk, they let their anger and sense of betrayal come out. One woman called it "a learning experience" but, as she kept talking, she recalled how the vinyl siding contractor had tricked her into signing a mortgage against her house. She said she was almost in tears when she realized it. But she didn't put up a fight, because she had signed the papers and the siding was already on her house: "Then you couldn't complain, could you? You couldn't say: 'Well, take it off.'"

Many of these scam victims seemed to think that they were all alone — that it was their fault and that they had somehow brought their problems on themselves. One woman who had been ripped off by a large national loan company told her lawyer that she didn't want to sue, even if she could win. "God will take care of it," she said.

But a lot of people have started to fight back. Legal Aid attorneys and private lawyers have begun filing big-dollar lawsuits against predatory financial companies, and community activists around the country have been organizing victims to speak out and compel media attention and legislative reforms. For instance, legislatures can compel enforcement of usury laws that limit how much interest a financial insti-

tution can charge. In Augusta, Ga., the Rev. Minnie Davis was able to organize more than 300 people to march on the state capital demanding that the state do something about Fleet Finance. Even though the subsidary of New England's largest bank was accused of ripping off black homeowners, it still took a while to get started, Davis said. "They were ashamed at first. Because nobody was saying anything. When other people start speaking out, they kind of overcome their shyness and say, 'That's happened to me too. You need to do something to help these people.'"

One older Atlanta homeowner, Dorothy Thrasher, testified before the Georgia legislature about how two vinyl siding salesmen had pressured her into signing a 23% mortgage with Fleet Finance. The legislature tightened regulation of the mortgage industry somewhat, but killed most of the reforms pushed by advocates for low-income homeowners. Despite that, Mrs. Thrasher thought it had been worth the trouble. "I feel like one day some good will come out of it. You can't keep mistreating people and have the problem ignored forever. God doesn't let good people suffer and suffer without no justice." ∎

Resources. Fringe Banking: Check-Cashing Outlets, Pawnshops, and the Poor, John P. Caskey, Russell Sage Foundation, 1994; "Dirty Deeds: Abuses and Fraudulent Practices in California's Home Equity Market," Norma Paz Garcia, San Francisco Regional Office, Consumers Union, October 1995; *Merchants of Misery: How Corporate America Profits from Poverty,* Michael Hudson, editor, Common Courage Press, 1996; "Sub-Prime Time," Adam Zagorin, *Time* magazine, Nov. 4, 1996.

ARTICLE 10   *November 1989*

SHAKING THE INVISIBLE HAND

THE UNCERTAIN FOUNDATIONS OF FREE-MARKET ECONOMICS

BY CHRIS TILLY

"It is not from the benevolence of the butcher, the brewer or the baker that we expect our dinner, but from their regard to their own interest...[No individual] intends to promote the public interest... [rather, he is] led by an invisible hand to promote an end which was no part of his intention."
Adam Smith, *The Wealth of Nations,* 1776

Seen the Invisible Hand lately? It's all around us these days, propping up conservative arguments in favor of free trade, deregulation, and tax-cutting.

Today's advocates for "free," competitive markets echo Adam Smith's claim that unfettered markets translate the selfish pursuit of individual gain into the greatest benefit for all. They trumpet the superiority of capitalist free enterprise over socialist efforts to supplant the market with a planned economy, and even decry liberal attempts to moderate the market. Anything short of competitive markets, they proclaim, yields economic inefficiency, making society worse off.

But the economic principle underlying this fanfare is shaky indeed. Since the late 19th century, mainstream economists have struggled to prove that Smith was right — that the chaos of free markets leads to a blissful economic order. In the 1950s, U.S. economists Kenneth Arrow and Gerard Debreu finally came up with a theoretical proof, which many orthodox economists view as the centerpiece of modern economic theory.

Although this proof is the product of the best minds of mainstream economics, it ends up saying surprisingly little in defense of free markets. The modern theory of the Invisible Hand shows that given certain assumptions, free markets reduce the wasteful use of economic resources — but perpetuate unequal income distribution.

To prove free markets cut waste, economists must make a number of farfetched assumptions: there are no concentrations of economic power; buyers and sellers know every detail about the present and future economy; and all costs of production are borne by producers while all benefits from consumption are paid for by consumers (see box for a complete list). Take away any one of these assumptions and markets can lead to stagnation, recession, and other forms of waste — as in fact they do.

In short, the economic theory invoked by conservatives to justify free markets instead starkly reveals their limitations.

THE FRUITS OF FREE MARKETS

The basic idea behind the Invisible Hand can be illustrated with a story. Suppose that I grow apples and you grow oranges. We both grow tired of eating the same fruit all the time and decide to trade. Perhaps we start by trading one apple for one orange. This exchange satisfies both of us, because in fact I would gladly give up more than one apple to get an orange, and you would readily pay more than one orange for an apple. And as long as

ASSUMPTIONS AND REALITY

The claim that free markets lead to efficiency and reduced waste rests on seven main assumptions. However, these assumptions differ sharply from economic reality. (Assumptions 1, 3, 4, and are discussed in more detail in the article.)

ASSUMPTION ONE: No market power. No individual buyer or seller, nor any group of buyers or sellers, has the power to affect the market-wide level of prices, wages, or profits.

REALITY ONE: Our economy is dotted with centers of market power, from large corporations to unions. Furthermore, employers have an edge in bargaining with workers because of the threat of unemployment.

ASSUMPTION TWO: No economies of scale. Small plants can produce as cheaply as large ones.

REALITY TWO: In fields such as mass-production industry, transportation, communications, and agriculture, large producers enjoy a cost advantage, limiting competition.

ASSUMPTION THREE: Perfect information about the present. Buyers and sellers know everything there is to know about the goods being exchanged. Also, each is aware of the wishes of every other potential buyer and seller in the market.

REALITY THREE: The world is full of lemons — goods about which the buyer is inadequately informed. Also, people are not mind-readers, so sellers get stuck with surpluses and willing buyers are unable to find the products they want.

ASSUMPTION FOUR: Perfect information about the future. Contracts between buyers and sellers cover every possible future eventuality.

REALITY FOUR: Uncertainty clouds the future of any economy. Futures markets are limited.

ASSUMPTION FIVE: You only get what you pay for. Nobody can impose a cost on somebody else, nor obtain a benefit from them, without paying.

REALITY FIVE: In a free market, polluters can impose costs on the rest of us without paying. And when a public good like a park is built or roads are maintained, everyone benefits whether or not they helped to pay for it.

ASSUMPTION SIX: Self-interest. In economic matters, each person cares only about his or her own level of well-being.

REALITY SIX: Solidarity, jealousy, and even love for one's family violate this assumption.

ASSUMPTION SEVEN: No joint production. Each production process has only one product.

REALITY SEVEN: Even in an age of specialization, there are plenty of exceptions to this rule. For example, large service firms such as hospitals or universities produce a variety of different services using the same resources.

swapping one more apple for one more orange makes us both better off, we will continue to trade.

Eventually, the trading will come to a stop. I begin to notice that the novelty of oranges wears old as I accumulate a larger pile of them and the apples I once had a surplus of become more precious to me as they grow scarcer. At some point, I draw the line: in order to obtain one more apple from me, you must give me more than one orange. But your remaining oranges have also become more valuable to you. Up to now, each successive trade has made both of us better off. Now there is no further exchange that benefits us both, so we agree to stop trading until the next crop comes in.

Note several features of this parable. Both you and I end up happier by trading freely. If the government stepped in and limited fruit trading, neither of us would be as well off. In fact, the government cannot do anything in the apple/orange market that will make both of us better off than does the free market.

Adding more economic actors, products, money, and costly production processes complicates the picture, but we reach the same conclusions. Most of us sell our labor time in the market rather than fruit; we sell it for money that we then use to buy apples, oranges, and whatever else we need. The theory of the Invisible Hand tells us a trip to the fruit stand improves the lot of both consumer and seller; likewise, the sale of labor time benefits both employer and employee. What's more, according to the theory, competition between apple farmers insures that consumers will get apples produced at the lowest possible cost. Government intervention still can only make things worse.

This fable provides a ready-made policy guide. Substitute "Japanese autos" and "U.S. agricultural products" for apples and oranges, and the fable tells you that import quotas or tariffs only make the people of both countries worse off. Change the industries to airlines or telephone services, and the fable calls for deregulation. Or re-tell the tale in the labor market: minimum wages and unions (which prevent workers from individually bargaining over their wages) hurt employers and workers.

FRUIT SALAD

Unfortunately for free-market boosters, two major shortcomings make a fruit salad out of this story. First, even if free markets perform as advertised, they deliver only one benefit — the prevention of certain economically wasteful practices — while preserving inequality. According to the theory, competitive markets wipe out two kinds of waste: unrealized trades and inefficient production. Given the right assumptions, markets ensure that when two parties both stand to gain from a trade, they make that trade, as in the apples-and-oranges story. Competition compels producers to search for the most efficient, lowest-cost production methods — again, given the right preconditions.

Though eliminating waste is a worthy goal, it leaves economic inequality untouched. Returning once more to the orchard, if I start out with all of the apples and oranges and you start out with none, that situation is free of waste: no swap can make us both better off since you have nothing to trade! Orthodox economists acknowledge that even in the ideal competitive market, those who start out rich stay rich, while the poor remain poor. Many of them argue that attempts at redistributing income will most certainly create economic inefficiencies, justifying the preservation of current inequities.

But in real-life economics, competition does lead to waste. Companies wastefully duplicate each other's research and build excess productive capacity. Cost-cutting often leads to shoddy products, worker speedup, and unsafe working conditions. People and factories stand idle while houses go unbuilt and people go unfed. That's because of the second major problem: real economies don't match the assumptions of the Invisible Hand theory.

Of course, all economic theories build their arguments on a set of simplifying assumptions about the world. These assumptions often sacrifice some less important aspects of reality in order to focus on the economic mechanisms of interest. But in the case of the Invisible Hand, the theoretical preconditions contradict several central features of the economy.

For one thing, markets are only guaranteed to prevent waste if the economy runs on "perfect competition": individual sellers compete by cutting prices, individual buyers compete by raising price offers, and nobody holds concentrated economic power. But today's giant corporations hardly match this description. Coke and Pepsi compete with advertising rather than price cuts. The oil companies keep prices high enough to register massive profits every year. Employers coordinate the pay and benefits they offer to avoid bidding up compensation. Workers, in turn, marshal their own forces via unionization — another departure from perfect competition.

Indeed, the jargon of "perfect competition" overlooks the fact that property ownership itself confers disproportionate economic power. "In the competitive model," orthodox economist Paul Samuelson commented, "it makes no difference whether capital hires labor or the other way around." He argued that given perfect competition among workers and among capitalists, wages and profits would remain the same regardless of who does the hiring. But unemployment — a persistent feature of market-driven economies — makes job loss very costly to workers. The sting my boss feels when I "fire" him by quitting my job hardly equals the setback I experience when he fires me.

PERFECT INFORMATION?

In addition, the grip of the Invisible Hand is only sure if all buyers and sellers have "perfect information" about the present and future state of markets. In the present, this implies consumers know exactly what they are buying — an assumption hard to swallow in these days of leaky breast implants and chicken a la Salmonella. Employers must know exactly what skills workers have and how hard they will work — suppositions any real-life manager would laugh at.

Perfect information also means sellers can always sniff out unsatisfied demands, and buyers can detect any excess supplies of goods. Orthodox economists rely on the metaphor of an omnipresent "auctioneer" who is always calling out prices so all buyers and sellers can find mutually agreeable prices and consummate every possible sale. But in the actual economy, the auctioneer is nowhere to be found, and markets are plagued by surpluses and shortages.

Perfect information about the future is even harder to come by. For example, a company decides whether or not to build a new plant based on whether it expects sales to rise. But predicting future demand is a tricky matter. One reason is that people may save money today in order to buy (demand) goods and services in the future. The problem comes in predicting when. As economist John Maynard Keynes observed in 1934, "An act of individual saving means — so to speak — a decision not to have dinner today. But it does not necessitate a decision to have dinner or to buy a pair of boots a week hence... or to consume any specified thing at any specified date. Thus it depresses the business of preparing today's dinner without stimulating the business of making ready for some future act of consumption." Keynes concluded that far from curtailing waste, free markets gave rise to the colossal waste of human and economic resources that was the Great Depression — in part because of this type of uncertainty about the future.

FREE LUNCH

The dexterity of the Invisible Hand also depends on the principle that "You only get what you pay for." This "no free lunch" principle seems at first glance a reasonable description of the economy. But major exceptions arise. One is what economists call "externalities" — economic transactions that take place outside the market. Consider a hospital that dumps syringes at sea. In effect, the hospital gets a free lunch by passing the costs of waste disposal on to the rest of us. Because no market exists where the right to dump is bought and sold, free markets do nothing to compel the hospital to bear the costs of dumping — which is why the government must step in.

Public goods such as sewer systems also violate the "no free lunch" rule. Once the sewer system is in place, everyone shares in the benefits of the waste disposal, regardless of whether or not they helped pay for it. Suppose sewer systems were sold in a free market, in which each person had the opportunity to buy an individual share. Then any sensible, self-interested consumer would hold back from buying his or her fair share — and wait for others to provide the service. This irrational situation would persist unless consumers could somehow collectively agree on how extensive a sewer system to produce — once more bringing government into the picture.

Most orthodox economists claim that the list of externalities and public goods in the economy is short and easily addressed. Liberals and radicals, on the other hand, offer a long list: for example, public goods include education, health care, and decent public transportation— all in short supply in our society.

Because real markets deviate from the ideal markets envisioned in the theory of the Invisible Hand, they give us both inequality and waste. But if the theory is so far off the mark, why do mainstream economists and policymakers place so much stock in it? They fundamentally believe the profit motive is the best guide for the economy. If you believe that "What's good for General Motors is good for the USA," the Invisible Hand theory can seem quite reasonable. Business interests, government, and the media constantly reinforce this belief, and reward those who can dress it up in theoretical terms. As long as capital remains the dominant force in society, the Invisible Hand will maintain its grip on the hearts and minds of us all. ∎

CHAPTER 3
Consumers

ARTICLE 11   *June 1991*

ENOUGH IS ENOUGH

WHY MORE IS NOT NECESSARILY BETTER THAN LESS

BY ALAN DURNING

"Our enormously productive economy... demands that we make consumption our way of life, that we convert the buying and use of goods into rituals, that we seek our spiritual satisfaction, our ego satisfaction, in consumption... We need things consumed, burned up, worn out, replaced, and discarded at an ever increasing rate."
         Victor Lebow, U.S. retailing analyst, 1955

Across the country, Americans have responded to Victor Lebow's call, and around the globe, those who could afford it have followed. And many can: Worldwide, on average, a person today is four-and-a-half times richer than were his or her great-grandparents at the turn of the century.

Needless to say, that new global wealth is not evenly spread among the earth's people. One billion live in unprecedented luxury; one billion live in destitution. Overconsumption by the world's fortunate is an environmental problem unmatched in severity by anything except perhaps population growth. Surging exploitation of resources threatens to exhaust or unalterably disfigure forests, soils, water, air, and climate. High consumption may be a mixed blessing in human terms, too. Many in the industrial lands have a sense that, hoodwinked by a consumerist culture, they have been fruitlessly attempting to satisfy social, psychological, and spiritual needs with material things.

Of course, the opposite of overconsumption — poverty — is no solution to either environmental or human problems. It is infinitely worse for people and bad for the natural world. Dispossessed peasants slash and burn their way into Latin American rain forests, and hungry nomads turn their herds out onto fragile African range land, reducing it to desert. If environmental destruction results when people have either too little or too much, we are left to wonder how much is enough. What level of consumption can the earth support? When does having more cease to add appreciably to human satisfaction?

THE CONSUMING SOCIETY

Consumption is the hallmark of our era. The headlong advance of technology, rising earnings, and cheaper material goods have lifted consumption to levels never dreamed of a century ago. In the United States, the world's premier consuming society, people today on average own twice as many cars, drive two-and-a-half times as far, and travel 25 times further by air than did their parents in 1950. Air conditioning spread from 15% of households in 1960 to 64% in 1987, and color televisions from 1% to 93%. Microwave ovens and video cassette recorders reached almost two-thirds of American homes during the 1980s alone.

Japan and Western Europe have displayed parallel trends. Per person, the Japanese today consume more than four times as much aluminum, almost five times as much energy, and 25 times as much steel as they did in 1950. They also own four times as many cars and eat nearly twice as much meat. Like the Japanese, Western Europeans' consumption levels are only one notch below Americans'.

The late 1980s saw some poor societies begin the transition to consuming ways. In China, the sudden surge in spending on consumer durables shows up clearly in data from the State Statistical Bureau: Between 1982 and 1987, color televisions spread from 1% to 35% of urban Chinese homes, washing machines quadrupled from 16% to 67%, and refrigerators expanded their reach from 1% to 20%.

Few would begrudge anyone the simple advantages of cold food storage or mechanized clothes washing. The point, rather, is that even the oldest non-Western nations are emulating the high-consumption lifestyle. Long before all the world's people could achieve the American dream, however, we would lay waste the planet.

The industrial world's one billion meat eaters, car drivers, and throwaway consumers are responsible for the lion's share of the damage humans have caused common global resources.Over the past century, the economies of the wealthiest fifth of humanity have pumped out two-thirds of the greenhouse gases threatening the earth's climate, and each year their energy use releases three-fourths of the sulfur and nitrogen oxides causing acid rain. Their industries generate most of the world's hazardous chemical wastes, and their air conditioners, aerosol sprays, and factories release almost 90% of the chlorofluorocarbons destroying the earth's protective ozone layer. Clearly, even one billion profligate consumers is too much for the earth.

Beyond the environmental costs of acquisitiveness, some perplexing findings of social scientists throw doubt on the wisdom of high consumption as a personal and national goal: Rich societies have had little success in turning consumption into fulfillment. Regular surveys by the National Opinion Research Center of the University of Chicago reveal, for example, that no more Americans report they are "very happy" now than in 1957.

Likewise, a landmark study by sociologist Richard Easterlin in 1974 revealed that Nigerians, Filipinos, Panamanians, Yugoslavians, Japanese, Israelis, and West Germans all ranked themselves near the middle of a happiness scale. Confounding any attempt to correlate affluence and happiness, poor Cubans and rich Americans were both found to be considerably happier than the norm.

If the effectiveness of consumption in providing personal fulfillment is questionable, perhaps environmental concerns can help us redefine our goals.

IN SEARCH OF SUFFICIENCY

By examining current consumption patterns, we receive some guidance on what the earth can sustain. For three of the most ecologically important types of consumption — transportation, diet, and use of raw materials — the world's people are distributed unevenly over a vast range. Those at the bottom clearly fall below the "too little" line, while those at the top, in the cars-meat-and-disposables class, clearly consume too much.

Approximately one billion people do their traveling, aside from the occasional donkey or bus ride, on foot. Unable to get to jobs easily, attend school, or bring their complaints before government offices, they are severely hindered by the lack of transportation options.

Another three billion people travel by bus and bicycle. Kilometer for kilometer, bikes are cheaper than any other vehicle, costing less than $100 new in most of the Third World and requiring no fuel.

The world's automobile class is relatively small: Only 8% of humans, about 400 million people, own cars. The automobile makes itself indispensable: Cities sprawl, public transit atrophies, shopping centers multiply, workplaces scatter.

The global food consumption ladder has three rungs. According to the latest World Bank estimates, the world's 630 million poorest people are unable to provide themselves with a healthy diet. On the next rung, the 3.4 billion grain eaters of the world's middle class get enough calories and plenty of plant-based protein, giving them the world's healthiest basic diet.

The top of the ladder is populated by the meat eaters, those who obtain close to 40% of their calories from fat. These 1.25 billion people eat three times as much fat per person as the remaining four billion, mostly because they eat so much red meat. The meat class pays the price of its diet in high death rates from the so-called diseases of affluence — heart disease, stroke, and certain types of cancer.

The earth also pays for the high-fat diet. Indirectly, the meat-eating quarter of humanity consumes nearly 40% of the world's grain — grain that fattens the livestock they eat. Meat production is behind a substantial share of the environmental strains induced by agriculture, from soil erosion to overpumping of underground water.

In consumption of raw materials, such as steel, cotton, or wood, the same pattern emerges. A large group lacks many of the benefits provided by modest use of nonrenewable resources — particularly durables like radios, refrigerators, water pipes, tools, and carts with lightweight wheels and ball bearings. More than two billion people live in countries where per capita consumption of steel, the most basic modern material, falls below 50 kilograms a year.

Roughly 1.5 billion live in the middle class of materials use. Providing each of them with durable goods every year uses between 50 and 150 kilograms of steel. At the top of the heap is the industrial world or the throwaway class. A typical resident of the industrialized fourth of the world uses 15 times as much paper, 10 times as much steel, and 12 times as much fuel as a Third World resident.

In the throwaway economy, packaging becomes an end in itself, disposables proliferate, and durability suffers. Americans toss away 180 million razors annually, enough paper and plastic plates and cups to feed the world a picnic six times a year, and enough aluminum cans to make 6,000 DC-10 airplanes. Similarly, the Japanese use 30 million "disposable" single-roll cameras each year, and the British dump 2.5 billion diapers.

THE CULTIVATION OF NEEDS

What prompts us to consume so much? "The avarice of mankind is insatiable," wrote Aristotle 23 centuries ago. As each of our desires is satisfied, a new one appears in its place. All of economic theory is based on that observation.

What distinguishes modern consuming habits, some would say, is simply that we are much richer than our ancestors, and consequently have more ruinous effects on nature. While a great deal of truth lies in that view, five distinctly modern factors play a role in cultivating particularly voracious appetites: the influence of social pressures in mass societies, advertising, the shopping culture, various government policies, and the expansion of the mass market into households and local communities.

In advanced industrial nations, daily interactions with the economy lack the face-to-face character prevailing in surviving local communities. Traditional virtues such as integrity, honesty, and skill are too hard to measure to serve as yardsticks of social worth. By default, they are gradually supplanted by a simple, single indicator — money. As one Wall Street banker put it bluntly to the *New York Times*, "Net worth equals self-worth."

Beyond social pressures, the affluent live completely enveloped in pro-consumption advertising messages. The sales pitch is everywhere. One analyst estimates that the typical American is exposed to 50-100 advertisements each morning before nine o'clock. Along with their weekly 22-hour diet of television, American teenagers are typically exposed to three to four hours of TV advertisements a week, adding up to at least 100,000 ads between birth and high school graduation.

Advertising has been one of the fastest growing industries during the past half-century. In the United States, ad expenditures rose from $198 per capita in 1950 to $498 in 1989. Worldwide, over the same period, per person advertising expenditures grew from $15 to $46. In developing countries, the increases have been astonishing. Advertising billings in India jumped fivefold in the 1980s; newly industrialized South Korea's advertising industry grew 35-40% annually in the late 1980s.

Government policies also play a role in promoting consumption and in worsening its ecological impact. The British tax code, for example, encourages businesses to buy thousands of large company cars for employee use. Most governments in North and South America subsidize beef production on a massive scale.

Finally, the sweeping advance of the commercial mass market into realms once dominated by family members and local enterprise has made consumption far more wasteful than in the past. More and more, flush with cash but pressed for time, households opt for the questionable "conveniences" of prepared, packaged foods, miracle cleaning products, and disposable everything — from napkins to shower curtains. All these things cost the earth dearly.

Like the household, the community economy has atrophied — or been dismembered — under the blind force of the money economy. Shopping malls, superhighways, and strips have replaced corner stores, local restaurants, and neighborhood theaters — the very places that help create a sense of common identity and community. Traditional Japanese vegetable stands and fish shops are giving way to supermarkets and convenience stores, and styrofoam and plastic film have replaced yesterday's newspaper as fish wrap.

All these things nurture the acquisitive desires that everyone has. Can we, as individuals and as citizens, act to confront these forces?

THE CULTURE OF PERMANENCE

The basic value of a sustainable society, the ecological equivalent of the Golden Rule, is simple: Each generation should meet its own needs without jeopardizing the prospects of future generations to meet theirs.

For individuals, the decision to live a life of sufficiency — to find their own answer to the question "how much is enough?" — is to begin a highly personal process. Social researcher Duane Elgin estimated in 1981 — perhaps optimistically — that 10 million adult Americans were experimenting "wholeheartedly" with voluntary simplicity. India, the Netherlands, Norway, Western Germany, and the United Kingdom all have small segments of their populations who adhere to a non-consuming philosophy. Motivated by the desire to live justly in an unjust world, to walk gently on the earth, and to avoid distraction, clutter, and pretense, their goal is not ascetic self-denial but personal fulfillment. They do not think consuming more is likely to provide it.

Realistically, voluntary simplicity is unlikely to gain ground rapidly against the onslaught of consumerist values. And, ultimately, personal restraint will do little if not wedded to bold political and social steps against the forces promoting consumption. Commercial television, for example, will need fundamental reorientation in a culture of permanence. As religious historian Robert Bellah put it, "That happiness is to be attained through limitless material acquisition is denied by every religion and philosophy known to humankind, but is preached incessantly by every American television set."

Direct incentives for overconsumption are also essential targets for reform. If goods' prices reflected something closer to the environmental cost of their production, through revised subsidies and tax systems, the market itself would guide consumers toward less damaging forms of consumption. Disposables and packaging would rise in price relative to durable, less-packaged goods; local unprocessed food would fall in price relative to prepared products trucked from far away.

The net effect might be lower overall consumption as people's effective purchasing power declined. As currently constituted, unfortunately, economies penalize the poor when aggregate consumption contracts: Unemployment skyrockets and inequalities grow. Thus arises one of the greatest challenges for sustainable economics in rich societies — finding ways to ensure basic employment opportunities for all without constantly stoking the fires of economic growth. ■

September 1997

MARKETING POWER

BY DAVID KIRON

On any given day, 18 billion display ads appear in magazines and daily newspapers across the United States. In consumer cultures like the United States, the urge to buy is sanctioned, reinforced, and exaggerated in ways so numerous, so enticing, so subtle, that ignoring them is not an easy option. The sales message is perhaps nowhere more vivid and insistent than on television. And with credit more widely available, buying is easy, its consequences distant. The cumulative impact on the psyche of all this urging and buying is never fixed as dissatisfaction recurs with each reminder that the goods we have are not good enough.

And the reminders are everywhere, the long tentacles of marketing now intrude upon nearly every aspect of modern life. From the perspective of economics, this is all for the best. Economic theory assumes that advertising is simply a benign provision of information that consumers use when they make decisions in the marketplace. But the reality is that marketers seldom offer consumers product information with which to make informed decisions. Instead marketers go for the consumer's jugular, targeting their beliefs, emotions, and desires. Manufacturers spend millions to place their products in movies, not to inform consumers, but to link their products with entertainment mega-hits. Nike pays sports stars like Michael Jordan and Tiger Woods to associate their success with its brand-name in the hope that consumer fascination with celebrities will carry to the Nike label. Marketers also take aim at the most basic of consumer desires, such as those for identity, status, and self-esteem, but offer little hope of satisfying them. Most consumers will never achieve the hard bodies displayed in ads for gym memberships, or the ruggedness of the Marlboro man, or the success enjoyed by shoe-promoting sports stars.

Advertising and the mass media together foster consumer culture. It is nearly impossible to avoid commercial messages in populated areas; whether one goes to the movies, enters a classroom, takes a bus, visits a museum, or opens a can of soup — the message to buy will be there as well. Advertising

THE TYPICAL ADULT SPENDS MORE TIME WATCHING TELEVISION THAN DOING ANYTHING ELSE BESIDES WORKING AND SLEEPING.

and media have become the essence of commercialism, the driving force behind the consumerist mentality.

DOES COMMERCIALISM PROMOTE THE PUBLIC GOOD?

Economic competition and the winner-takes-all structure of many markets prompted per capita advertising expenditures (in the United States) to quadruple between 1935 and 1994. But it is far from clear that the volume and nature of contemporary advertising is desirable from a consumer standpoint. Enormous amounts of money are spent on ads, rather than enhancing the quality of products. In 1994, ad expenditures (in all different media, including newspapers, magazines, television, and billboards) in the United States totalled $148 billion — equal to what the nation spent on higher education in 1990.

When advertising, television, and credit cards were first introduced, consumers were led to believe that each would further the public good. In the mid-1920s, commercial sponsorship of entire radio programs was widely accepted as a public service and marketers argued that the radio medium should not be debased by advertisements for specific products. In 1940 David Sarnoff, president of the Radio Corporation of America (RCA, then owner of NBC, the National Broadcasting Company), predicted that mass distribution of commercial television would unify the nation and enhance the individual. In the late 1950s, Bank of America promoted credit cards as a service that would permit upstanding middle-class citizens to achieve the American Dream.

Today, however, instead of facilitating cultural goals such as national unity, commercial media tend to dominate consumer culture. Consider the role of television viewing in the United States, where more homes have televisions than indoor plumbing or telephones. The typical adult spends more time watching television than doing anything else besides working and sleeping — turning on the set for an average of four hours a day. Robert Putnam, a professor of political science at Harvard University, recently discovered a significant correlation between the abrupt arrival of television, when household ownership of televisions exploded from 9% in 1950 to 90% in 1959, and the beginning of a dramatic decline in civic participation, as measured by membership trends in organizations such as Parent Teacher Associations (PTAs) and bowling leagues.

From the perspective of economic theory, televisions simply provide a service to consumers, no differently than other appliances. Mark Fowler, a chairman of the Federal Communications Commission during the Reagan administration, once described televisions as toasters with pictures.

This point of view, however, is contradicted by survey evidence which shows that watching television affects the way consumers see the world. Adults who watch more than an average amount of television tend to exaggerate the wealth of others, to hold disproportionately conventional views on politics and society, and to suffer a mean-world syndrome which combines feelings of insecurity with a belief that violence is the solution to life's problems.

> PRODUCERS NOT ONLY MANUFACTURE GOODS THAT SATISFY DESIRES, BUT THEY ALSO (INDIRECTLY) *CREATE* DESIRES FOR THOSE GOODS.

Although economists assume that consumers are willing to pay for what they want and that they are knowledgeable participants in the market, it may be impossible to be fully informed about the range of services provided by television. Many innovations in media technologies, such as VCRs, cable and the internet, have led to new, unforeseen uses of televisions and enhanced the home as an entertainment center. However, these developments have also brought hidden costs to consumers. Once free from advertising, most home video rentals, cable programming, and many internet websites carry unwanted commercial messages. Moreover, commercials are confusing to children. Young children (up to six years old) cannot understand that they are watching a sales message and cannot determine when a program stops and when a commercial begins.

DO MARKETS OFFER WHAT CONSUMERS WANT?

Consumer demand theory implies that economic activity does not shape consumer preferences. But as John Kenneth Galbraith argued long ago, advertising in wealthy countries creates tastes and desires for goods that contribute little to human well-being. Galbraith was one of the first economists to point out that producers not only manufacture goods that satisfy desires, but they also (indirectly) *create* desires for those goods.

Today, however, leading critics of advertising emphasize a different problem from the one Galbraith emphasized — some wants, even if they are not created by economic activity, may be impossible to satisfy through the market. Everyone wants to be beautiful, yet few consumers will ever attain the promise of beauty suggested by the painfully thin models displayed in many fashion ads.

Living in a culture where image is everything means that consumers are constantly bombarded with information about the things they need in order to be socially acceptable and successful. The confusion that results hits some more than others. For instance, the ideal beauty image promoted by many thin female models in various media has contributed to higher rates of anorexia among white as compared to black women.

Ideal images of feminine beauty affect women differently across nations as well. White American women tend to follow current trends in U.S. media, which gratuitously promote the appeal of the busty female, by having cosmetic surgery to enlarge their breasts. But in France the media emphasizes other aspects of the female form. Not surprisingly, French women who want to change the appearance of their breasts tend to have breast reduction surgery. One of the most damaging effects of commercialism is its impact on the poor. Commercial images help create consumption standards that everyone must achieve in order to gain respect, leaving many poor persons unable to afford the badges of respectable membership in consumer culture. The true life tales of school children being beaten or killed for their new leather jackets or name brand sneakers are powerful reminders of the influence of markets on consumer identities among the young and the poor.

A TAX ON DESIRE

The availability of credit makes possible much of today's high consumption levels, which are more than twice the levels of forty years ago. According to the authors of *Marketing Madness: A Survival Guide for a Consumer Society*, "The average cardholder carries eight to ten credit cards, owes about $2,500, and pays about $450 in interest annually." Some credit companies even reward taking on debt by awarding discounts and prizes on unpaid balances. In 1992, Americans spent $27 billion in finance charges alone. Instead of simply paying for the things they want, consumers pay for wanting what they want; a veritable tax on desire.

> AS CONSUMPTION PER PERSON HAS MORE THAN DOUBLED (AFTER CORRECTING FOR INFLATION), SO HAS THE NUMBER OF PERSONAL BANKRUPTCIES.

Until the late 1950s, the ability to acquire consumer debt was determined primarily by bank fiat. Consumers had to prove that they were good risks in face-to-face confrontations with loan officers, and were forced to wait for banks to process their applications each time they wanted a loan. After World War II, sporadic efforts were made to introduce credit cards, which would allow consumers to have more control over the lending process. The first major initiative, a fiasco, was undertaken in 1958 by the Bank of America in Fresno, California, before the bank was technically equipped to monitor credit use and avoid abuses. The success of the credit card as an institution awaited successful adaptation of technological innovations such as the computer to the specific requirements of credit card banking.

Between 1958 and 1970, 100 million credit cards were dispersed across the United States. With its mass distribution, the feel of the card and the spontaneity of credit transactions soon became common place. Yet as consumption per person has more than doubled (after correcting for inflation), so has the number of personal bankruptcies, which tripled between 1985 and 1994. Greater accessibility to credit is certainly a factor in this trend. It is easy to confuse the availability of credit with greater purchasing power; flexibility in payback schedules offers the illusion of immediate ownership. Credit card abuse is so pervasive that in San Francisco chapters of Debtors Anonymous hold 45 meetings a week.

In traditional economic models, rational consumers take on debt in order to purchase items that have a long lifetime, such as homes, autos, and appliances, and to balance fluctuations in their incomes. However, these models do not explain what really happens in the economy. They cannot explain why many people do not foresee or simply ignore the consequences of finance charges on unpaid balances. In 1992 Americans charged over $400 billion, while close to 900,000 people went brankrupt. It is hard to believe that rational planning would lead to so many bank-ruptcies. Like advertising, credit promises fulfillment but often delivers heartbreak.

The economic model of consumer behavior implies that an ideal life is one that is all consumption and no work. This alone should give us pause. And if we also take into account that emphasizing consumption as the primary route to happiness draws our attention from the economy's effects on the environment, we should pause a moment longer. But silence should not be our response to the seeming inevitability of consumer culture.

Alternatives exist for both consumers and producers. On the consumer side, some individuals are opting for less work and less consumption to have more time with their families; others are living more simply, more conscientiously; others are living in co-operatives with their friends and consuming less as a collective. On the producer side, the work week can be shortened, job security can be increased, and corporations can become more socially responsible in their dealings with the environment. However, none of these changes will fundamentally alter consumer culture, unless we also realize that commercialism creates the illusion that we can buy our happiness in the marketplace. ∎

Resources: Marketing Madness: A Survival Guide for a Consumer Society, Michael Jacobson and Laurie Ann Mazur, 1994; *A Piece of the Action: How the Middle Class Joined the Money Class*, Joseph Nocera, 1994); *The Consumer Society*, Neva Goodwin, Frank Ackerman, and David Kiron, 1997.

Editor's Note: Granted with permission from *The Consumer Society* edited by Neva R. Goodwin, Frank Ackerman, and David Kiron ©Island Press, 1997. Published by Island Press, Washington, D.C. and Covelo, CA. For more information, contact Island Press directly at 1-800-828-1302, info@islandpress.org (E-mail), or www.islandpress.org (website).

GOOD HEALTH FOR SALE

BY BARBARA EHRENREICH

Those clear blue skies! The cool triumph of that goddess-like face! Rush out to the nearest physician, is the message, and get yourself a little of this!

Time was when the pharmaceutical companies were content to market to the physicians themselves — hosting them, for example, at free weekend-long "seminars" at important margarita-producing sites. But doctors are a rushed and harried bunch these days, struggling to survive in their HMOs. Only the consumers — still known in the medical business by the archaic term "patients" — have the time to savor a well-crafted commercial and decide whether it suits their needs.

Hence the sudden expansion of "direct-to-consumer" prescription drug advertising, which began, innocently enough, with Rogaine, and extends now to remedies for everything from high blood pressure and prostate problems to fungus and migraines. Pharmaceutical companies spent $35 million on it in 1987 and almost ten times more — $308 million — in '94. And whatever the pills do, at least the advertising works: In 1989, 45% of doctors said they had patients who were able to specify, by brand name, exactly what they wanted prescribed. By 1995, 93% of doctors were encountering such medically gifted patients.

But why go to a doctor if you already know what you need? When an ad works, when it touches you in that deep subconscious layer of the brain where the ad-receptors are located, you don't want to diddle around with appointments and insurance forms and long waits on cold plastic seats. It gets irritating, in fact, that you have to go through this odd ritual — undressing in front of strangers, answering personal questions — just to get hold of some product that a nice voice on TV has already told you that you need.

Then there's the cost. Drug prices, already giddily high, are rising at more than twice the rate of inflation. This makes sense when you realize that pharmaceutical companies, just like presidential candidates and breakfast cereals, have to spend hundreds of millions a year on high-concept prime-time commercials. But when you're already facing $90 or more for a little vial of chemical comfort, that $50 surcharge for a doctor's prescription begins to look like an inexcusable shakedown.

So the pressure will inevitably grow to cut the doctors out of the loop. We're already being groomed by the medical companies in the skills of kitchen-table diagnosis. Take that indefinable malaise you were feeling: Now you can go to a drug store and, without any prescription at all, pick up a testing kit that will allow you to determine whether the problem is pregnancy or diabetes or possibly AIDS. So what are you paying the doctor for — $50 worth of bedside manner?

Think of it as the ultimate market-based health reform: A system in which consumers will decide what they need and then go out and get it, unimpeded by the need to support some gray-templed fellow with a serious golf habit. Americans currently spend billions a year on visits to physicians, and, despite the nice neighborly locution, most of these "visits" are purely bureaucratic formalities required to renew our antihistamine prescriptions. Why not go the way of Mexico and so much of the Third World and let consumers fill their shopping carts with beta-blockers and serotonin-uptake inhibitors as impulse demands? We don't, after all, require anyone to have a note from a fashion consultant before going home with a salmon-colored leisure ensemble.

There is of course the issue of safety. The drug with the most appealing packaging or cunning commercial could conceivably put an end to one's entire medical shopping career. But the truth is we're not doing so well on the safety front now, even with doctors manning the medical checkpoints. About 2 million people are hospitalized each year, and 140,000 actually die, as a result of dire reactions to drugs that were duly prescribed. Besides, if prescriptions are such an indispensable safeguard, why are the drug companies rushing to make their antacids and analgesics available over the counter, where we can O.D. on them to our hearts content?

Sadly, in a health system dominated by mega-corporations, the physician is fast becoming an evolutionary throwback. Today, the insurance companies that manage "managed care" don't even trust a doctor to monitor a routine blood pressure problem without some low-level bureaucrat looking over his or her shoulder for deviations from "cost effectiveness." And any loyalty the medical profession may have had from the long-suffering public evaporated last year when the AMA made a deal to let the Republicans cut Medicare without cutting doctors' fees. As for threatening us with serious trouble if we don't stop smoking and take off 15 pounds — well, what are spouses for?

So, Physician, heal thyself — is the message from Madison Avenue — and patients, heal thyselves too. Health reformers used to fantasize about networks of neighborhood clinics filled with nurturing, culturally sensitive, holistic providers. But in a health system ruled increasingly from Wall Street, where the only vital signs of interest are profits and market-share, doctor-free drug shopping may be the best we can hope for. ■

May/June 1994

MARKETING GREEN

ARE YOU GETTING WHAT YOU ASK FOR?

BY DAVID LEVY

"The Dow Chemical Company is committed to continued excellence, leadership and stewardship in protecting the environment. Environmental protection is a primary management responsibility as well as the responsibility of every Dow employee." So begins Dow's environmental policy statement. Yet the same company is responsible for the toxic waste in 38 Superfund sites (the worst areas in the nation, targeted for cleanup by federal law). And it is among the biggest corporate contributors to political action committees with anti-environmental agendas.

For its part, Chevron publishes an impressive annual Report on the Environment, detailing its efforts to reduce pollution — printed on recycled paper, of course. But Chevron was named one of the ten worst companies of 1992 by *Multinational Monitor* because of its dismal environmental record.

If we listened to advertisements, corporate annual reports, or the many new "environmentally friendly" labels on supermarket products, we might think that many large corporations have seen the green light of environmentalism. Even business schools are joining the bandwagon, spreading the message that being green is good for business. Should we read these as signs that the powerful energies of capitalism are now turning toward solving environmental problems?

The truth is that the 300 million tons of hazardous waste generated by U.S. industry each year are not about to disappear. Many companies seem to be showing a commitment to reducing pollution, but only where they need to meet legal requirements or where there is a clear financial payoff — and the financial benefits of environmental responsibility are often far from clear. While the multinational firm 3M (Minnesota Mining and Manufacturing) touts its 3P — "Pollution Prevention Pays" — program, for much of corporate America business as usual is the 4P program: profits, pollution, public image, and politics.

Some of America's largest industrial companies, particularly those with a high public profile, have developed programs to reduce pollution generated in their production processes. The managerial philosophy behind these efforts reflects the Japanese concept of "lean production": fix problems at their source. Rather than install expensive "end of the pipe" equipment to cut pollution, the new approach is to cut pollution at its source by improving the production process itself. This lowers waste disposal costs, liability, and might save on raw materials and energy too. Chevron started a program in 1987 called SMART (Save Money and Reduce Toxics). Chevron claims that in its first three years, its facilities reduced hazardous waste by 60% and saved more than $10 million in disposal costs.

What have these efforts achieved? Many programs are little more than declarations of intent. Even the claims of pollution reduction need close examination. They are hard to verify and may refer to new capacity that uses new, less polluting technology but still adds to total emissions. For instance, 3M initiated its "Pollution Prevention Pays" program to encourage product reformulation, process modification, equipment redesign, and resource recovery. The company claims that as a result of more than 2,000 projects, it has reduced its worldwide output of pollutants by nearly 450,000 tons while saving $420 million over the 15 years since the 3P program began in 1975. An analysis of 3M's overall level of emissions shows that they are still rising, however — just more slowly than the rate of growth of output. In addition, 3M has been cited and fined numerous times in the latter 1980s by the EPA, OSHA, and the Nuclear Regulatory Commission, and it has paid millions of dollars to settle lawsuits over environmental, health and safety practices.

Some companies proudly boast about going "beyond compliance" in their efforts to reduce pollution. The most well-known case is DuPont's unilateral commitment to phase out production of ozone-depleting CFCs faster than required by the Montreal Protocol. DuPont's decision, announced with great fanfare in March 1988 to the surprise of its competitors and many in the environmental community, won it an award from the EPA for stratospheric ozone protection. Yet DuPont's action appears to be part of a strategic move to dominate the market for CFC substitutes.

It is not as if DuPont gave up on CFCs easily. DuPont has been a leader in the CFC market since a DuPont chemist developed the chemicals in 1928 and began marketing them under the trade-name Freon in 1931. DuPont vigorously fought the ban on CFCs in aerosol sprays, taking out double-page newspaper and magazine advertisements to warn that "to act without the facts—whether it be to alarm consumers, or to enact restrictive legislation — is irresponsible." As late as February 1988, Du Pont was claiming that "scientific evidence does not point to the need for dramatic CFC emission reductions."

But as the evidence mounted during the 1980s on damage to the ozone layer caused by CFCs, and the Montreal Protocol set specific target dates for an international phaseout of CFC production, DuPont invested considerable money in HCFCs, a CFC substitute that damages the ozone layer to a lesser extent. Du Pont actually lobbied for the 1989 Helsinki declaration that brought up the phaseout of CFCs to the year 2000, hoping that it would have a headstart in the market for CFC substitutes. But then, during the consideration of a provision in the 1990 Clean Air Act that would phase out HCFCs, Du Pont returned to its old games to protect its new investment: the company led industry's successful lobbying efforts to push back that deadline to 2030.

GREEN MARKETING

Consumer concern for environmental issues has grown considerably over the past decade. The Michael Peters Group, a design and new products consulting firm, found in a 1989 survey that 89% of Americans are concerned about the environmental impact of the goods they purchase, more than half do not buy certain products for environmental reasons, and 78% would pay more for products in biodegradable or recyclable packaging.

> MANY COMPANIES SEEM TO BE SHOWING A COMMITMENT TO REDUCING POLLUTION, BUT ONLY WHERE THEY NEED TO MEET LEGAL REQUIREMENTS OR WHERE THERE IS A CLEAR FINANCIAL PAYOFF.

Corporations, however, seem to be more concerned with what image they project than with the real impact of their products. Perhaps the most notorious case of deceptive "green marketing" is the degradable garbage bags affair. Chevron ran television advertisements for its "degradable" Glad Bags with images of children laughing and skipping as they carried green garbage bags across a litter-strewn meadow. As the children put the trash into bags, a Native American in full ceremonial dress intones, "Take what you need, but always leave the land as you found it."

A Greenpeace study of "biodegradable" plastic products concluded that the manufacturers of products tested, including the garbage bags, could not support their claims. The products needed sunlight and air to degrade, both of which are lacking in most landfills. Moreover, if the products did break down, they did not really degrade but only turned into plastic particles, which released potentially toxic additives and colorants. The report quoted an anonymous employee of Mobil, manufacturer of Hefty "degradable" bags, saying "Degradability is just a marketing tool...We're talking out of both sides of our mouths when we want to sell bags. I don't think the average customer knows what degradability means. Customers don't care if it solves the solid waste problem. It makes them feel good." This cynical attitude finally caught up with Mobil. The Federal Trade Commission began investigating, and in 1990 Mobil was hit with seven lawsuits from states charging the company with consumer fraud and deceptive advertising.

GREEN PROFITS?

Proponents of corporate environmentalism argue that profit-seeking firms will respond to consumers who are increasingly concerned about environmental issues, and, second, that improving environmental performance is profitable, at least in the long run. The problem with the first argument is that most consumers can't make good decisions if corporate green advertising is their main source of information. Moreover, in the absence of green taxes that would make prices reflect more closely the full environmental cost of products, those that are less detrimental to the environment are relatively expensive, and consumers are not willing to pay a significant premium for them. In any event, many of the most polluting industries sell their output to other firms, not to consumers.

Although advocates of corporate environmentalism claim that being green is compatible with profits, the evidence for this is very thin. Despite the examples cited by Bruce Smart in his book *Beyond Compliance* of companies reaping profits from their environmental efforts, environmentalists cannot rely on this being the case. Environmental degradation is essentially an "economic externality," meaning that companies do not bear the cost of the damage and therefore will not take it into account when making decisions. Chevron's written policy makes it clear that environmental expenditures are judged in business terms: "Discretionary environmental, health and safety expenditures should be managed prudently to enhance Chevron's long term competitive position."

CORPORATE SPIN DOCTORING

The misleading advertisements for degradable plastic bags are part of a much wider corporate effort to influence the media and public debate. One way that corporations exert their power while avoiding the public spotlight is through front organizations with benign-sounding names. The U.S. Council for Energy Awareness, whose stated goal is to "build understanding, acceptance, and support for nuclear power among policy makers, opinion leaders and the public," is financed by the nuclear industry, with a board composed of representatives from General Electric, Bechtel, Westinghouse, and other nuclear power interests. Corporate fronts often use their own "experts" to peddle views that portray environmentalists as extreme and irrational.

The corporate response to concerns about Alar, which surfaced in early 1989 after the Natural Resources Defense Council (NRDC) published the results of a two year study linking Alar in apples to a risk of cancer in children, is an example of this technique. By late 1989, a series of articles began to appear in influential media with headlines like "Doctor Says Alar Fear Needless" and "Consumer Health Advocate Fights 'Ban Everything' Trend." These articles were authored by or based on the opinion of Dr. Elizabeth Whelan, a real medical doctor but hardly a consumer health advocate. Dr. Whelan was executive director of the American Council on Science and Health, a group almost entirely funded by the food, drug, and chemical industries, including Dow and Uniroyal Chemical, the maker of Alar.

At times, corporations can exert their influence directly through ownership of the media. In March 1987, NBC broadcast a special documentary, "Nuclear Power: In France it works." NBC is owned by GE, America's second-largest nuclear energy company, so it was no surprise that the documentary was more like an advertisement for the industry. According to ad copy for the program, "French townspeople welcome each reactor with open arms." Even PBS is not immune to the power of corporate money; many programs on nature and the environment are underwritten by companies with less than admirable records. The list includes a series of National Geographic Specials funded by Chevron, the Living Planet by Mobil, and Conserving America by Waste Management Inc., one of the most frequently fined companies in EPA history.

THE GREEN POLITICAL MACHINE

In addition to shaping public debate, some corporations try to influence environmental regulations by targeting politicians. ARCO's donation of $862,000 to the 1988 Republican campaign was one of the more blatant attempts to affect policy — and the Bush administration complied by inserting into the Clean Air Act a provision favoring a type of reformulated gasoline made by ARCO. ARCO then promoted this gasoline using the mind-bending slogan "Let's drive away smog." Bush's national energy strategy also proposed to open Alaska's Arctic National Wildlife Refuge to oil drilling — it is surely no accident that ARCO is the second largest oil producer in Alaska. The Center for Economic Priorities (CEP) in New York has calculated a "Greendex" representing the environmental soundness of corporate PAC contributions. In contrast to their professed concern for the environment, about 75% of the companies studied gave to congresspeople with poor environmental voting records.

Despite Vice-President Gore's reputation as an environmentalist, corporate power to influence Congress and the executive branch does not seem to have diminished much with the arrival of the Clinton administration. Although some were hopeful when Clinton dismantled Dan Quayle's old Competitiveness Council, which had systematically blocked regulations deemed harmful to industry, and set up a new Council for Sustainable Development, the new council is still a platform for protecting corporate interests.

Appointees include a vice-president of Dow, the chair of Chevron, and former EPA head William Ruckleshaus, now chair and CEO of BFI, the country's second largest waste hauler. Corporate influence seems to have paid off in the demise of the proposal for a broad-based energy tax, the recent compromises on Pacific Northwest forestry policy, and the November 1993 decision to approve the use and sale of dairy foods derived from Bovine Growth Hormone (BGH), a decision taken under pressure from Monsanto, producer of the artificial hormone.

If corporations are increasingly acting out of fear of the pinch of environmental regulations at the national level, they are extending their reach to the international arena. Under the auspices of GATT, corporate committees are setting international standards for safe levels of chemical residues in food and agricultural products — and if a country wants to set stricter standards, a GATT panel can strike the standards down as a violation of free trade.

ENVIRONMENTALISM, INC.

Mainstream environmental organizations increasingly depend on corporate sources for funding, leading many to worry about the influence that corporate money can buy. The large ones, with the exception of Greenpeace, typically receive less than 25% of their budgets from individual memberships and contributions. The annual reports of the Audubon Society, the National Wildlife Federation (NWF), and the Sierra Club feature long lists of corporate donors including well known polluters such as GE, Chevron, Dupont, Waste Management, ARCO, Dow, Exxon, Mobil, and Monsanto.

Corporate funding is an investment, and environmental organizations are under pressure to ensure that it is a profitable one. In 1982, the NWF established a Corporate Conservation Council to promote "mutually agreeable" policy proposals, and in 1989 went even further when it offered a seat on its board of directors to Dean Buntrock, the head of Waste Management, Inc.

Although some corporate managers are making sincere and substantial efforts to reduce pollution, these efforts are dwarfed by the magnitude of environmental problems. The lack of alternative technologies and the need to justify expenditures in terms of profitability limits how far companies will go. Many seem to think that it's easier and cheaper to clean up their image than the environment. By adopting the rhetoric of environmentalism and exerting influence over the media and public policy, corporations are attempting to market themselves and their products as "green" while evading calls for more stringent environmental regulation and enforcement.

The language of corporate environmentalism masks the inherent contradictions between private capital and the environment, promoting the naive idea that with goodwill, a bit of education, and playing around with economic incentives, all will be well. Ultimately, corporations are economic institutions pursuing private gain, and environmental solutions require community decisions that take into account non-economic values. ∎

CAN WE BUILD A NEW AMERICAN DREAM?

The Center for a New American Dream is a new nonprofit organization whose goal is to promote "sustainable consumption." The Center seeks to change the ways North Americans produce and consume, in order to lessen our harmful impact on the natural environment while improving our quality of life as individuals, families and communities.

It was founded by environmentalists and social activists concerned that the traditional American Dream, which defines success and status through ever-expanding possessions, is socially, economically and environmentally unstable. In January 1997, it opened its national office in Burlington, Vermont. Dollars and Sense asked Barbara Brandt, author of Whole Life Economics, to interview the Center's executive director, Ellen Furnari, to learn more.

QUESTION: The Center is an unusual kind of social change organization, because you are attempting to bring about broad social and economic changes by focusing on lifestyles — on individuals' everyday activities of buying and consuming.

ELLEN FURNARI: In the long term we will also be involved with public policy. For example, some issues we are thinking about now concern the design of urban communities — we are looking into promoting more public transportation — and eliminating perverse tax subsidies that promote environmentally destructive logging or fossil fuel depletion. But we are starting out by encouraging individual change, because we want more Americans to understand the connections between the typical American lifestyle and bigger social and environmental problems.

For example, the race to "keep up with the Joneses" pushes many Americans to work longer hours so they can earn enough to consume all the "right things." This leaves little time for getting together as a family, or for community or civic participation, and this diminishes the quality of our community and family life. The average American now spends six hours a week shopping and only 40 minutes a week playing with children — and the average couple only spends about 12 minutes per day talking together!

Also, the Earth can't support the current level of U.S. consumption and waste, especially if it were extended to the rest of the world. Environmentalists have estimated that we would need about three earths to support the entire global population at the current U.S. levels of consumption and resource use — and about nine earths to absorb the wastes and toxins generated. The U.S. is seen as a model by so many other people, and the media is busily promoting our materialistic and consumption-oriented lifestyle all around the globe. So if we can change our consumption habits here, that will send a new message to the rest of the world.

Q: But is there enough interest in reducing consumption here in the U.S.? Isn't materialism and the desire to express ourselves through our possessions deeply ingrained in the American psyche?

FURNARI: There's clearly significant interest. A number of recent polls show that large numbers of Americans are now concerned that our society has become too materialistic — our lives have gotten out of balance. They are especially concerned about materialistic values in our young people. Many Americans now say that what's really important to them are satisfying relationships with family and friends, making a contribution to their community, enjoying nature and expressing their spirituality.

The problem is that most of us are not living according to what we really value. It's not that people want to go back to the Stone Age; they don't want to give up material things. But they want more of a balance between material things and those non-material things which give real meaning to life. People feel that our lives have gone too far in the direction of materialism, so there is now a new interest in living more simply. A small percentage of Americans have already started making these changes, and the numbers willing to make these kinds of changes is growing. Our data base lists several thousand individuals, organizations, publications and so forth around the U.S. already actively promoting sustainable consumption.

Q: What about the criticism that this movement to consume less is only relevant to white upper-middle-class Americans?

FURNARI: Our consumption-oriented lifestyle is related to issues of social and economic justice. It widens the gap between the super-rich and the super-poor, both in North

America and internationally, and this division is unsustainable. For the sake of equity, the people who consume the most will have to reduce their consumption the most. The Center doesn't dictate how much people should cut back, but says we must begin talking about this problem.

Also, our materialistically focused culture is especially brutal to lower-income communities. It's hard enough to be poor because you don't have material necessities, with all the extra work and stress that entails. But it's especially cruel to have the whole culture bombard you with the message that you're only a worthwhile person if you buy this or that. And all that waste and pollution generated by our consumer culture has to go somewhere. In most cases it is dumped in or near poor communities, often communities of color. Municipalities tend to locate landfills and toxic waste dumps in low-income neighborhoods, and in fact, one out of every five African-Americans and Latinos live in a community with one or more toxic waste sites.

Q: Has the Center done specific outreach to lower-income communities or communities of color?

FURNARI: In the next year we plan to hold two special constituency meetings, one with people who organize in low-income communities, and another with labor unions. There's so often conflict between labor and environmentalists, for example on the issue of jobs. We want to make sure that there is no wedge driven between environmentalists and labor around the issue of sustainable consumption.

Q: Talking about jobs — that brings up another familiar question. If we reduce our consumption, won't that shrink our economy and increase unemployment?

FURNARI: This is a very important question that we as a society need to discuss openly. Where do we want our economy to expand? Where do we want it to contract? *How* do we want it to grow? Do we want — or need — to grow? Can we redistribute instead of grow?

Even the May/June 1997 issue of *Dollars and Sense* on the environment never asked these questions. You had a good article on green consumers but we need to redeploy the market both to support better products and to fight the ethos of consumption. For example, even if you bought shirts made of organic cotton and sewn by union labor with good wages and safe working conditions, we still need to ask the question, "How many shirts do you need? How often do you need to buy a shirt?" And what about children's toys? Do we really need to buy every new baby 25 stuffed animals? And do all the gadgets and appliances that fill our homes and closets really save us time? Maybe they just make more work for us because we have to clean them and maintain them, and then we need a bigger house to store all these things!

Even if all our businesses were producing everything with a minimum of waste and pollution, and recycling everything, we should still be consuming less overall. Even if the auto industry came out with a car that gets 70 or 80 miles per gallon, people should still be using more public transportation instead of so many private automobiles.

So we at the Center are saying that we need to look at what are the things we can consume more of, for example the arts. And what are the worst things we now consume, which we absolutely should consume less of? And what are the implications of these kinds of questions for employment, distribution, etc.? It makes no sense to reduce consumption unless you also deal with equity issues.

Luckily for us and our planet, the kinds of things people really long for, such as friendship, community, and spiritual meaning, are low-consumption items.

Q: How are you getting your message out?

FURNARI: For the first two years we are focusing on public education. We especially want to promote individual awareness and change around two points. One: How can we bring our lives back into balance with our values and with the Earth? And two: How much is enough? Our goal is to reach over 1,000,000 Americans with these two questions. ∎

Resources: "Yearning for Balance" action kit, and "How Much is Enough?" study guide, Center for a New American Dream, 156 College St., 2d floor, Burlington, Vt. 05401; 802-862-6762; www.newdream.org.

CHAPTER 4
Firms and Competition

September 1989

TO MAKE A TENDER CHICKEN
TECHNOLOGICAL CHANGE AND COSTCUTTING TAKE THEIR TOLL

BY BARBARA GOLDOFTAS

In 1983 Donna Bazemore took the best-paying job she could find in northeastern North Carolina — gutting chickens for Perdue Farms. At first she slit open carcasses; later she became a "mirror trimmer" on the night shift. As the birds moved by on the assembly line, a federal inspector next to her examined their far sides in a mirror. He pointed out unacceptable tumors, bruises, and other "physical defects," which Bazemore sliced off with huge scissors.

While the job paid better than the minimum wage she might have earned elsewhere, the conditions were grueling. Bazemore worked in 90-degree heat as the chickens sped by, 72 to 80 a minute. Strict work rules limited bathroom breaks. The primarily black, female work force faced sexual harassment and racism from the white male supervisors. And the women endured a slew of medical problems, ranging from skin rashes to cuts to swollen, painful hands and arms.

Several months after becoming a mirror trimmer, Bazemore noticed that she had no feeling in several fingertips. The numbness progressed to pains shooting up the inside of her arm — symptoms of carpal tunnel syndrome, a potentially disabling disorder caused by overly repetitive movements.

Even after surgery, the trouble continued. "I had no strength in my hands," she says. "I couldn't do the littlest tasks around the house, like sweep a floor or stir for long periods of time. I couldn't write six or seven words without having to rest my hand."

Bazemore is one of thousands of workers hurt by their jobs in poultry processing plants — the polite term for slaughterhouses. "Work in poultry plants by every stretch of the imagination is horrible," says Artemis (her full name). She has worked for two different companies in northern Arkansas, a region thick with poultry plants. "It's stressful, demanding, noisy, dirty. You're around slimy dead bodies all the time. And it's very dangerous."

According to its trade journal, *Broiler Industry,* the industry makes "staggering" profits. Demand for poultry has grown steadily for decades, and U.S. consumers now eat more chicken and turkey than red meat. Production increased by 67% in just 10 years, from 12 billion pounds in 1977 to about 20 billion pounds in 1987.

The industry's growth and profitability have in large part come at the expense of poultry workers who, according to the Bureau of Labor Statistics, suffer twice the average private sector rates of illness and injury. As poultry processing expanded, it grew increasingly concentrated. Firms converted to large-scale assembly-line operations, ultimately speeding up and deskilling individual jobs. The resulting breakneck pace and repetitive motions tax workers' hands and arms — and can ultimately cripple them.

A CHICKEN IN EVERY POT

The poultry industry of 50 years ago hardly resembled the one that ConAgra, Tyson Foods, and Perdue now dominate. Small farmers raised most chickens and turkeys, sending them to private, local slaughterhouses. The birds were smaller and more expensive than those sold today. People ate less poultry and usually bought it whole.

In the 1940s, poultry scientists created new breeds of birds that grew faster and did not waste away in crowded conditions. The innovations made large-scale operations both feasible and efficient. In the 1940s and 1950s, giant "integrators," which already owned slaughterhouses, animal feed mills, and hatcheries, bought out the small chicken farms as well.

Since the 1960s, processing has undergone a similar transformation. Mechanizing parts of their operations enabled firms to increase the volume and size of their plants. The industry also grew more consolidated. In 1977, the top four firms slaughtered just 20% of all chickens killed in the United States. By 1987, their portion had nearly doubled to 38%. During that same period, poultry companies used the gimmick of name-brand poultry to secure a larger share of the retail market. They began selling directly to the fast-food and retail outlets, and they introduced new, expensive products that required further processing.

A typical poultry plant now processes tens of thousands of chickens each day. One by one, live birds are hung by the feet on a moving line of hooks called shackles and mechanically stunned, decapitated, and scalded to remove the feathers. They are quickly gutted and then cut into parts, packaged whole, or sped through a deboning line.

Throughout the plant, workers perform simple, highly repetitive jobs. They draw out guts, pull livers, cut wings and gizzards, pop thigh bones. Most do a single, defined movement — cutting, slicing, lifting birds onto the shackles, or pulling breast meat from the bone with their fingers. They may repeat this motion 25, 40, 90 times a minute, hour after hour. "They treat you as if you were a machine, plugged in, running on electricity," says Rita Eason, another former Perdue worker.

Like Bazemore, many workers do their jobs in conditions of extreme heat or cold. Processing involves both ice and scalding water, and plant temperatures reportedly vary from 26 to 95 degrees. Bazemore's department lacked ventilation, despite the heat, and in other departments, she says, "people wear three, four, five pair of socks and long underwear all year. And they're still cold."

Although the work is fast and hard, the companies allow few scheduled breaks, usually just lunch and two 10- or 15-minute rests each day. At many plants, a strict disciplinary system keeps workers in line — literally. Returning late from a break or missing part of a day, regardless of the reason, brings an "occurrence" or "write-up." After a certain number of write-ups, workers are "terminated."

"If you had to go to the bathroom more than once in two or three hours, they would threaten to write you up," says Brenda Porter, who worked at a Cargill plant in Buena Vista, Georgia, for 12 years.

Afraid to ask permission to leave the line, or forbidden to leave, workers sometimes urinate, vomit, and even miscarry as the chickens pass by. Although it has been nine years since Eason worked at Perdue, she remembers clearly seeing "a grown woman stand on the line and urinate right on herself. She was too scared to move. But then she got so cold she walked out and went home."

A constant risk of illness and injury compounds the harsh day-to-day conditions in the plants. Common ailments include warts, infections from bone splinters, and

POULTRY WORKERS ORGANIZE

Three-fourths of poultry processing happens in Arkansas, Georgia, Alabama, and North Carolina. The warm climate allows year-round production, and the poultry firms also prefer the southern labor climate — cheap and largely unorganized.

For many workers, poultry jobs are steadier and easier than field work. And the companies pay more than convenience stores and fastfood joints, usually between $4.50 and $6.00 an hour.

The price of the job, though, is high — a worker's safety and health — and even in anti-union areas, workers are starting to organize. At the Cargill plant in Buena Vista, Georgia, workers say the Retail, Wholesale, and Department Store Union (RWDSU), which survived a recent decertification drive there, gives them a say about their health.

"A lot of people are afraid to speak up, afraid to get fired," says Felton Toombs, who was fired three months after having carpal tunnel surgery in 1988. "You need someone to speak up for you when something goes wrong."

In northeastern North Carolina, the Center for Women's Economic Alternatives (CWEA) teaches workers that they should not have to choose between their job and their health. Organizers offer clinics about repetitive motion injuries, and they have helped hundreds of Perdue workers get medical care and workers' compensation. Workers are now asking to be sent to the doctor, says former Perdue worker Bazemore. "A couple months ago, they were losing fingers and arms and they would never complain."

rashes from the chlorine water used to wash birds contaminated with feces. Workers often lose fingernails and toenails, and they suffer injuries from the knives, saws, and machinery.

The speed and repetition of the work cause the most serious problems. Performing the same action for hours and hours makes poultry workers highly susceptible to debilitating conditions of the nerves, muscles, and tendons. These cumulative trauma disorders, also called repetitive motion injuries, occur among a wide range of workers, from letter sorters to textile workers to typists. According to the Bureau of Labor Statistics, the disorders were the fastest-growing occupational disease of the 1980s.

Carpal tunnel syndrome, which damaged Bazemore's arms, is the most severe such disorder. When the tendons passing though a narrow channel in the wrist — the carpal tunnel — are overused, they swell and press on the nerve that controls feeling in the hand. The result can be painful — and permanently disabling.

Although Mary Smith only worked at Cargill for seven months, her brief stint at the Buena Vista plant left her with hands that hurt day and night. She started in March 1988, trimming bruises and tumors from chicken skin. The pain began in June. "At first they would swell. The nurse said it was normal; I had to get used to the job," she says. "They started hurting real bad and getting numb, especially at night. I'd wake up, shake them, lay them on the pillow. It didn't do no good."

She has not worked since last September but, says Smith, "I still have problems holding things. It hurts to wash dishes, take clothes out of the machine. My arm hurts at night, hurts all day. I get so frustrated sometimes, I feel like just cutting it off." She is hardly alone. At least 14 of her co-workers have had surgery for carpal tunnel syndrome. Union stewards at the plant estimate that more than a third of the workers there have trouble with their hands.

THE BREAKNECK PACE AND REPETITVE MOTIONS OF POULTRY PROCESSING TAX WORKERS' HANDS AND ARMS — AND CAN ULTIMATELY CRIPPLE THEM.

THEY WEAR OUT

While gutting and cutting chickens was never easy, poultry work became even harder as the industry expanded. During the 1960s and 1970s, firms increased their productivity by replacing workers with machines. A skilled worker, for example, could slaughter about 66 birds a minute, while a killing machine beheads five times as many — five a second. To meet the recent rise in demand, the plants sped up production, and workers now work at a faster pace for longer hours. Between 1975 and 1985, output per worker increased by 43%.

The U.S. Department of Agriculture (USDA), which regulates slaughterhouses, facilitated the speed-up. Federal inspectors check each bird before and after slaughter, working no faster than the rate set by the agency. Since 1979, USDA engineers have pared down the inspection time allowed for each bird. Upper limits jumped from 57 to 70 birds a minute for two inspectors, even reaching 91 for some high-speed plants.

Safe-food advocates worry about contaminated birds and rising rates of salmonella infections, but the speed-ups have also been critical to the 150,000 workers who process poultry. The changes constituted a "policy shift toward de facto deregulation," says Tom Devine of the Government Accountability Project, a whistleblower support group in Washington, D.C. that has worked with former USDA inspectors. "The idea was to keep the USDA seal of approval but get inspectors out of the way of faster line speeds."

The agency simply determines how quickly inspectors can work "comfortably," says Patrick Burke of the USDA's Food Safety and Inspection Service. "They wear out if the rate's too fast." Asked about how the speed-up might affect other workers, whose "comfort" is not monitored, Burke says that the USDA "can't legally do anything with plant employees."

The new, lucrative products of the 1980s — filleted breasts, poultry patties, chicken nuggets — have made poultry work even more physically demanding. Workers who cut or pull the meat from the bone use quick, repetitive motions that are particularly trying on their wrists and hands. Even Cargill spokesman Greg Lauser acknowledges that the "more intensive processing operations tend to have a greater incidence of repetitive motion injuries."

Many workers suffering from repetitive motion injuries have a hard time getting treatment because of hostile management, untrained nurses, and doctors who know little about their medical problems. "When you tell people you're hurting, they don't really believe you," says Perdue worker Rose Harrell, who was bounced from doctor to doctor before being diagnosed with carpal tunnel. "I told the plant manager that I didn't mind working, but my hands hurt. 'What you telling me for,' he said. 'I can't stop your hands from hurting.'"

Workers and union officials at plants throughout the South describe similar circumstances. "At Cargill [in Buena Vista] when a worker notices her hands are hurting, she'll be given Advil and told that she's just breaking them in," says Jamie Cohen, health and safety director for the Retail, Wholesale, and Department Store Union (RWDSU), which represents the plant's work force. "The previous nurse apparently even told some people, 'Go back and take the pain like the rest.'"

Workers also report being fired after they developed "hand problems." "The procedure is to keep you from going to the doctor instead of sending you to the doctor," says Zelma Ghant, a union steward at the Buena Vista plant who accompanies workers to the nurse. "Instead of facing the problems, the company tries to scare people. When a person is persistent, they find a way to terminate them, to set an example for the rest: If you don't keep quiet, this will happen to you."

Ignoring cumulative trauma disorders can aggravate them, though. Untreated, temporary damage can become permanent, and even a short delay can make a difference. Companies could help limit damage by giving employees less strenuous tasks or letting them rotate jobs. Instead, some workers report being given work that only makes their injuries worse.

Unfortunately, poultry companies have a built-in incentive to ignore injuries — it keeps workers' compensation costs down. Until recently they showed very low rates on their OSHA "200 logs," where they record work-related injuries and illnesses. The disorders are "underreported," says Roger Stephens, federal OSHA's sole ergonomist, who studies how the design of a workplace affects workers. "The reporting just doesn't go on."

Benny Bishop, plant manager of Southland Poultry in Enterprise, Alabama, says there are "few injuries" to report. "Every injury that has been reported has been recorded," he claims. RWDSU representative Linda Cromer, who worked on a recent union drive there, agrees that the past five years of Southland's OSHA logs show "virtually no repetitive motion injuries listed." But, she adds, "we hear about it on every house call."

In a written statement sent to a congressional hearing on cumulative trauma disorders in early June, Perdue Farms claims that "grossly inaccurate media reports have created undue concern" about these disorders. Yet an internal memo from the Perdue personnel department this past February tells a different story. In response to a worker's complaint, it states that it is "normal procedure for about 60% of our work force" at the Robersonville plant to go to the nurse every morning to get pain killers and have their hands wrapped.

Perhaps in an effort to shake its reputation of ineffectualness, OSHA recently levied huge fines against meatpackers and poultry companies for failing to report repetitive motion injuries. But on both the federal and state level, OSHA has been slow to respond to the cause of repetitive motion injuries — the very nature of poultry work.

"I think there will have to be limits on the physical demands employers can make of employees," says Steve Edelstein, a North Carolina attorney who handles compensation cases for injured workers. "People shouldn't have to feel pain every day just to make a living." He says that OSHA historically overlooked the design of assembly-line work, focusing instead on safety standards and a narrow definition of illness and injury.

Companies could make some changes immediately, says Sarah Fields-Davis, director of the Center for Women's Economic Alternatives, a worker advocacy group in Ahoskie, North Carolina. "Redesigning tools and keeping scissors sharp so people don't have to use their backs to cut doesn't cost that much," she says. "Neither does rotating workers" or giving them longer breaks.

Former Perdue worker Donna Bazemore believes that companies like Perdue should retrain workers disabled by poultry work. After a woman develops carpal tunnel, they should "realize that it's going to be hard for [her] to make a living," she says.

"We're not advocating that Perdue leave," says Fields-Davis. "We just want the company to become more responsive to — and responsible for — the people who are making them rich." ■

POULTRY COMPANIES HAVE A BUILT-IN INCENTIVE TO IGNORE INJURIES — IT KEEPS WORKERS' COMPENSATION COSTS DOWN.

July/August 1995

CO-OPs, ESOPs, AND WORKER PARTICIPATION

BY REBECCA BAUEN

In contrast, worker co-operatives, in which the employees have both full ownership, and control over management decisionmaking, are a true break with traditional corporate structures. As such, studies have shown that not only do they generate more employee satisfaction, but production efficiency often improves greatly. While still a tiny fraction of American companies, worker coops are steadily demonstrating their viability in the marketplace.

In 1991 the 130 employees of Market Forge, an industrial cooking equipment manufacturer in Everett, Massachusetts, were threatened with loss of their jobs. The Chicago-based conglomerate that owned the 95 year-old plant intended to sell it to a firm in Georgia and move operations there. When the union, United Steel Workers (USW) Local 2431, successfully halted the move, the company threatened bankruptcy.

But in 1993, after two and a half years of negotiations, the workers bought their plant. With the help of the USW the employees were able to assess whether the firm would be a good investment before purchasing it. Said Dave Slaney, Vice President of the Steelworkers local, "We created a financing structure which allows employees to own 100% of the shares and have full control: each employee has one vote to decide on management salaries, their own pay raises, firing the management, as well as plant relocation."

The Market Forge buyout was accomplished through the increasingly common tool of an Employee Stock Ownership Plan (ESOP). But 100% ownership by workers is rare for ESOPs. In almost all cases employees own a small fraction of the stock, and so have little decision-making power.

ESOPs are one of two mechanisms that many corporations are encouraging as solutions to meager rates of productivity growth. The second mechanism is employee participation plans, which allow workers to have input into how their jobs are structured and how companies are run.

Business leaders hope that ESOPs and participation schemes will raise productivity by reducing workers' alienation from their jobs. But both of these mechanisms are management-inspired, and neither, on its own, gives employees real power within their workplaces. As a result they have generally failed to yield serious productivity improvements.

ESOPS ARE NOT WHAT THEY SEEM

There are approximately 9,500 U.S. companies with ESOPs—including Hallmark, Avis, and United Airlines — covering over 10 million employees, who control over $150 billion in corporate stock. And they are growing at a rate of 300,000 to 600,000 new participants a year, according to the National Center for Employee Ownership (NCEO), an Oakland-based non-profit.

In most ESOP corporations, employees are offered stock as part of a benefits package, and accrue increasing rights to shares with seniority. Some companies substitute ESOPS for pensions altogether — despite the riskiness for employees of having their retirement invested in the fate of the company.

Veronica Manson of NCEO explains that ESOPs are popular with corporations because of the tax benefits. In fact ESOPs were invented by a corporate investment banker in 1974. ESOPs allow a company to set up a trust fund for employees and borrow money to buy shares. The company then makes a tax deductible contribution to the plan to enable it to repay the loan.

Besides large corporations, small family-owned firms are also turning to ESOPs. Traditionally, when a company's founder wants to retire and cash out, the owner sells the company to a large firm, or goes out of business altogether. The alternative is to sell to the workers and get a tax break.

Many stock ownership plans offer employees the right to vote for the board of directors. But, unlike the Market Forge case, employees rarely comprise a majority of the stockholders. NCEO reports that less than one-third, or about 2,500 companies, form ESOPs for philosophical reasons; to really share ownership. A top manager in one of the country's leading ESOP investment firms admits, "ESOPs are the antithesis of workplace democracy." The Horatio Alger strategy of benefitting individuals, rather than collective groups of workers, is the operative one.

At first glance, ESOPs seem to offer a win-win strategy; the individual employees gain by the financial success of the company, and the corporation gains tax benefits. Yet the cards are stacked: the company's financial success is only a possibility, while the tax benefits to the corporation are guaranteed. "Employee owners" are still employed by CEOs and outside stockholders, who continue to both reap profits and make the majority of decisions about the future of the firm.

PARTICIPATIVE MANAGEMENT: ANOTHER DIVERSION

Another strategy that appears to offer increased democracy in the workplace is participatory management. Invented by management consultant Edward Deming in the 1950s, employee participation's purpose is to increase productivity and employee motivation.

How work is organized is a key to productivity. By setting up flexible work teams and inviting production workers to contribute to product design, management found new ways to remain profitable in an increasingly competitive global market. By appealing to workers' "higher order" need for meaning through increased participation, corporations avoided compensating them financially for their extra efforts. Yet, for most employees, increased involvement has resulted in few real changes.

Most Fortune 1000 participatory management programs allow employees to give input — but only to make suggestions, not decisions. In order to make good decisions, workers need information. Yet in 25% of these firms, employees have no access to information on the company's overall performance — even though that information is public. Half don't regularly inform employees of their teams' unit operating costs, which would help them evaluate their own performance.

Both employee participation programs and ESOPs are management-inspired models. In ESOPs, employees gain individual stock benefits, but the ratios between the highest and lowest wage levels do not change, and most profits still go to non-employee stock owners. Increased participation through teams may make work more "meaningful," but offers little real power. In both, employees remain at the whim of management and stockholders.

WORKER COOPS: A DEMOCRATIC ALTERNATIVE

Participation alone doesn't lead to greater productivity. Rather, having real decision-making power does, according to studies tracked by the NCEO. And participation without ownership tends to be short-lived or ambiguous. Ownership seems to provide the fuel to keep participation going. On the other hand, ownership alone affects performance little if at all. A 1987 U.S. General Accounting Office (GAO) study found that ESOPs had no impact on profits.

But firms that are *managed in a participatory way and are employee-owned* increase their productivity growth rate by 52% per year, according to the same GAO study. NCEO confirms, "We can say with certainty that when ownership and participative management are combined, substantial growth results. Ownership alone and participation alone, however, have, at best, spotty or short-lived results."

Worker-owned cooperatives are a model that combines and extends the benefits of both ESOPs and participation plans. Ownership of the firm belongs solely to those who work there rather than to those who can afford to buy stock. Employees are not subject to the whims of the chief executive officer or board. Instead, the worker-owners elect the board, who in turn hire management and control capital.

Economic benefits — regular pay and net profit — are distributed equitably to workers, not to external shareholders according to the number of shares purchased. Decision-making power also belongs to workers. Each person has the right to one vote based on their work in the company, not on the number of shares owned. And, by combining economic ownership with participation in significant decisions, worker-owned cooperatives have proven to be more productive than traditional businesses.

Dick Gilbert (one of the founding owners of Stone Soup, a worker-owned restaurant in Asheville, North Carolina), myself, and others recently conducted a survey of coops throughout the nation. It provides the most comprehensive information available on worker-owned cooperatives in the U.S. today.

WORKER-OWNED COOPERATIVES ARE A MODEL THAT COMBINES AND EXTENDS THE BENEFITS OF BOTH ESOPs AND PARTICIPATION PLANS.

There are nearly 150 such businesses (not including consumer-owned coops, such as most food coops), primarily concentrated on the west and east coasts. Some are in manufacturing, others in retail trade, while most are in services such as printing, restaurants and health care. Like traditional businesses, these firms must develop marketable products, gain access to financing, and compete in the market while at the same time attempting to model economic justice through shared ownership.

While some of those employed in coops are attracted by the ownership structure, many just need the jobs. Cooperative Home Care Associates (CHCA) in the Bronx currently employs 300 low-income Latina and African American women, 80% of whom previously had been receiving some sort of public aid. Offering women the opportunity for ownership, as well as higher wages and better advancement opportunities than are normal in this "ghettoized" industry, they believe that high quality care will result. Success has led to franchising home care cooperatives in Boston, Philadelphia and rural Connecticut.

Following CHCA's success in home care services, Boston's ICA Group, a non-profit providing technical assistance to worker-owned firms, is encouraging coop development in low-income communities in five other industrial sectors: retail franchises, temporary employment, environmental products and services, childcare and private security services.

ICA chose these industries based on its analysis of the market — minimal barriers to entry, growth potential, access to capital, and the potential to employ a significant number of low income people. Job quality — opportunities for liveable wages and advancement — was also an important consideration.

SO, WHY THE SMALL NUMBER?

Skeptics conclude that their small numbers indicate that worker-owned firms are inefficient organizations, and that the challenges of democratic control by ordinary workers must lead to a greater failure rate than conventional business. This conclusion is wrong.

Worker-owned cooperatives have no greater failure rate than conventional businesses. Yet, because they are unique, they attract more attention and appear to fail more often. External market forces cause some of those failures that do occur. Stone Soup, for example, faltered when seven new restaurants opened in Asheville's downtown.

COOPS' DEMOCRATIC STRUCTURE MAKES IT MORE DIFFICULT FOR THEM TO ACCESS FINANCING.

Failures also take place due to the difficulty that traditional business services and conventionally-trained individuals have in relating to cooperatives. Coops' democratic structure makes it more difficult for them to access financing, or to attract managers who are both competent and understand democratic participation. In addition, most workers have little or no prior experience in education or employment that prepares them for cooperative business practices.

Gerry Mackie, former director of Hoedad, the largest of the Northwest's Forest Workers Cooperatives, believes capitalizing new worker-owned cooperatives is more difficult than traditional businesses. In many industries, cooperative members can't finance all the costs themselves through individual investments, and locating outside money without voting rights is difficult. Venture capitalists are unwilling to forfeit these rights. Traditional banks are wary of the unusual cooperative structure and hesitate to make equity or working capital loans.

Carol DiMarcello of the ICA Group disagrees with Mackie, stating, "Money does exist for groups to start worker-owned cooperatives, through intermediary groups such as ICA, which makes loans nation-wide, as well as other regional and local credit unions." Foundations are increasingly supportive of non-profits starting worker-owned cooperatives as a means to create economic self-sufficiency for economically deprived groups. New York's Cooperative Home Care Associates continues its work through foundation support.

"Finding managers who understand cooperative structures and are willing to work in them, at a rate lower than they could make in conventional firms, is more difficult than financing," says DiMarcello. In addition to traditional business skills, managers need to understand the cooperative's unique internal capital accounting system (which tracks workers' initial investment as well as their share of profits and losses), cooperative problem-solving, and democratic information sharing.

Others, like Dick Gilbert of Stone Soup, believe cooperation is difficult to teach and maintain, particularly in industries with high turnover rates, like restaurants. Stone Soup managed to reduce its annual turnover rate to 50% (half the workers leave each year), far less than the industry's average of 600% (workers last only two months on average). But it was still difficult to share information, build trust, make collective decisions, cooperate in conflict resolution, and run the business.

To maintain the democratic nature of these groups, they need to instill and practice democratic management. Gilbert, along with a handful of worker-owners and adult educators around the country, is organizing educational programs to teach the culture and history of cooperation as well as the technical aspects of running and managing worker-owned businesses.

"Given our acculturation, we're probably more comfortable in authoritarian structures and carrot and stick motivators," Gilbert says. "This isn't the way it should be. We need to build models which are different and gain an understanding of how it's done."

In the United States today, there is greater capacity than ever before to promote worker-owned cooperatives. There are increasing numbers of financing mechanisms such as community development banks, revolving loan funds, foundations, and union pension funds. We also have more savvy at cooperative business development, and more technical assistance organizations like the ICA Group in Boston, Praxis in Philadelphia, and NCEO in Oakland. We have learned through our own history and international experiments what contributes to building networks of cooperatives. We still need to develop education for economic cooperation in schools and universities, as well as in our places of work.

As we find ourselves lured by the promise of reorganizing traditional workplaces, we should not be seduced by the economic benefits of ESOPs to individuals, or by employee participation schemes. Although interest in them is widespread, they are diversions from a broader goal. Instead, we should move beyond management's strategies and create new ways to equitably share control and the economic rewards of our labor. ■

Resources: Industry Sector Assessment for Community Economic Development Replication Strategy, The ICA Group, 1994 (20 Park Plaza, Suite 1127, Boston, MA 02116); *Employee Ownership and Corporate Performance*, National Center for Employee Ownership, undated (1201 Martin Luther King Jr. Way, Oakland, CA 94612).

ARTICLE 18   *September 1992*

THE QUALITY MOVEMENT

IS IT DEFECTIVE?

BY DAVID LEVINE

At Ford, "Quality is Job 1." IBM managers wrote a book about their quality movement and sponsored a PBS television series. *Business Week* published a special issue on "The Quality Imperative." Quality gurus such as Edward Deming, J.M. Juran, Phil Crosby, and Kaoru Ishikawa lecture and consult around the globe.

Under pressure from Japanese competitors whose defect rates may be a tenth of theirs, hundreds of the U.S.'s largest companies are adopting quality programs. The programs at firms as different as Hewlett Packard, Ford, and Motorola have led to dramatic increases in quality and productivity.

Managers, consultants, and unions have variously described the quality movement as:
- a set of techniques to reduce the defect rates in manufactured products;
- a way of simultaneously increasing customer and worker satisfaction, while increasing profits; or
- a management speed-up that *makes* workers work harder, but is unlikely to improve the quality of U.S. products.

In the United States the management speed-up description has more truth than the others at present. But, if U.S. management can change its behavior sufficiently, the movement could succeed here as it has in Japan.

WHAT IS THE QUALITY MOVEMENT?

In the early 1950s the American Edward Deming lectured in Japan on how to use statistical methods for quality control. Kaoru Ishikawa and other engineers and managers quickly coupled Deming's statistical tools with changes in Japanese workers' roles. These included training workers in problem-solving techniques and giving them leeway to design and implement solutions. The quality movement emphasized reducing waste, which includes defective parts, time spent on inspections, and high levels of inventory. Quality practices worked well in Japan due to compatible labor relations. Many large Japanese corporations, for example, avoid layoffs, giving workers confidence that if they improve efficiency they will not lose their jobs.

Management's "empowerment" of production employees has been equally important to quality's success. Upper management gives production workers more responsibility and authority, while reducing the number of managers and inspectors. Workers play a large role in designing how products are made, and in many cases are allowed to redesign their own jobs. This improves morale and productivity, and frees up engineers' time, greatly increasing the speed of developing new products. That speed makes Japanese companies formidable competitors in computer-controlled machine tools and other rapidly-innovative industries.

But Japan's quality movement has problems and contradictions. One concerns who shall participate in quality-improvement activities. Ishikawa stresses that workers will be more creative if they participate voluntarily, without "coercion from above." Yet he also argues that "If there are six persons in one workplace... Participation by all six is imperative."

In most large Japanese companies the second principle is dominant. Participation in quality activities is formally voluntary, but employees (and their bosses) are given low performance ratings if they do not participate, and meetings usually take place on workers' own time.

The quality movement has other major drawbacks for Japanese workers. Quality's focus on eliminating all waste has contributed to high levels of job stress. Some

Japanese wives have sued companies for the "death from overwork" of their husbands.

Japanese companies rarely extend the benefits of high levels of training and job security to women and older employees (over 55). Few workers in small companies get these benefits either.

The quality movement — at its best — helps companies produce products that have few defects and match customers' desires. A company can organize work in many ways to satisfy these goals at a reasonable cost.

At laboratories and special restaurants, food engineers employed by McDonald's, Inc., experiment. They alter recipes and try new combinations of flavorings. The engineers carefully track customers' responses as they vary salt, temperature, seconds of frying, and other variations, to determine the "one best way" to cook a hamburger.

In contrast, McDonald's hamburger flippers do not experiment. They follow the recipes and processes that the engineers design. The workers cannot alter their recipes to match local tastes or the fresh produce which is available. Their job is routine, and quite boring.

Like assembly lines or data processing offices around the globe, McDonald's expects defects. Managers and quality inspectors try to catch most of these defects before they reach the customers. Since no inspector is perfect, McDonald's employs a world-wide corps of inspectors of inspectors, and inspectors of inspectors' inspectors.

BACK TO THE U.S.A.

After a series of setbacks in the 1980's, Cummins Engine Co. adopted quality techniques. Cummins now finds production defects in 1% of its engines rather than the 10% of earlier years, and warranty costs have fallen 20% since 1989.

Motorola suffered through several bad years at the hands of Japanese competitors. Since devoting itself to quality in the mid-1980's, the company has slashed defects from 6,000 to 40 per million.

The U.S.'s top three automakers have cut their defect rates from 7 per car in 1981 to 1.5 today, close to the 1.1 rate in Japanese cars. Ford was the first U.S. automaker to focus on quality, bringing in Deming in 1981. Ford used one technique, "design for manufacturing," and reduced the number of parts in its V-8 engine by 25%.

Workers can appreciate quality practices for several reasons. Most like to do a good job and to satisfy customers, with whom they identify. When the pursuit of quality is practiced correctly, workers learn new skills and enjoy more autonomy. They can perform their own quality control, influence their immediate work environment, and make decisions about how to increase quality. Employee satisfaction and productivity increase, leading to lower turnover and higher take-home pay.

Quality requires managers who reward experimentation and recognize that most experiments do not work.

Employees must feel confident that bosses will view their mistakes as sources of learning, not examples of failure. Even *Business Week* argues that empowering workers is crucial to success, "because it's the employees themselves who generally find the best solution."

But such empowerment violates long-standing American management practices, such as not listening to workers or giving them a role in decisionmaking. As a result, in most companies the quality movement is likely to go the way of Zero Defects, quality circles, quality of work life, and other short-lived management fads.

A study of 584 companies reported in the *Wall Street Journal* found that "among most U.S. companies, virtually no quality-boosting practices have reached... meaningful levels." Bill Sheeran, a vice president at General Electric's appliance operations, has said that quality circles failed because companies "didn't empower employees to carry through with it." And quality management has failed at a number of U.S. auto plants, such as General Motors' plant in Van Nuys, California.

In many factories, managers have burdened workers with the added task of filling in SPC charts that track machine performance, without rewarding workers for their efforts. In one auto parts plant, for example, only engineers were trained to analyze data from the charts, and they rarely did. The workers found that even if they entered numbers at random, no one complained. When SPC occurs without empowerment, it is little more than a speed-up.

Without the cooperation of the employees, SPC loses its potential for improving quality. But managers are more likely to punish American workers than reward them for trying to increase quality. Management treats each report of a quality problem as an admission of failure, or a criticism of management. Thus, employees are often afraid to share their ideas. One think-tank, the American Quality Foundation, found that "70% of American workers are afraid to speak up with suggestions or to ask for clarification." These fears are particularly acute for the four-fifths of American workers who are not in unions and so have no protection against unjust dismissals.

Everyone is in favor of quality. If corporations would empower workers and share with them the benefits of higher productivity, quality practices could increase the competitiveness of American enterprises without lowering the living standards of workers. But due to the intransigence of management, the movement has had only modest effects at most American factories and offices. Until American managers take the desires of workers and customers seriously, quality will remain an elusive goal. ■

Resources: David I. Levine, "Japan's Other Export," *Dollars & Sense,* Sept., 1990; Juran, J.M., ed., *Juran's Quality Handbook,* 4th edition, 1988; *Business Week,* 10/25/92; *Wall Street Journal* 5/14/92.

September/October 1996

WORKER PARTICIPATION

IS IT WORTH THE PRICE?

BY ROBERT DRAGO

"Worker participation" is shorthand for "giving workers greater influence over managerial decisions." Such participation can range from "low level" decisions like choosing the color of the lunchroom walls to "high level" decisions like voting for the president of the firm. Since most companies would rather have workers dealing with wall color than selecting CEOs, worker participation is not always what managers and consultants might have you believe.

Worker participation brings both good news and bad news. The good news is, first, that when firms advocate participation they are admitting that capitalist management is typically authoritarian and arbitrary — and so is often bad for people and even for profits. For example, when a small clothing manufacturer in Massachusetts introduced a worker participation program, stitchers gained the right to go to the bathroom without raising their hands and getting permission from the supervisor. Since the workers were already on piece rates, the firm lost no money in the process and the supervisor's headaches were reduced. More generally, many of the largest firms in the United States have been able to cut layers of management as they finally admitted that front-line employees are actually capable of thinking and taking initiative.

A second piece of good news is that some worker participation programs involve genuine elements of democracy in the workplace. For example, at the Saturn automobile factory in Tennessee, workteams elect their supervisors, control the layout of the line, and perform all hiring and firing decisions. Through their United Automobile Workers local, Saturn workers also exert significant control over the design of the car, personnel policies, marketing, training and technology.

Many left observers would like to think that Saturn will become the norm for production practices in the United States or, better still, that the high levels of participation at Saturn might lead workers to demand control over the big money issue — investment. And that leads us to the bad news, as neither of these outcomes seem likely to occur.

The current context is not favorable to workers. Managers have known for decades that worker participation could lead to productivity improvements and a more satisfied workforce, but most U.S. companies avoided it like the plague. Now these same firms openly embrace autonomous workteams, getting rid of supervisors through worker participation programs, and so forth.

The key to understanding this change of strategy is that managers have workers so scared and fearful for their job security that they feel safe in turning workers loose on the shop floor. If workers don't use their new-found "freedom" to help increase profits, the corporation will replace the workers, moving the jobs elsewhere in the United States or abroad.

The U.S. workplace is now disposable, and workers are being given the "opportunity" to prevent job loss through worker participation programs. Even at Saturn, Mike Parker and Jane Slaughter (1994) found that fear of job loss was a major factor in motivating workers.

Another piece of bad news, closely related to the first, is that the fastest-growing worker participation programs are all low level, such as autonomous workteams. Yes, workers are being given more control over production lines, quality issues, customer relations and issues of supervision. But the opportunities for high level participation in decisions like pay scales, overall employment or job security are dwindling.

This is hardly an accident. On the one hand, since the purpose of most current worker participation programs is to increase profits, why involve workers in issues which cost money? On the other hand, the major tools which workers have used over the years to "participate" in high level issues — trade unions — have been decimated by many of the same firms that so proudly trumpet their worker participation programs, including Hewlett-Packard, IBM and General Electric.

Worker participation has some good points, particularly in terms of getting supervisors off the backs of workers. But, at least in the United States, it has not addressed the big issues — corporate downsizing, jobs, wages and investment. Take it for what it's worth. ∎

Resources: The New American Workplace, Eileen Appelbaum and Rosemary Batt, 1994, ILR Press; *Working Smart*, Mike Parker and Jane Slaughter, Labor Notes, 1994, Detroit.

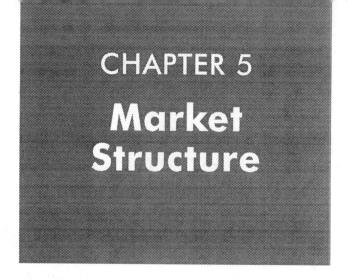

ARTICLE 20   *July/August 1989, revised March 1995*

IS SMALL BEAUTIFUL?
IS BIGGER BETTER?

SMALL AND BIG BUSINESS BOTH HAVE THEIR DRAWBACKS

BY CHRIS TILLY

Beginning in the late 1980s, the United States has experienced a small, but significant boom in small business. While big businesses have downsized, small enterprises have proliferated. Should we be glad? Absolutely, declare the advocates of small business. Competition makes small businesses entrepreneurial, innovative, and responsive to customers.

Not so fast, reply big business's boosters. Big corporations grew big because they were efficient, and tend to stay efficient because they are big — and thus able to invest in research and upgrading of technology and workforce skills.

But each side in this debate omits crucial drawbacks. Small may be beautiful for consumers, but it's often oppressive for workers. And while big businesses wield the power to advance technology, they also often wield the market power to bash competitors and soak consumers. In the end, the choices are quite limited.

BIG AND SMALL

Is the United States a nation of big businesses, or of small ones? There are two conventional ways to measure business size. One is simply to count the number of employees. By this measure, small businesses (say, business establishments with less than 20 employees) make up the majority of businesses (Table 1). But they provide only a small fraction of the total number of jobs.

The other approach gauges market share — each firm's share of total sales in a given industry. Industries range between two extremes: what economists call "perfect competition" (many firms selling a standardized product, each too tiny to affect the market price) and monopoly (one business controls all sales in an industry). Economy-wide, as with employment, small businesses are most numerous, but control only a small slice of total sales. Sole proprietorships account for 73% of established businesses, far outnumbering corporations, which are 19% of the total (the remainder are partnerships). But corporations ring up a hefty 90% of all sales, leaving sole proprietors with only 6%. It takes a lot of mom and pop stores to equal General Motors' 1993 total of $138 billion in sales.

Industry by industry, the degree of competition varies widely. Economists consider an industry concentrated when its top four companies account for more than 40% of total sales in the industry (Table 2). At one end of the spectrum are the chewing gum, beer, and aircraft industries, where four or five firms account for most U.S. production.

No market comes close to meeting the textbook specifications for perfect competition, but one can still find industries in which a large number of producers compete for sales. The clothing and restaurant industries, for example, remain relatively competitive. Overall, about one-third of U.S. goods are manufactured in concentrated industries, about one fifth are made in competitive industries, and the rest fall somewhere in between.

BEATING THE COMPETITION

Those who tout the benefits of small, competitive business make a broad range of claims on its behalf. In addition to keeping prices low, they say the quality of the product is constantly improving, as companies seek a competitive edge. The same desire, they claim, drives firms toward technological innovations, leading to productivity increases.

The real story is not so simple. Competition does indeed keep prices low. Believe it or not, clothing costs us less — in real terms — than it cost our parents. Between 1960 and 1995, while the overall price level and hourly wages both increased fivefold, apparel prices didn't even triple. And small businesses excel at offering variety, whether it is the ethnic restaurants that dot cities or the custom machine-tool work offered by small shops. Furthermore, however powerful small business lobbies may be in Washington, they do not influence the legislative process as blatantly as do corporate giants.

But those low prices often have an ugly underside. Our sportswear is cheap in part because the garment industry increasingly subcontracts work to sweatshops — whether they be export assembly plants in Haiti paying dollar-a-day wages, or the "underground" Los Angeles stitcheries that employ immigrant women in virtual slavery. Struggling to maintain razor-thin profit margins, small businesses cut costs any way they can — which usually translates into low wages and onerous working conditions.

"There is a rule of survival for small business," Bill Ryan, president of Ryan Transfer Corporation, commented some years ago. "There are certain things you want to have [in paying workers] and certain things you can afford. You had better go with what you can afford." Bottom line, workers in companies employing 500 or more people enjoy average wages 30% higher than their counterparts in small businesses.

Part of this wage gap results from differences other than size — unionization, the education of the workforce, the particular jobs and industries involved. But University of Michigan economist Charles Brown and his colleagues controlled for all these differences and more, and still found a 10% premium for big business's employees. A note of caution, however: Other recent research indicates that this wage bonus is linked to long-term employment and job ladders. To the extent that corporations dissolve these long-term ties — as they seem to be rapidly doing — the pay advantage may dissolve as well.

Small business gurus make extravagant claims about small businesses' job-generation capacity. An oft-quoted 1987 report by consultant David Birch claimed that businesses with fewer than 20 employees create 88% of new jobs. The reality is more mundane: over the long run,

TABLE 1
SMALL BUSINESS NATION?
Most businesses are small, but most employees work for big businesses

Company size (number of employees)	Percent of all firms	Percent of all workers
1-4	55%	6%
5-9	20	9
10-19	12	11
20-49	8	16
50-99	3	13
100-249	2	16
250-499	0.4	9
500-999	0.2	7
1,000 or more	0.1	13

Source: County Business Patterns, 1993.

Note: "Businesses" refers to establishments, meaning business locations

TABLE 2
WHO COMPETES, WHO DOESN'T

Industry	Percent of sales by top four firms
Chewing gum	96%
Malt beverages	87
Cereal breakfast foods	87
Greeting card publishing	85
Aircraft	72
Soaps and other detergents	65
Blast furnaces and steel mills	44
Electronic computers	43
Machine tools, metal cutting types	31
Bolts, nuts, rivets, and washers	16
Women's and misses' dresses	6
Wood pallet skids	4

Source: 1987 Census of Manufacturers, Subject Series MC87-S-6

businesses with 19 or fewer workers account for about one quarter of net new jobs. One reason why Birch's statistics are misleading is that new small businesses are created in great numbers, but they also fail at a high rate. The result is that the *net* gain in jobs is much smaller than the number created in business start-ups.

For companies in very competitive markets, the same "whip of competition" that keeps prices down undermines many of competition's other supposed benefits. The flurry of competition in the airline industry following deregulation, for example, hardly resulted in a higher quality product. Flying became temporarily cheaper, but also less comfortable, reliable, and safe.

Technological innovation from competition is also more myth than reality. Small firms in competitive industries do very little research and development. They lack both the cash needed to make long-term investments and the market power to guarantee a return on that investment. In fact, many of them can't even count on surviving to reap the rewards: only one-third to one-half of small business startups survive for five years, and only about one in five makes it to ten years. A 1988 Census Bureau survey concluded that in manufacturing, "technology use is positively correlated with plant size." Agriculture may be the exception that proves the rule. That highly competitive industry has made marked productivity gains, but its research is supported by the taxpayer, and its risks are reduced by government price supports.

Of course, the biggest myth about competition is that it is in any way a 'natural state' for capitalism. In fact, in most markets the very process of competing for high profits or a bigger market share tends to create a concentrated, rather than a competitive, market structure. This process occurs in several ways. Big firms sometimes drive their smaller competitors out of business by selectively cutting prices to the bone. The smaller firms may lack the financial resources to last out the low prices. In the 1960s, several of IBM's smaller competitors sued it for cutting prices in a pattern that was designed to drive the smaller firms out of the market. Large corporations can also gain a lock on scarce resources: for example, large airlines like United and American operate the comprehensive, computerized information and reservation systems that travel agents tap into — and you can bet that each airline's system lists their own flights first.

Other firms eliminate competitors by buying them out — either in a hostile takeover or a friendly merger. Either way, a former competitor is neutralized. This strategy used to be severely limited by strict antitrust guidelines that prohibited most horizontal mergers — those between two firms that formerly competed in the same market. The Reagan administration's team at the Justice Department, however, loosened the merger guidelines significantly in the early 1980s. Since that time, many large mergers between former competitors have been allowed to go through, most notably in the airline industry.

THE POWER OF CONCENTRATION

Concentration, then, is as natural to market economies as competition. And bigness, like smallness, is a mixed bag for us as consumers and workers. For workers, bigness is on the whole a plus. Whereas competition forces small businesses to be stingy, big firms are on average more generous, offering employees higher wages, greater job security, and more extensive fringe benefits. In one 1986 survey, 100% of businesses with 500 or more workers provided health insurance; only 55% of smaller firms did so. Large firms also provide much more employee training. The strongest unions, as well, have historically been in industries where a few firms control large shares of their markets, and can pass along increased costs to consumers — auto, steel, and tires, for example. When profits are threatened, though, firms in concentrated markets also have more resources with which to fight labor. They are better able to weather a strike, oppose unionization, and make agreements with rivals not to take advantage of each other's labor troubles. In addition, large companies, not surprisingly, score low on workplace autonomy.

What about consumers? Corporations in industries where there are few competitors may compete, but the competitive clash is seldom channeled into prolonged price wars. The soft drink industry is a classic example. David McFarland, a University of North Carolina economist, likens soft drink competition to professional wrestling. "They make a lot of sounds and groans and bounce on the mat, but they know who is going to win," he remarked.

Coke and Pepsi introduce new drinks and mount massive ad campaigns to win market share, but the net result is not lower prices. In fact, because competition between industry giants relies more on product differentiation than price, companies pass on their inflated advertising expenses to consumers. In the highly concentrated breakfast cereal market, the package frequently costs more than the contents. And of every dollar you pay for a box, nearly 20 cents goes for advertising.

It takes resources to develop and market a new idea, which gives large corporations distinct advantages in innovation. The original idea for the photocopier may have come from a patent lawyer who worked nights in his basement, but Xerox spent $16 million before it had a product it could sell. RCA invested $65 million developing the color television. RCA could take this gamble because its dominance in the television market ensured

> THE VERY PROCESS OF COMPETING FOR HIGH PROFITS OR A BIGGER MARKET SHARE TENDS TO CREATE A CONCENTRATED, RATHER THAN A COMPETITIVE, MARKET STRUCTURE.

that it would not be immediately undercut by some other firm.

But market dominance can also translate into complacency. The steel industry illustrates the point. A few major producers earned steady profits through the 1950s and 1960s but were caught off-guard when new technologies vaulted foreign steel-makers to the top of the industry in the 1970s. Similarly, when IBM dominated the computer industry in the 1960s and early 1970s, innovation proceeded quite slowly, particularly compared to the frantic scramble in that industry today. With no competitors to worry about, it was more profitable for IBM to sit tight, since innovation would only have made its own machines obsolete.

And large corporations can also put their deep pockets and technical expertise to work to short-circuit public policy. In the 1980s, when Congress changed corporate liability laws to make corporate executives criminally liable for some kinds of offenses, General Electric's lobbyists and legal staff volunteered to help draft the final regulations, in order to minimize the damage.

Big businesses sometimes hide their lobbying behind a "citizen" smokescreen. The largest-spending lobby in Washington in 1986 was Citizens for the Control of Acid rain. These good citizens had been organized by coal and electric utility companies to oppose tighter pollution controls. Along the same lines, the Coalition for Vehicle Choice (now, who could be against that?) was set up by Ford and General Motors in 1990 to fight higher fuel efficiency standards.

CONCENTRATION OR CONGLOMERATION

Over the last couple of decades, the mix of big and small businesses has changed, but the changes are small and—at first glance — contradictory. Over time, employment has shifted toward smaller firms, though the shift has been subtle, not revolutionary. Meanwhile, the overall level of industry-by-industry sales concentration in the economy has increased, but only slightly. As older industries become more concentrated, newer, more competitive ones crop up, leaving overall concentration relatively steady. In his book *Lean and Mean*, economist Bennett Harrison points out that there is actually no contradiction between the small business employment boomlet and big firms's continued grip on markets. Big businesses, it turns out, are orchestrating much of the flowering of small business, through a variety of outsourcing and subcontracting arrangements.

But if industry-by-industry concentration has changed little over the decades, conglomeration is a different matter. Corporate ownership of assets has become much more concentrated over time, reflecting the rise in conglomerates — corporations doing business in a variety of industries. Five decades ago, the top 200 firms accounted for 48% of all sales and 30% of all manufacturing value added in the U.S. economy. By the early 1980s, the 200 biggest firms controlled 60% of sales and over 40% of value added.

Most mainstream economists see these groupings as irrelevant for the competitive structure of the economy. Antitrust laws place no restrictions on firms from different industries banding together under one corporate roof. But sheer size can easily affect competition in the markets of the individual firms involved. A parent company can use one especially profitable subsidiary to subsidize start-up costs for a new venture, giving it a competitive edge. And if one board of directors controls major interests in related industries, it can obviously influence any of those markets more forcefully.

A case in point is the mega-merger of Time Inc. and Warner. The resulting conglomerate, Time Warner Inc., controls massive sections of the home entertainment business, bringing together Time's journalists, film and television producers, and authors, and Warner's entertainment machine, which includes Home Box Office, the nation's largest pay television channel. The conglomerate can influence the entertainment business from the initial point — the actors, writers, and directors — up to the point where the finished products appear on people's televisions via cable. Conglomeration also multiplies the political clout of large corporations. No wonder Disney and others are joining Time-Warner in hopping on the conglomeration bandwagon.

CHOOSE YOUR POISON

Competition, concentration, or conglomeration: The choice is an unsavory one indeed. Opting for lots of tiny, competing firms leaves labor squeezed and sacrifices the potential technological advantages that come with concentrated resources. Yet the big monopolies tend to dominate their markets, charge high prices, and waste countless resources on glitzy ad campaigns and trivial product differentiation. And the big conglomerate firms, while not necessarily dominant in any single market, wield a frightening amount of political and economic power, with budgets larger than those of most countries.

Of course, we don't have much to say about the choice, no matter how much "shopping for a better world" we engage in. Market competition rolls on — sometimes cutthroat, other times genteel. Industries often start out as monopolies (based on new inventions), go through a competitive phase, but end up concentrating as they mature. As long as bigness remains profitable and the government maintains a hands-off attitude, companies in both competitive and concentrated industries will tend to merge with firms in other industries. This will feed a continuing trend toward conglomeration. Since bigness and smallness both have their drawbacks, the best we can do is to use public policies to minimize the disadvantages of each. ∎

Resources: Lean and Mean: The Changing Landscape of Corporate Power in the Age of Flexibility, Bennett Harrison, 1994; *Employers Large and Small*, Charles Brown, James Hamilton, and James Medoff, 1990.

THE MEDIA MEGA-MERGERS

BY EDWARD S. HERMAN

In 1951, the distinguished jurist, Learned Hand, said "The hand that rules the press, the radio, the screen and the far-spread magazine rules the country."

Recent years have seen this ruling hand further centralized. In 1989 Time, Inc. and Warner Communications merged, creating the world's largest media complex. The cable TV power Viacom acquired Paramount Communications in 1994 and Blockbuster Video in January 1995. Following soon after were the almost simultaneous announcements in July 1995 that Disney would buy Capital Cities/ABC, and Westinghouse would gobble up CBS.

That same July Viacom sold its 1.1 million-subscriber cable system to Tele-Communications Inc. (TCI), the largest U.S. cable company, for $2.3 billion. Only a month later, Time Warner offered to acquire Turner Broadcasting Systems for $8.5 billion.

This recent wave of giant mergers has sharply increased media concentration in the United States. With opportunities for mergers enlarged by the 1996 Telecommunications Reform [sic] Act, we can anticipate further concentration.

A notable feature of the biggest recent mergers is that the firms dominating this process are not media companies in a strict sense: Disney is avowedly a "family entertainment communication company" in the business of selling theme parks, toys, movies, and videos. Its focus, in the words of CEO Michael Eisner, is on the provision of "non-political entertainment and sports." Time Warner has a similarly wide spectrum of business interests and a comparable marketing orientation. Disney and Time Warner are what Herbert Schiller calls "pop cultural corporate behemoths."

Westinghouse, by contrast, has long been primarily a nuclear power and weapons producer, with its media interests only 10% of sales revenue. With the Westinghouse takeover of CBS, two of the three top networks are controlled by large firms in the politically sensitive nuclear power/weapons industries (the other is NBC's owner General Electric, which, along with Westinghouse, is one of the top 15 U.S. defense contractors).

These developments threaten the survival of independent and critical programming, which have become merely appendages to entertainment and weapons-seller complexes. Conflicts of interest in news production within the complexes already abound (see accompanying box). The global and marketing focus of the new complexes will exacerbate the conflicts with news reporting and analysis and cause the public sphere to continue eroding.

In addition, as monopoly power increases both horizontally (among the providers of programming, for example) and vertically (such as through program producers merging with broadcasting networks), this will enhance their power to exclude rivals and impose higher prices on consumers.

The bases of the new merger wave are twofold. First, perceptions by managers of the dominant media firms that combining forces will yield new business opportunities. And second, a more permissive political and regulatory environment that has allowed and even encouraged mergers.

BUSINESS OPPORTUNITIES

The economic underpinnings of the recent mega-mergers have been the rapid growth of the entertainment business at home and abroad and the new global horizons of media entrepreneurs. Business Week noted in 1994 that "Europe and Japan used to mock America by calling it a 'Mickey Mouse' economy. Well, they're right. By any yardstick Mickey and his friends have become a major engine for U.S. economic growth. Since the economy turned up in 1991, entertainment and recreation — not health care or autos — have provided the biggest boost to consumer spending." Forecasters are predicting continued high growth rates in entertainment, recreation, and communication outlays over the next five years.

Global entertainment and media markets have been growing even faster than domestic markets, and companies like Disney and Time Warner, with huge stakes in foreign markets, plan to use these assets to increase their reach overseas. The European motion picture industry, for example, is suddenly reviving, but "what is sparking the growth is investment by the big American film studios like Walt Disney and Warner Brothers," who are behaving, according to Jeremy Thomas, chairman of the British Film Institute, "like when you have a predator fish in a pond." Rupert Murdoch and his rivals are enthralled with the prospects of the opening Chinese market, and are aggressively positioning themselves with alliances, mergers and satellite stations in pursuit of this and other Asian markets.

The growing global market has been a huge windfall for U.S. "content" producers of movies, TV shows, popular music, videotapes and cassettes. Owners of old movies and cartoons (e.g., Ted Turner) have seen the market value of their properties rise accordingly. Owners of cable channels with access to growing foreign audiences have been anxious to affiliate with content suppliers (producers or owners of films, syndicated TV shows, and cartoons). And content providers have been eager to gain assured access to means of reaching audiences — channels, stations, and distribution networks. Disney wanted Capital Cities/ABC in good part for the access that Cap Cities could provide. Time Warner wanted Turner in large measure for his marketable content in CNN, his Cartoon Channel, cartoon stocks and capacity to produce new shows.

Beyond secure access, the vertical mergers (Disney-Cap Cities; Time Warner-Turner) allow what are euphemistically called "synergies," which in practice means "cross-selling." The merger participants have been enthusiastic over the prospect that, for example, Disney could not only show its films and TV programs on ABC, but that Disney theme parks and toys could be promoted on ABC and on Cap Cities' ESPN (sports channel). Conversely, ABC's and ESPN's programs could be promoted in theme parks, and the entire system could buy advertising globally on favorable terms. According to the Wall Street Journal, Disney head Eisner and Cap Cities head Murphy anticipated other synergies, such as "promotion of the Disney Channel during Disney-produced Saturday morning cartoon shows and the use of Disney's syndication muscle to sell ABC-owned and produced programs."

Viacom has successfully used its Blockbuster video stores to push Paramount movies, and in the summer of 1995, Time Warner mobilized its Six Flags theme park and its Warner retail store system to promote its movie "Batman Forever." ABC's news magazine's program "Prime Time Live" has several times profiled personalities and stars on other ABC programs — cross-selling in the guise of infotainment. Financial analyst James Reidy notes that Murdoch "had set a standard that other studios now want to follow by using his network to create value for shows Fox owned....Only a network can create value by making a program a hit. Even if you don't have very good ratings, you can still showcase a program and then sell it in Bulgaria or someplace." Jerome Dominus, of the J. Walter Thompson ad agency, agrees: the "promotional capabilities of a network" can build audiences for new shows by plugging them during existing hits or "event" programming like the Olympics.

All of these "synergies" are what economists call "pecuniary" as opposed to "real" economies from mergers. That is, they involve financial and marketing advantages to the private firm, but no real cost reductions that would benefit society. There is also an exclusionary aspect to cross-selling synergies: a book that Time Warner publishes because of its synergistic potential as a movie and with spinoff toy and video sales not only receives massive advertising, it also benefits from promotion on Time Warner TV shows and in its magazines, at the expense of possibly superior books

that don't meet the synergistic standard. There may be a corruption of the reviewing process in favor of the privileged books. And Westinghouse or GE may regard their power to suppress or edit programs critical of nuclear power and the military budget as one of the "synergistic" merits of network control.

For Westinghouse, owning CBS provides few cross-selling opportunities. Its only related holdings are TV and radio stations, a number in the same markets as those held by CBS. This horizontal fusion might afford some small real economies in the sharing of services like news reporters (or closing overlapping stations) in common markets — but these hypothetical benefits must be weighed against the reduction in competition in these markets.

Real economies are hard to locate in the giant mergers. It is interesting that the dominant political opinion-makers have not objected to growing centralization of power in a strategic industry, and one where diversity of viewpoints is acknowledged to be important for a democratic society. This lack of concern exists despite the absence of evidence that these mergers will improve social efficiency.

> THE DOMINANT POLITICAL OPINION-MAKERS HAVE NOT OBJECTED TO GROWING CENTRALIZATION OF POWER IN A STRATEGIC INDUSTRY.

REGULATORY CAVE-IN

The Disney-Cap Cities merger was made possible by the FCC'S ending of the financial syndication ("fin-syn") rules. These rules had limited network ownership of the rights to syndicate programs produced for them, prevented the networks from owning program producers, and blocked Hollywood studios from owning networks. As one commentator noted: "Hollywood's titans seem to be trying to buy broadcast outlets for one major reason: They can."

But the mega-mergers also rest on a broader collapse of political and regulatory opposition to increased media concentration. This partially reflects the political climate of greater deference to the demands of business and "competitiveness." The media are substantial political funders, but a more important consideration is the politicos' fear of the raw propaganda power of media barons.

In Great Britain, Rupert Murdoch's role in causing Labor's past electoral defeats led the new Labor Party leader Tony Blair to abandon his party's 1992 campaign pledge that the Monopoly Commission would investigate Murdoch's "unacceptable concentration of power" (he holds a 35% share of weekday newspaper circulation, among other interests). Instead, Blair travelled to Australia to meet with Murdoch, and persuade him of his credentials for office.

In the United States, Murdoch's book deal with Newt Gingrich, preceded by a discussion of Murdoch's media regulatory problems, merely added icing to an already rich cake of Republican mega-media solidarity. Equally interesting in 1995 was the ease with which Murdoch got the Clinton-era Federal Communications Commission (FCC) to let him retain his Fox network — despite Murdoch's admission that his 1986 application to buy TV stations failed to make clear de facto (and illegal) foreign ownership.

The Reagan-Bush years witnessed a steady erosion of antitrust limits on mergers and FCC concern over issues of market power. The new laxity was intellectually grounded in a Chicago-School faith that the market automatically serves the public interest. This was reinforced by the claims that new media forms like cable, direct satellite-based TV transmissions, and videotapes, were breaking down any broadcast station and network monopoly power. It also

---

MEDIA POLITICAL BIAS: THE TIP OF THE ICEBERG

Time Warner

— In 1973, Warner Modular, a subsidiary of one of Time Warner's predecessors, Warner Publishing, issued a book titled *Counter-Revolutionary Violence*, by Noam Chomsky and this writer. The top brass of Warner Publishing disapproved of the book, and reacted by cancelling all advertising, refusing to sell the book, and closing down the subsidiary. One of the officers involved, Steven Ross, was the organizer and first CEO of Time Warner.

Paramount Communications

— In 1979, Mark Dowie's *Corporate Murder* was dropped by Simon and Schuster, a subsidiary of Paramount's predecessor, Gulf & Western. A Simon & Schuster editor told Dowie that the president of the book company simply disliked the anti-corporate thrust of the book.

Bantam, Bertelsmann, Disney

— Marc Eliot's book, *Walt Disney: Hollywood's Dark Prince*, was killed in 1991 by Bantam, a subsidiary of Bertelsmann. Apparently its critical stance angered Disney officials. At the same time, Bantam and Disney had a major contract in which Bantam would publish children's book versions of Disney movies for supermarket sale. That and other contracts would be jeopardized by publication of the book.

---

rested on increased globalization, and the alleged need to allow U.S. media enterprises to meet the new global competition. The argument was reinforced by the strong positive contribution that communications industries make to the U.S. balance of payments. For the Clinton administration, with its heavy emphasis on trade expansion, the media giants represented the national interest and were to be given support.

The FCC has never forcefully defended the public interest. No station, for example, has ever been deprived of its license due to low quality programming, and the FCC has gradually adapted its policies to broadcaster demands. Concerning the degradation of children's programming, Action for Children's Television pushed for changes from 1969 onward. But its appeals were not met under either Democratic or Republican rule. In "liberal" administrations the FCC acknowledges a problem, carries out studies demonstrating this, and sometimes asks the broadcasters to voluntarily do something about it; whereas in 1983 the Republican-controlled FCC found that the broadcasters had no responsibility whatsoever to children.

During the Reagan-Bush years, the Fairness Doctrine was ended, the time between broadcast station license renewals was increased to five years, and ownership rules were amended to allow more concentrated holdings and cross-ownership. From 1953 until the Reagan years, ownership limits were fixed by the "7-7-7" rule (7 AM, 7 FM, and 7 TV stations per owner), and cross-ownership of newspapers and broadcasting stations within the same market was barred (with over a hundred exceptions grandfathered, however). These limits were raised to 12-12-12 in 1985, with TV station owners allowed to reach 25% of the national population. The ownership limits for radio were raised to 24-24 in 1992 with rights to acquire multiple stations in each market.

The 1996 Telecommunications Reform Act removes the national ceiling on radio station ownership and allows as many as eight stations to be acquired in the largest single markets. The ceiling on TV station ownership was raised to allow a single owner to reach 35% of the national audience. Merger guidelines have also been softened, and giant mergers have been approved as a matter of course. GE was allowed to acquire NBC in 1986, in a regression from the 1967 intervention by the Justice Department that prevented ITT from buying ABC. Justice took this action partly on grounds of conflict of interest between ITT's international business interests and objective performance of the news media.

In 1948, Paramount was forced to divest its movie theaters on the ground that this gave the movie maker the ability to exclude its rivals from Paramount's distribution network. The same issues are present now, as potential cable entrants, fearing exclusion from program supply, are suing Time Warner and Turner, while independent program makers worry about access to Time Warner-Turner and affiliated TCI cable channels and networks.

But the climate of opinion and law has changed to such a degree that the Disney-Cap Cities merger breezed through the FCC, with seven waivers for combinations of media properties in single markets. "I think its great that a major network like ABC would be thinking of combining resources with a family-oriented company like Disney," said Republican Commissioner Rochelle Chong. The vertical monopoly power implicit in such a marriage didn't bother her, nor did it influence the FCC as a whole.

The new political warmth toward giant mergers is reflected in the quick approval that the Justice Department gave to the Westinghouse-CBS merger, while the FCC granted Westinghouse 19 permanent or temporary waivers of agency rules that limit broadcaster concentration. The FCC acted despite Westinghouse management's lack of experience relevant to CBS's managerial problems, a conflict of interest similar to that which halted ITT's attempt to acquire ABC in 1967, and in the face of liberal advocacy group criticisms of Westinghouse's poor record in children's educational programming. The FCC claimed in a news release that "the overall public interest benefit of the transaction outweigh any diminution in diversity and competition."

BIGNESS AND MONOPOLY POWER

For many years, containing business size in order to preserve the economic basis of a political democracy, was considered a primary purpose of antitrust law. That notion is no longer operative, for liberals like FCC head Reed Hundt, as well as conservatives.

On the basis of the old, democratic standard, bigness, especially when obtained by merger rather than internal growth, should require proof of real economic advantage to society, not merely corporate pecuniary advantage based on cross-selling. None of the great media mergers from 1989 to the present meet this standard.

On more conventional antitrust principles, mergers should not be allowed where they enhance market power and reduce competition, actual or potential, in already concentrated markets. The giant mergers of 1989-1996 also fail this test, in one or more of three ways. First, competition will necessarily be reduced and tighter oligopolies created by the mergers. For example, the Time Warner-Turner merger, with Malone's TCI a substantial owner of the merged company, will tighten the bonds between the two top cable powerhouses (TCI and TW), and between them and a leading cable channel supplier (Turner).

Second, they remove major rivals who were well-positioned to enter into the niches filled by the merger itself. Cap Cities was in a strong position to enlarge its production of content in competition with Disney, as Cap City head Murphy acknowledged in pre-merger days ("The only thing the studios bring to the creative process is money,

and we've got that too"). Meanwhile, Disney was strong enough to enter the distribution field by building up its own network of stations. The merger ended this important basis of potential competition.

Third, the mergers weaken the position of outsiders in selling programs, getting channels introduced, and entering the distribution field. Malone of TCI prevented the powerful GE from starting a 24-hour news channel in the mid-1980s by refusing to carry it on his cable system. He has been able to favor right-wing cable channels like Paul Weyrich's Empowerment Channel, and the large number in which he has a financial interest, while literally destroying the liberal "90s Channel" by limiting its exposure and imposing discriminatorily high prices for admission. Only the phone companies are serious potential rivals to cable companies and over-the-air broadcasters, and they are likely to enter slowly and in alliances with existing oligopolists. Even these powerful firms are worried enough about access to programming from the Time Warner-Turner combine to sue to prevent the merger or assure protection against exclusion. The recent mergers are almost certain to elicit further defensive mergers, yielding a tightened oligopoly of very large firms with great market power.

WITH EACH MAJOR MERGER, FROM TIME AND WARNER IN 1989 TO THE PRESENT, THERE HAVE BEEN SHARP CUTBACKS IN NEWS BUREAU STAFF.

ENTERTAINMENT AND THE PUBLIC SPHERE

Companies like Disney, Time Warner and Viacom openly proclaim themselves to be first and foremost, bottom-line oriented entertainment companies. They are selling movies, TV shows, books, magazines, theme park amusements and toys to the public, searching for "added value" in cross-selling among these marketed products. "Creativity" is producing books, movies, videos and spin-off toys based on the salable qualities of Forest Gump, Dumb and Dumber, and The Lion King. Disney's Lion King represents the ideal toward which the entertainment complexes aspire: The movie was "the hub of a marketing program that connects its book, movie, recording and theme park units." There were a million books quickly shipped to retailers, hundreds of thousands of sound tracks issued pushing Lion King to the top of the Billboard charts, tie-ins with Toys "R" Us and Kodak, and Disney retail store promotions, all producing an estimated $1 billion in profits over a short time span.

By contrast with The Lion King and Looney Tunes, news, public policy debates, and public interest programs have little "synergistic" potential and do not sell well abroad. With each major merger, from Time and

Warner in 1989 to the present, there have been sharp cutbacks in news bureau staff, partly reflecting the pressure of heavy debts to cut costs, but also reflecting the drive for profits.

When broadcasting began in the 1920s, and later when rights to the public airwaves were being debated, both broadcasters and politicians claimed that radio and TV would not merely amuse and divert. They would provide a public service, by educating, showing quality children's programs, and being a forum for news and debates on public issues. With the growth of advertising, however, the commercial media gradually sloughed off public service in favor of the more saleable entertainment. (The commercial interests welcomed the coming of public broadcasting in 1967, as it took them off the hook for abandoning public service.) The triumph of the entertainment complexes culminates the displacement of the public sphere with mainly light entertainment.

Entertainment complexes neglect public service programming because their social benefits can not be captured in revenue. In contrast, the social costs associated with sex and violence will be ignored because they enlarge audiences and profits. Thus, a cultivation of anti-social distraction and systematic neglect of citizenship-enhancing programming is built-in to the ongoing merger movement.

TRIUMPH OF CONSERVATISM

The entertainment-media complexes are generally run by men of exceedingly conservative bent and rigorously bottom-line orientation. NBC is controlled by GE, which sponsors the rightwing-oriented McLaughlin Group on PBS and has long supported conservative thinktanks and causes. Rupert Murdoch recently provided $3 million in start-up funding for a new rightwing journal, The Standard, and his support of conservative politicos and causes is well-known. John Malone, president of TCI, the largest cable system, and a fan of Rush Limbaugh, has joined with Murdoch in sponsoring a new news channel to offset an alleged "left bias" in the rest of the news media. Malone has also sponsored a new program, Damn Right!, run by the extreme rightwing Wall Street Journal editorial writer David Asman (a consistent apologist for state terror in Guatemala and El Salvador in the 1980s).

Shortly after Disney agreed to acquire Cap Cities/ABC, a rare bird in the form of liberal talk show host Jim Hightower was dropped by ABC. With the new media giants in place, we may expect an already-shrivelled public sphere to be further ideologically cleansed.

WHO OWNS THE AIRWAVES?

The profit-making companies licensed to use the airwaves were given those rights in exchange for a commitment to serve the "public interest, convenience, and necessity." The quoted phrase did not mean serving up entertainment programs to pull in large audiences for advertisers. Nevertheless, while the broadcasters have successfully sloughed off any public service responsibilities, they maintain free access to the airwaves, even while the remaining airspace is auctioned off at sky-rocketing prices. The broadcasters are even today fighting for, and expecting to receive, additional channels without charge in supposed compensation for their costs in moving to digitalized TV.

The market value of the airwaves now in use for cellular, phone, broadcast, and satellite transmission is estimated at $200 to $300 billion. Taxed or leased at a moderate rate of 5%, these public assets would yield government revenue of $10 to $15 billion per year. Turned over to an authority that would distribute that sum to nonprofit community and public broadcasting stations, public service could be revived and a public sphere could be rehabilitated.

But an adequate policy response to ongoing trends, consistent with the preservation of a democratic society, would also entail a far reaching effort to democratize the media. Not only would the mega-mergers be disallowed, the existing structures of power would be attacked, global combines would be dismantled, and the system would be biased toward local and non-commercial control. It will be difficult to maintain a democratic political order with an increasingly concentrated, centralized mass media buried within global entertainment complexes. As James Madison stated back in 1822, "a popular government without popular information, or the means of acquiring it, is but prologue to a farce or a tragedy, or perhaps both." ■

Resources: "Media Ownership and Control," Herbert Schiller, in *Media Ownership and Control in an Age of Convergence*, International Institute of Communications, 1996; "Demonopolize Them!," Marc Crispin Miller, *EXTRA!*, Nov./Dec. 1995; "Info-bandits," Jim Naureckas, *In These Times*, March 4-17, 1996; "The Externalities Effects of Commercial and Public Broadcasting," Edward Herman, in *Beyond National Sovereignty*, Nordenstreng and Schiller, 1993; "Murdered Books," Jon Wiener, *Nation*, May 31, 1993.

November/December 1996

SUPERMARKET BUYOUT MANIA

BY MARC BRESLOW

One day last summer I walked into my favorite local supermarket, the Purity Supreme in Medford, Massachusetts. But the shelves were half empty, and there were signs saying the store would be closing in a few days. Along with shoppers like me, store employees were caught by surprise. "They gave us one week notice of the layoff," said Mark, a part-time worker at the store.

Losing this store was my rude introduction to the brave new corporate world that has transformed the grocery business. A corporate buyout — the latest in a series — led to the store's closing.

Similar buyouts have rippled through supermarket chains in New England and other parts of the United States in recent years. In each case, local chains were sold to mega-corporations seeking profitable outlets for their spare cash.

Purity's saga is representative. A chain with 55 stores in three states, it had begun as a family business, Purity Markets, owned by Leo Kahn. It first merged with the Supreme supermarket chain, to form Purity Supreme, which was later sold to Supermarkets General, headquartered in New Jersey. But the chain really entered the revolving door of takeovers when Freeman Spogli, a California-based investment firm, bought Purity Supreme for $300 million in 1991. Then in April 1995 Stop & Shop, the largest supermarket operator in New England, bought the chain from Spogli.

"It was good way back when Leo Kahn owned the company and everyone was treated as family," said Sue Waystack, who worked in the Saugus, Mass. Purity for 22 years. "But it went from a family-oriented store to just a conglomeration... After the Kahn sale, it just kept getting bigger. They were only concerned about profits, not the people."

The new buyers, and the trade press, regularly claim that such buyouts will be good for everyone. Bigger corporations can exercise economies of scale, and bring more cash flow to the stores, modernizing them and better serving consumer needs. Workers will benefit from more profitable stores.

But the evidence is less one-sided. As with mergers in other industries, the buyers often milked the stores for their cash, then resold them in weakened condition, leading to more concentration in the grocery market and higher prices. Throughout the 1980s and 1990s, buyouts often meant threats to job security and loss of union protection for workers.

BUILDING EMPIRES

The Purity Supreme buyout story does not end with Stop & Shop. Stop & Shop itself had been bought out in 1988 for $1.2 billion by Kohlberg, Kravis, & Roberts (KKR), the predominant leveraged-buyout (LBO) artists in the United States. KKR pulled off the largest LBO in history in 1989, buying RJR Nabisco (itself a combination of a food company and the nation's second-largest lung-cancer promoter, R.J. Reynolds) for $24.7 billion. Among KKR's other acquisitions were Beatrice Foods ($6.3 billion), Borden ($2 billion), and Jim Walter Homes (known for ripping off moderate-income families by selling them shoddily-constructed houses, $2.4 billion).

KKR's partners would assert that the purpose, and result, of its LBO's is to force slothful corporate executives to make their firms more efficient. But the main beneficiaries are the partners themselves, who collect millions of dollars in fees regardless of whether buyouts succeed or fail. The investor group that KKR put together for the RJR Nabisco deal, for example, eventually sold its shares for virtually the same price that it had paid years earlier. But KKR reportedly collected nearly $500 million in transaction, advisory, and other fees.

In an LBO, a small group of investors gains control of a company by buying out the other stockholders. They usually do so by using the value of the company itself as collateral to raise money (by obtaining bank loans or selling high-yield corporate bonds), with which they pay off the stockholders. The end result is replacement of stock (to whose owners the company is not obligated to pay out profits immediately) with debt (which must be repaid on a fixed schedule).

This often leaves the company with huge interest payments on its loans, forcing it to focus on short-term profits rather than long-term development. Not only may employees and consumers be badly served, but even stockholders may lose out. *Business Week* argued in 1995 that there is "strong evidence that mergers and acquisitions, at least over the past 35 years or so, have hurt more than helped companies and shareholders."

Economists Walter Adams and James Brock, discussing the merger wave of the 1980s, found that "merger-mania undermines efficiency in production... obstructs technological advance, and... subverts international competitiveness." On average, the 6,000 mergers studied by economists David Ravenscraft and F.M. Scherer led to lower profits and reduced efficiency.

Supermarkets are a particularly attractive target for buyouts since, in contrast to many other industries, they offer dependable cash flow. While consumers may cut their purchases of autos or computers during a recession, they will continue to buy food.

Before gobbling up Stop & Shop, in 1986 KKR had bought Safeway, one of the nation's largest supermarket chains with more than 1,000 stores, primarily on the East and West coasts, for $5.3 billion. In 1995 KKR spent $1.15 billion to buy Bruno's Inc., based in Birmingham, Alabama, and operator of Food World, Foodfair, and Piggly Wiggly stores.

In March of 1996, KKR resold Stop & Shop (including the Purity Supreme stores) to Royal Ahold, a Dutch conglomerate that already owned 650 stores throughout the United States, including the Mayfair (based in New Jersey), Bi-Lo (southeastern U.S.), Edwards (New York), Finast (Ohio), Giant and Tops (Buffalo) chains. Meanwhile, foreign companies also bought other leading chains in New England. A large British firm, J. Sainsbury, bought Shaw's supermarkets, with 101 stores. Star Markets had been sold to American Stores, based in California, in 1984. But American, under pressure from its own debt load, resold Star in 1994 for $285 million to Investcorp, based in the Middle East oil-producing nation of Bahrain.

CONSUMERS

Both the Federal Trade Commission (FTC) and the Massachusetts Attorney General took an interest in the sale of Purity Supreme to Stop & Shop in 1995, worrying that the dominant chain's acquisition of 55 more stores would increase concentration in the grocery business. Such an increase in monopoly power could lead both to higher prices and to less choice for consumers, if Stop & Shop chose to close Purity stores that were near existing Stop & Shops.

One rule-of-thumb used by economists to warn of the potential for abusing consumers is when the top four firms

Buyouts Unlimited

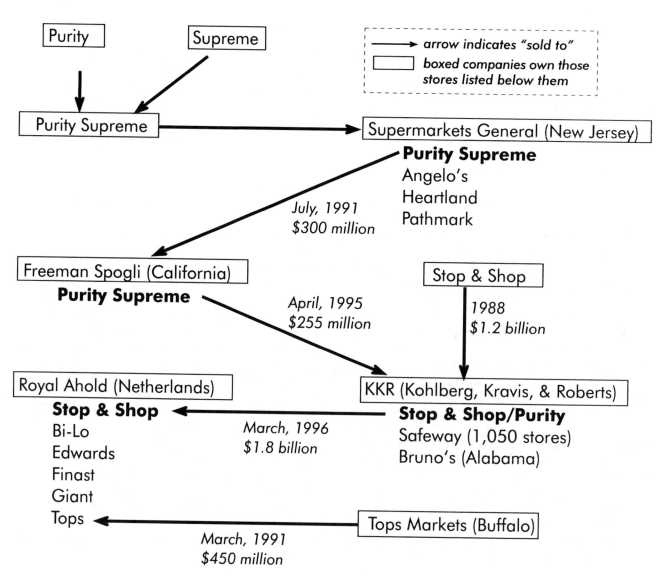

in an industry have more than 40% of total sales. Such concentration levels for supermarkets have been a problem in cities throughout the United States, such as Denver (94%), Miami (87%), Cleveland (77%), Philadelphia (72%), and Los Angeles (59%). As of the early 1990s, the Boston market was less concentrated than many others, with a four-firm ratio of 48%.

During Ronald Reagan's presidency, the federal government virtually abandoned antitrust enforcement, allowing supermarket mergers (among others) to proceed unhampered, according to economist Ronald Cotterill of the University of Connecticut. One study of this period found that grocery chains that had undergone LBO's charged significantly higher prices than other chains, says Cotterill.

In recent years the FTC has been more active in regulating merger activity. After months of negotiation, Stop & Shop (alias KKR) reached a settlement with the government agencies in November 1995, agreeing to divest 17 stores in the Boston metropolitan area and Cape Cod. The FTC argued that these sales would adequately protect food shoppers.

Perhaps the FTC is right. But Stop & Shop could resell the 17 stores to only a few other regional supermarket chains, and I'm not convinced that we consumers will be well served. Most of the stores were to be sold to Star Market, which itself is a major player in the Boston retail food business.

Food shopping depends greatly on convenience, so that to be meaningful, competitors must be within walking distance or a few minutes driving time of where people live. Even before the buyout, my shopping choices were few. Besides Purity, there was a small, overpriced Foodmaster, a Star Market that had wider selections but was overcrowded and expensive, and an inconveniently located Stop & Shop. KKR sold the Medford Purity to — you guessed it — Star Market, a concession to the FTC that I found little comfort in. And for the past several months the store has been sitting idle.

WORKERS

Employees also have little to cheer about from buyouts. The 1980s wave of LBOs "was predicated on strapping the companies with so much debt that their only option to pay off the debt was to bust the union," says Ronald Cotterill.

KKR was heavily involved throughout the country. "They sold out to people who could not afford the high price, and they failed... So it goes non-union, and this threatens other union operations," says Howie Forman, research director for the United Food and Commercial Workers union (UFCW). "This had a very negative effect on the the UFCW... We have had to forego wage increases for fear that companies would go into bankruptcy."

Purity workers described how recent management turmoil harmed them at the store level. Mike Rourke, a full-timer with 23 years seniority, had been a department manager. But after the chain was sold twice to larger companies, "I was put on night shift stocking shelves."

"During Freeman's years... Everything became a payroll issue, the bottom line was everything. There were massive layoffs back then," says Mike Evangelifta, who had been a bakery manager and shop steward in the Saugus, Mass. Purity. "After the sale to Stop & Shop, prices were raised above those in the nearby Stop & Shop... They took a store that had been doing $300,000 a week and dropped it down to $110,000. It had been a fairly successful store, but they annihilated us."

Boston-area UFCW locals say that they were able to protect most of their members who worked at Purity. Stop & Shop, with 36,000 employees, is itself unionized, and agreed to observe the Purity contract. But while wage rates for full-time workers were maintained, the large proportion of supermarket workers who are part-timers were not so lucky. Many who had seniority faced sharp pay cuts from $9 or $10 an hour to $6.60, the maximum pay allowed by Stop & Shop for part-timers. And Star Market is non-union, so hundreds of workers will lose their union protection.

> MANY PART-TIMERS WHO HAD SENIORITY AT PURITY FACED SHARP PAY CUTS FROM $9-$10 AN HOUR TO $6.60.

Perhaps I'm being too hard on Stop & Shop, KKR, and Royal Ahold. Maybe bigness really does offer advantages, and the new Star Market in Medford, whenever it actually reopens, will be better than the old store. Maybe Royal Ahold will do wonders with its Stop & Shops, proving that ownership of a thousand supermarkets throughout the United States somehow will benefit consumers. Maybe the stores will flourish, and there will be more jobs, with rising wages, for the workers.

But I remain unconvinced. After all, they said the same thing when the banking behemoth, Fleet Financial, bought Shawmut, the Boston-based bank where I had my checking account. (KKR, by the way, is a major stockholder in Fleet.) Within months they had closed the former Shawmut branch down the street from the *Dollars & Sense* office, saying it would be no problem to go to the Fleet branch a mile or two away.

I wasn't too discouraged at first, because there was still an ATM conveniently located on my route home from work. But soon afterwards they demolished that ATM. So now I'm looking for a new bank, and a new supermarket, although both are likely to require longer driving times — so perhaps Exxon and Mobil will be the real winners from the new merger wave. ∎

Resources: "The Case Against Mergers: Even in the '90s, most still fail to deliver," *Business Week*, 10/30/95; "Barbarians Revisited," *Business Week*, 4/3/95; *Dangerous Pursuits*, Walter Adams and James W. Brock, 1989.

September/October 1995

TRUCKERS' TRAVAILS

THE IMPACT OF ECONOMIC DEREGULATION ON THE TRUCKING INDUSTRY

BY MIKE BELZER

The open road may be their chief terrain, but American truckers have found themselves riding a roller coaster over the last few decades. Unfortunately, since the peak in 1973, the overall movement has been down. While unions (mainly the Teamsters) represented about 60% of all truck drivers twenty years ago, they represent less than 25% of drivers today. Wages, once among the highest in American industry, have plummeted.

While employment in the trucking industry has increased 3.9% per year since the early 1980s, real earnings dropped 27% between 1978 and 1990, a decline of nearly $10,300 in yearly wages (in 1995 dollars). This was 3.5 times the average decline in earnings among all manufacturing and service workers, who lost $2,900 per year. If real wages had remained constant for truckers during this period, the average trucker would have earned about $120,000 more than he did.

The recent tumble reversed an earlier trend toward better wages and conditions. Trucking employees improved their lot steadily during the 1950s and 1960s. Though truckers originally earned wages comparable to those of ordinary manufacturing workers, the successful unionization and collective bargaining efforts of many early Teamster leaders moved their wages into the range of auto and steel workers.

Truck drivers' wages rose steadily until 1965. During this time, Teamster leader Jimmy Hoffa held wage increases down in some areas, such as the East, where wages already were high. Meanwhile, he brought wages up in other areas, such as the Mountain States and the South, where wages had been notoriously low. Although Hoffa didn't need social science to tell him, this wage convergence, or "solidarity wage," produced higher average wages as employers could not play one terminal, city, or region against another.

Real wages remained stable until 1970, when labor unrest rocked the nation. Hoffa went to jail and Teamster leaders, jockeying for power by promising better contracts to members whose votes they needed, produced a 20% real wage increase in only three years. Chicago Local 705 led the nation. It rejected the pattern set by the National Master Freight Agreement and struck for 13 weeks, winning a $1.65 raise. Not to be outdone, Teamsters General President Frank Fitzsimmons went back to the national table for $1.85.

These wage increases, along with generally increased concern about simultaneous inflation and economic stagnation, fueled political support for deregulation. Many economists made the argument that the wage increases were pushing prices up and creating inflation, and the only way to restrain it was by reducing the economic regulation of industries and the labor market, making it harder to unionize new operations or to maintain unionization in existing ones. In short, we could characterize the deregulation movement as a thinly-veiled attack on collective bargaining itself.

During the late 1970s and early 1980s the government restructured the regulatory environment of the trucking industry. Before economic deregulation, trucking companies operated within a framework determined explicitly by the Interstate Commerce Commission (ICC). The ICC restricted entry into each market in order to prevent "destructive competition"; it sanctioned rate bureaus that allowed carriers (i.e., trucking firms) to set prices; it required public carriers (called "common carriers") to accept any shipment within certain guidelines; and it disallowed discount rates that did not cover costs, making it impossible for carriers to encroach on each other's business by using cutthroat rates designed to lure business away from competitors by taking an initial loss. After deregulation, the ICC lost its authority to set and enforce these regulations, and the market took over. Carriers began to cut each other's throats by discounting rates broadly.

In 1994, the trend toward deregulation became even more pervasive, as Congress extended the relaxation to the state level, unleashing competition among carriers that specialize in transporting goods within state borders. This "intrastate deregulation" quickly launched a new shakeout among regional carriers, and many local carriers are now facing extinction.

With these changes, trucking wages started a slide from which they have never recovered. Widespread rate cutting and competition among carriers produced strong downward pressure on wages, since unlike fuel or equipment, wages were a variable cost easy to cut. Currently, average real wages in trucking are no better than in the late 1950s.

Even worse, the Teamsters' decades-long campaign to equalize wages for truck drivers, regardless of region or product hauled, came apart at the seams under relentless economic pressure, compounded by its own corrupt leadership. Now, while drivers for firms such as United Parcel Service (UPS) and other unionized national carriers earn top dollar, non-union drivers for long-haul carriers work extremely long hours for near-minimum wages. Large differences between carriers and among labor markets give employers the ability to move work to low-wage areas, or to subcontract union work to low-wage non-union employees and operations.

This wide variance in wages and conditions has put union employees on the defensive. Any job action by Teamster drivers runs the risk of attracting low-paid non-union drivers who might have no compunction about taking their jobs at a fraction of the wage. The union has held up to this pressure so far, mounting recent strikes with some success. Still, "double-breasting" by unionized carriers — the development of non-union subsidiaries doing virtually the same work — gives the carriers tremendous leverage that they cannot afford not to use.

WHERE DID THE MONEY GO?

We might expect that trucking company owners benefitted from labor's pains, but the truth is much more complicated. Even though drivers' wages took a nose-dive, trucking company revenues have not kept pace with expenses. In fact, average profits declined more than 22% from 1977 to 1990.

The industry experienced a shakeout, with some big winners and many big losers. In the largest two classes of interstate general freight carriers, Class I and Class II, so many firms have gone bankrupt that, according to the Teamsters, there are about half the number than before deregulation. As of the summer of 1993, more than 140 carriers employing more than 175,000 workers had gone out of business since the passage of the Motor Carrier Act of 1980 inaugurated deregulation. Regulatory change dislocated more than half the employees in the industry. Deregulation, which was ostensibly meant to foster competition, has actually led to concentration.

WHERE DID THE BUSINESS GO?

Existing large carriers picked up part of the business. The interstate trucking business has become approximately four times as concentrated since deregulation. The four largest carriers that existed before deregulation doubled their share of the revenue (see table). United Parcel Service alone earned nearly $1 billion in profits in 1994.

The rest of the business went to a virtually new industry that deregulation created. Before economic deregula-

A TRUCKER'S VIEW

It's been 18 years since I began driving a tractor-trailer, all for the same company, a Northeastern retail outfit with a fleet of about 50 rigs. Times were good in the days before deregulation. We ran a lot of miles and made pretty good money back then. I'm glad I was able to get in a few years before freight rates dropped and our company began pinching pennies.

It didn't take long to see changes after deregulation went into effect. First, one LTL outfit after another folded. The odds seem really stacked against the union companies. The big guys like Consolidated Freightways and Roadway have spun off non-union subsidiaries. During the last truckers' strike, the big boys shifted their freight to the subsidiaries. Several non-union outfits have recently sprung up and look like they're doing well.

Probably the biggest beneficiary of deregulation is JB Hunt, who operates one of the biggest fleets in the country. You see their trucks everywhere — cream-colored cabs, white trailers. Hunt slashed rates, driving out most of the smaller carriers. The owner was quoted as saying that if he made $5 a day on each truck, he was happy. Considering he has over 1,000 trucks, that's a lot of money. He's successful on sheer size alone. Most of the drivers are new, straight out of training school. Early Hunt advertisements claimed a first-year driver could make $40,000 a year. Now they're advertising $22,000. Sorry, but that's not much money to live in a truck 2-3 weeks at a time away from your family.

What's more, safety has been compromised by deregulation. Drivers have always been pushing too hard and falling asleep, since the Roman chariots. But now drivers have to stay on the road longer to make a dollar. Instead of letting them get home fairly often, companies keep their drivers moving — they don't make money on idle trucks.

— Frank Arpino

tion, general commodities carriers hauled a mix of truckload (TL) and less-than-truckload (LTL) freight. A truckload shipment weighs 10,000 pounds or more, while a less-than-truckload shipment weighs in under that threshold. This means that a single load of LTL shipments may include 30 or more shipments, while a single TL load probably includes only one or two shipments.

While an LTL firm must maintain an extensive network of pick up and delivery drivers and terminals, along with a staff of dock workers, a TL firm needs only a truck and a telephone, as all of its pick ups and deliveries directly connect shippers and receivers. Because it allowed rate freedom, deregulation induced carriers to specialize in either truckload shipments or LTL shipments. The market split into truckload, in which firms can afford to charge lower rates, and LTL, in which firms face much higher costs.

> TDU'S EFFORTS TO STOP CONCESSIONS, ALONG WITH THEIR BROAD ATTACK AGAINST ABUSES OF POWER BY TEAMSTER LEADERS, HELPED PRODUCE THE GROUNDSWELL THAT LED TO CHANGE.

This new TL business grew out of the historically non-union specialized freight and contract carrier sectors, and stripped existing common carriers of their TL shipments. This almost entirely non-union industry developed during an era extremely hostile to organized labor. What's more, current labor law makes it nearly impossible to organize the long-haul TL business. For instance, more and more states have made union shops illegal, and TL firms can choose to locate their main offices in those states. Workers displaced from other declining industries during the 1980s and 1990s have drifted into long-haul TL trucking, only to find low wages and onerous conditions. Many former employees of bankrupt trucking companies have also found their way into truckload, making around half their previous salary despite working much longer hours.

Just how low are wages? Recent research suggests long-haul TL drivers typically work 80 to 100 hours per week, far in excess of the 60 hour legal limit. Since the Fair Labor Standards Act exempts employees of interstate trucking companies, drivers find that they earn about minimum wage while they work the equivalent of two or three full-time jobs.

These low wages and hard conditions in some sectors of the trucking industry have made trucking an occupation of last resort. Turnover in unionized carriers remains very low, but turnover in non-union long-haul carriers typically runs about 200% annually (companies may need to hire two or three drivers yearly just to keep one truck on the road). Through the recent economic boom, some long-haul trucking companies had to refuse work and left trucks parked in their yards because they could not find enough drivers to do the job. Even in the recession during the early 1990s, these truckers complained of a driver shortage: an inability to recruit, hire, train, and retain drivers who could both do the job and pass stringent drug and other screening required by law.

THE UNION VIEW

The Teamsters continue to represent most unionized trucking industry employees. But a large section of the Teamsters' core industry, general freight, has undergone a wrenching restructuring (about half of trucking employees work in general freight). Teamster employees have rarely voted the union out, although this has occurred in isolated carriers that permanently replaced striking employees. But the development of a large non-union truckload industry has diluted the Teamsters' strength.

Census data indicate overall unionization in trucking has declined from about 60% to 25%. In general freight, the growth of large LTL and package carriers (Consolidated Freightways, Yellow Freight System, Roadway Express, and UPS) has helped offset the loss of union jobs caused by the massive shakeout that deregulation produced. Most LTL carriers, especially national ones, have long traditions of collective bargaining. While data is fragmentary (see endnote), it appears that unionization in general freight is about 65%.

The union's influence remains strong, and the best way workers can assure their well-being is by becoming members, either by organizing or joining a unionized firm. While a driver's wages depend partly on which segment of the industry he is working in and also on the market share of his employer, a full half of wage differences can be explained by the presence (or absence) of unionization by the Teamsters.

CORRUPTION AND REFORM

Charges of corruption and abuses of power have dogged the Teamsters for decades. But recently, a strong reform movement, Teamsters for a Democratic Union (TDU), has mobilized rank-and-file Teamsters to fight corruption and abuse, along with the concessionary contracts that characterized the deregulatory era. Immediately after Congress passed the Motor Carrier Act of 1980, carriers began to demand that contracts be reopened and sought major give-backs.

During the 1980s, the Teamsters allowed major changes in work practices, such as flexible starting times and flexible work weeks, that ended the Monday through Friday work week and the regular morning starting time. Many contracts also froze wages, diverted automatic cost-of-living adjustment wage increases to benefit plans, created a lower wage for new hires, and used Employee Stock Ownership Plans and profit sharing plans to hide wage cuts. TDU's efforts to stop concessions, along with their broad attack against abuses of power by Teamster leaders, helped produce the groundswell that led to change.

Since the union elected Ron Carey as president in 1991, it has taken a hard line on contract negotiations, resulting in high profile strikes such as that over the National Master Freight Agreement during the Spring of 1994. While bargaining results may be uneven, it appears that a broad cross section of trucking employees have gotten the message that the Teamsters are again the kind of organization that won them a reputation for toughness in the past. And while the drastic wage increases of the early 1970s proved unwise, the new Teamsters are struggling against formidable obstacles to restore the solidarity wage established by the end of the Hoffa years.

For the first time, a strong organizing drive in LTL has borne fruit as hundreds of employees of Overnite, the largest non-union LTL carrier, have voted for union representation. Though the Teamsters have won some campaigns and lost others, the National Labor Relations Board has found that Overnite committed such egregious violations of labor law that it has issued bargaining orders in several cases.

While the Overnite campaign is not over, the fact that the Teamsters have successfully won several such elections may signal the beginning of a long overdue recovery. ▪

THE SHAKEOUT SINCE DEREGULATION
Market Concentration of Class I General Freight Carriers

Carrier	1977	1982	1987	1990
Consolidated Freightways	4.0%	5.0%	6.4%	5.7%
Roadway	4.9%	5.6%	6.5%	5.4%
Yellow	3.7%	4.4%	7.1%	6.2%
Total Big Three	**12.6%**	**15.0%**	**20.0%**	**17.3%**
UPS	15.1%	23.7%	33.0%	31.9%*

Source: Computer data files of 1977, 1982, 1987, and 1990 Motor Carrier Annual Reports, American Trucking Associations. Market includes all LTL and TL Class I general freight carriers. *UPS data missing for 1990; somewhat higher 1991 revenue used for calculation.

Note: Many of the non-union subsidiaries of some of these and other companies either do not report or report as part of their larger holding companies, while some carriers refuse to comply with legal reporting requirements. Therefore, this data may overstate unionization levels.

Resources: From the same author: "Labor Law Reform: Taking a Lesson from the Trucking Industry." Proceedings of the 47th Annual Meeting of the Industrial Relations Research Association. Washington, DC. January 6-8, 1995. Madison, Wisconsin: Industrial Relations Research Association, forthcoming. "Collective Bargaining in the Trucking Industry: Do the Teamsters Still Count?" *Industrial and Labor Relations Review* 48:4 (July 1995). "The Motor Carrier Industry: Truckers and Teamsters Under Siege," *Contemporary Collective Bargaining in the Private Sector*, edited by Paula B. Voos. Madison, Wisconsin: Industrial Relations Research Association. 1994. *Paying the Toll: Economic Deregulation of the Trucking Industry.* Washington, D.C.: Economic Policy Institute, 1994.

ARTICLE 24   *September/October 1993*

JACK AND ME

I WAS DOWNSIZED — GE GOT RICH

BY LAURIE DOUGHERTY

For Jack Welch, CEO at General Electric Company (GE), competitiveness is a driving obsession. Allies and enemies, us and them, winning and losing are his personal themes, and they run throughout the new book on GE's rise to power, *Control Your Destiny or Someone Else Will.* But it is not only corporate competitors whose destinies Welch seeks to determine. He is the controlling force, the "someone else" of the title for a few hundred thousand American people — a few million, if you count the families and communities of GE employees and former employees.

This book is an insider's view from the top down. Noel Tichy, of the University of Michigan School of Business, has been a consultant to GE and other Fortune 500 firms for many years, and for two years he ran GE's executive training program. Co-author Stratford Sherman writes from the vantage point of *Fortune*'s editorial board. While they claim to have talked with hourly workers and union officials, none show up on their list of sources. They do, however, cite interviews with dozens of GE management personnel as well as 110 hours of interviews with Welch himself. Beating the drum for the "GE Revolution," the authors mimic the manic quality of Welch's public statements, his obsession with speed, and his generally hyperactive behavior.

I also have an insider's view, a view from the factory floor. I worked at GE's Appliance Park in Louisville, Kentucky off and on from March 1974 to July 1991. In those 17 years, I was laid off so much, I accumulated barely 10 years actual seniority. Several hundred of us who were hired there at the tail end of the post-World War II boom in 1973-74 spent our adult lives on a roller coaster ride through the U.S. economy, rocked by the GE revolution.

My response partakes of a deep and bitter rage. I went from wearing a "GE is Me" T-shirt to studying the political economy of deindustrialization. I am aware that to focus on a personality can mask the structural and systemic forces at work in the economy, but there is a telling detail in the index to this book: under Welch, John F., Jr. (Jack), the last entry reads, "see also General Electric." Jack Welch embodies the zeitgeist, the spirit of global capitalism. As a friend of mine at GE said, "No one should have that much power."

WINNING IS EVERYTHING

Faced with the volatile economy of the late 20th century, Welch moved to protect GE's bottom line no matter what the human cost. In 1992, the company's net after tax earnings were $4.7 billion. Welch himself was the third most highly paid CEO in the United States with total compensation worth $14.9 million, according to the *Boston Globe.* Without apology Tichy and Sherman quote from *Fortune*: "'That image — rude havoc revealing a Darwinian truth — is Welch in a nutshell.'"

To Tichy and Sherman, there are necessary trade-offs between the financial performance of the corporation and the trauma imposed on employees. The GE Revolution follows a formula that Welch devised soon after he became CEO. Each GE business must achieve the #1 or #2 market share for its product lines or the company will "fix, sell or close" it. In addition, Welch requires the company's quarterly earnings increases to be 1.5 to 2 times the growth in Gross National Product (GNP). Tichy and Sherman explain: "These paired demands forced many GE managers... to drastically slash costs. GE designed a self-sustaining process that in the short run forced layoffs, and eventually purged GE of almost all its substandard operations."

GE financed its restructuring with a company-wide fund established from the sales of assets (from those sectors which did not measure up). The remaining businesses would therefore reap the benefit of cost-cutting measures while the corporate fund absorbed severance costs. The demand to be #1 or #2 is no bluff. Since 1981 GE has either sold or swapped Housewares (small appliances like toasters), Consumer Electronics (TVs, VCRs, etc.), Utah International (a mining division), Central Air Conditioning, Aerospace, and over 100 smaller divisions and product lines.

In *Control Your Destiny* a point that recurs often is that customer satisfaction provides job security. More and more, GE is abandoning its traditional customer base as less of the company's operations are geared to consumer goods: by 1991, less than 10% of company profits came from such sales. "[T]he most important customers... were not householders buying electric can openers at less than $20 a pop." In the authors' view, Welch envisions GE as "primarily a vendor of items selling for $1 million or more: jet engines, turbines, credit card processing services, high impact plastics sold in bulk."

In addition to dramatic divestitures, the company's incessant tinkering with production elements has upset the lives of workers. The company's rationale for this constant turmoil is the wolf of competition at the door. Pressure pervades the company at all levels. According to Tichy and Sherman, Welch "often makes operating executives prepare a few simple slides...[with] the answers to a few basic questions such as these: What does your global competitive environment look like? In the last three years, what have your competitors done? In the same period, what have you done to them? How might they attack you in the future? What are your plans to leapfrog them?"

THE BODY COUNT

The authors describe three dimensions of Welch's systematic transformation of the company: technical, reallocating human and capital resources; political, restructuring the chain of command within the company; and cultural, winning hearts and minds.

The most visible component of Welch's program falls into the "technical" category: the downsizing and delayering (removing layers of management) of the employee population. Taking into account the buying and selling of whole businesses and divisions, attrition, early retirement under heavy pressure, and layoffs, the net effect is 170,000 fewer employees in 1992 than the 420,000 when Welch took the helm in 1981.

At the factory level, through employee publications, bulletin boards, huge graphic displays, and "informative meetings," GE inundates its employees with information on market share, economic indicators, and slogans. On a recent visit back to Louisville, I saw the following on bulletin boards and banners: "Beat Whirlpool." "Watch out Canada. AP1 [Appliance Park, Building 1] is exporting washer and dryers to Canada." "One team... better and faster than anyone else in the world."

What makes it take is fear — a pervasive insecurity rooted in the body count. The business press didn't nickname Welch "Neutron Jack" for nothing: like a neutron bomb, he eliminates people but leaves the buildings standing. When I was a kid in the 1950s, I remember watching GE Theater on TV. Ronald Reagan was the host and enthusiastic spokesman for the company. He showed pictures of GE's new Louisville, Kentucky showcase facility, Appliance Park— "Where Progress is our Most Important Product." When I began working at Appliance Park in early 1974, there were close to 23,000 employees. Today there are about 9,000. Along with several hundred others, I was laid off indefinitely five times before I finally moved back to Massachusetts in 1991 and declined recall. What Karl Marx called the disposable reserve army of the unemployed, GE calls surplus.

There are also countless short term layoffs, extended vacation shutdowns, a day here, a week there of "lack of work." But never a lack of rumors. Going to the bathroom could be a strange trip indeed. Every now and then, along with tales of murder, mayhem and romance gone awry, the grapevine would have us sold off to the Japanese. To that I'd mutter, "Maybe we'll be better off."

The appliance division underwent extensive reshaping that included upgrades of many areas to automated systems and robotics, rendering many jobs obsolete. Parts production, sub-assembly, and even whole model lines moved from one GE factory to another or to outside vendors, often outside the United States. The company bought Roper, a smaller appliance manufacturer, closed factories in Maryland and Chicago, and opened a state of the art factory in Mexico in 1991 to build its new line of gas ranges. On the *same day* in October 1990 that the company announced yet another impending layoff of several hundred people, a full page article in the company newspaper outlined GE's strategy for dominating the global appliance market. A reporter for the Louisville *Courier-Journal* who has covered Appliance Park for years remarked in a discussion

'FATIGUE AND DISCOMFORT' DON'T BEGIN TO TELL THE TALE OF THE BUILDING, WHICH HAS NOT SEEN MUCH OF GE'S MODERNIZATION SCHEMES. IT LOOKS LIKE AN ORTHOPEDIC WARD.

with some GE employees: "Laying you off is *part* of GE's global strategy."

In January of this year, GE alarmed its Appliance Park employees yet again. With much fanfare and heavily hyped cost/revenue/earnings projections, GE threatened to retool for its new washing machine design at a GE facility outside of Louisville or to out-source production altogether, putting the GE logo on a product bought from another manufacturer. The company implied that such a loss (1,500 jobs) would put the rest of the Park in jeopardy, perhaps reducing its operations below a viable level.

Subsequent negotiations involved the union at both the local and international levels and officials from Louisville, Jefferson County, and the state of Kentucky. In return for a commitment to invest $70 million in its Home Laundry division, GE won $19.5 million worth of tax abatements from the state over 20 years, $2 million in concessions from the city and county, and work rule changes from the union. Even so, the new design will still involve a 600-job cutback at projected production levels, a payroll savings which will quickly offset the amount invested.

> IF JACK WELCH REALLY BELIEVES IN THE BOUNDARYLESS COMPANY, HE'LL SPEND SOME TIME WORKING ON AN ASSEMBLY LINE.

While visiting Louisville in May of this year, I picked up a copy of the employee newspaper. No longer *Park News for Appliance Park Employees*, *GEA Today* covers all of GE's appliance facilities. The front page article, "Leading the Fight for Appliance Park Profitability," contained a picture of a smiling Jack Welch in shirt and sweater beside a smiling Norm Mitchell (President of IUE Local 761) in rolled-up shirtsleeves at a Save the Park team meeting.

Mitchell, President of Local 761 of the International Union of Electrical Workers (IUE), which represents most hourly workers at Appliance Park, is convinced that the threat to shut down washer production (and possibly the whole Park) is no bluff. He told the Louisville *Courier-Journal* that he and other local board members were "'sticking their political necks out' to mobilize the work force in favor of company demands." On January 15, 1993, company and union officials presented a united front appeal to the entire work force. The company officials stressed Welch's program for worker involvement and the "soft" values that nurture participation and loyalty, but the bottom line was still fear.

RIPPING OFF REVOLUTION

The political part of the process described in *Control Your Destiny* took place in the upper reaches of the corporate hierarchy: heads rolled at the VP and middle management

levels, and the rhetoric of competitiveness suddenly cut close to home for many who had previously treated it as an abstraction. In one of his few disagreements with Welch, Tichy points out that in 1985 the company was at a crossroads and Welch underestimated the "depth of resistance" among the troops. Whether or not he correctly understood the state of morale, Welch was clear from the start about the measures he was willing to take to prevent backsliders from undermining him.

As the authors put it, "To consolidate his power, Welch seized the revolutionary's three main levers of control: the police, the media, and the schools." Could Lenin have said it any better? The phrase "GE revolution" is the authors', but it's based on Welch's own remarks. The word "revolution" appears in two chapter titles, and the last 70 pages of the book are a "Handbook for Revolutionaries." Harvard Business School Professor and GE consultant Len Schlesinger called GE's employee involvement program "one of the biggest planned efforts to alter people's behavior since Mao's Cultural Revolution."

Tichy claims to be a "professional agent of change." In his Ph.D. dissertation in social psychology, he included research on Saul Alinsky, Ralph Nader, the Black Panther Party, and radical anarchists. He offers this background as a qualification to participate in the process of developing "transformational leadership" at GE. For an executive training session Tichy developed a process he called visioning, using Martin Luther King's "I Have a Dream" speech to stimulate managers to envision their own dreams for their GE projects. (There are things we really should have thought to copyright, my friends.)

Welch's cultural strategy toward his lower-level employees involves both rhetoric and formal worker involvement programs. While making decisions based on market share, Welch has espoused softhearted values intended to liberate the energies and talents of GE employees so they will contribute loyally and enthusiastically to the company's goals. The main practical vehicle for GE's cultural revolution is "Work-Out," its employee involvement program. Work-Out brings employees into problem-solving forums with the goal of improving productivity.

When I worked at Appliance Park, Work-Out was in its infancy. When I visited recently, it was more of a presence. There are mixed feelings among the workers. There is a lot of training going on, on company time. Some friends I spoke with were getting into it: speaking up in a meeting, acting as a Business Team leader, working on a committee, feeling part of a team. But there was also fear that this was a ploy to undermine the union, or that all the time spent in training sessions and meetings would lead to lost production, an excuse for the company to shut the Park down.

The authors mention benchmarking: comparing performance to an objective standard. I have benchmarks of my own. To evaluate Work-Out, I'll follow the planned retooling of AP1 for the new GE washer. From the perspective of ergonomics (the application of design factors to the workplace to increase productivity by minimizing fatigue and discomfort),

AP1 is currently a disaster area. "Fatigue and discomfort" don't begin to tell the tale of the building, which has not seen much of GE's modernization schemes. It looks like an orthopedic ward. People work taped, wrapped, in casts, and slings. Often so many workers are on light duty there is a real problem keeping the lines running.

If production workers participate in the redesign of jobs and processes before the new washer goes into production, then "Work-Out" will have merit. Computer simulations and time study analyses don't get it. The only way to know what a job is doing to your body is to do it. Informal job reorganization goes on all the time as people learn each other's jobs and trade off or recombine job elements. Start-up of the new GE washer should be a test case for Work-Out as a vehicle for worker involvement in process design, with the goal of improved working conditions as well as increased productivity.

GE UNBOUND

"Boundarylessness" is Welch's word for one big happy company. He becomes positively poetic on the subject. The idea is to break down barriers between divisions within the company, between people within the company, between the company and its outside suppliers and customers, indeed between nations. If Jack Welch really believes in the boundaryless company, he will spend a fair amount of time working on an assembly line. Appliance Park will do, in August when the temperature is 95 degrees and the humidity about 98%. When the competition gets heavy, or the economy declines, he will take the hit with the rest of us, distributing some of the hardship among the shareholders and the executive suite rather than sacrificing GE employees to his obsession with ever-higher earnings. Is this a fantasy? I am not the one who wrote: "A boundaryless organization will ignore or erase group labels such as 'management,' 'salaried' or 'hourly,' which get in the way of people working together."

Under Welch, the shareowners have been well looked after. While some business analysts argue that Welch's obsession with short-run performance is gutting the company of productive capacity and the research and development infrastructure needed to compete over the long haul, since 1988 the bottom line has increased from $3.4 billion to $4.7 billion, a gain of 39%. Earnings per share rose from $3.75 to $5.51, a 50% increase. Dividends per share rose 58% from $1.46 to $2.32.

My bottom line reads differently. It became clear in a conversation with a friend. I worked on the same line with her years ago, but didn't see her very often as we both got laid off and bumped around numerous times. Once in a while we'd run into each other and catch up. In the fall of 1990 we were threatened with yet another layoff. I stopped by to talk to her one day. I can see her house now: a small subdivision house near GE, neat as a pin and decorated for Halloween for the two kids she is raising by herself. A state of mind had kicked in — part panic and part attitude. The proportion varies from person to person, from hour to hour. That day we were both very, very angry. She told me, "I am not going to lose this house." That is my benchmark for financial performance. If she still has her house, a lot of other measures will fall in place.

But even the great god Welch, head honcho of the boundaryless empire that *Forbes* ranks as the most powerful corporation in the United States, has worries. He predicts "ferocious price competition" for the 1990s due to overcapacity and a worldwide shortfall in demand. His greatest concern, though, is government: "I have to worry about whether government policies here will allow us to deliver the productivity we need to win on a global basis.... I don't want to see governments meddling in industrial policy — bureaucrats picking winners and losers." Evidently, picking winners and losers is his prerogative. ■

Resources: *Control Your Destiny or Someone Else Will: How Jack Welch is Making General Electric the World's Most Competitive Company*, by Noel M. Tichy and Stratford Sherman, New York, Currency Doubleday, 1993. GE Annual Reports, 1986-1992.

November/December 1994

IT'S NOT WORKING

LOW-WAGE JOBS MAY NOT BE THE ANSWER FOR THE POOR

BY CHRIS TILLY AND RANDY ALBELDA

Most current welfare reform proposals assume that all single mothers can simply work their way out of poverty — that it's a matter of will. President Clinton's "two years and out" time limit on benefits before mandatory work, along with the renewed emphasis on job search and short-term training programs, arises from an increasingly common determination to have poor women lift themselves up by their bootstraps.

For many single mothers, this strategy cannot work. In the absence of universal child care, health care, and an abundance of good jobs, welfare plays a crucial role as a safety net. And even if the government were to offset the daunting demands of caring for children, provide health care, and brighten the limited opportunities at the bottom of the labor market, large numbers of single mothers would continue to require public assistance.

It's not for want of trying that single mothers have not been able to make ends meet. They work for pay about as many hours per year, on average, as other mothers: about 1,000 hours a year (a year-round, full-time job logs 2,000 hours). But less than full-time work for most women in this country just doesn't pay enough to feed mouths, make rent payments, and provide care for children while at work.

Not all single mothers are poor — but half of them are (compared to a 5% poverty rate for married couples). For poor single mothers, the labor market usually doesn't provide a ticket off of welfare or out of poverty. That's why AFDC (Aid to Families with Dependent Children, the program known as welfare) works like a revolving door for so many of them.

Heidi Hartmann and Roberta Spalter-Roth of the Institute for Women's Policy Research (IWPR) report that half of single mothers who spend any time on welfare during a two-year period also work for pay. But that work only generates about one-third of their families' incomes. In short, work is not enough; like other mothers, they "package" their income from three sources: work in the labor market, support from men or other family members, and government aid. "Mothers typically need at least two of those sources to survive," says Spalter-Roth.

THE TRIPLE WHAMMY

While all women, especially mothers, face barriers to employment with good wages and benefits, single mothers face a "triple whammy" that sharply limits what they can earn. Three factors — job discrimination against women, the time and money it takes to care for children, and the presence of only one adult — combine to make it nearly impossible for women to move off of welfare through work alone, without sufficient and stable supplemental income supports.

First, the average woman earns about two-thirds as much per hour as her male counterpart. Women who need to rely on AFDC earn even less, since they often have lower skills, less work experience and more physical disabilities than other women. Between 1984 and 1988, IWPR researchers found, welfare mothers who worked for pay averaged a disastrous $4.18 per hour. Welfare mothers with jobs received employer-provided health benefits only one-quarter of the time. AFDC mothers are three times as likely as other women to work as maids, cashiers, nursing aides, child care workers, and waitresses — the lowest of the low-paid women's jobs.

Second, these families include kids. Like all mothers, single mothers have to deal with both greater demands on their time and larger financial demands — more "mouths to feed." A 1987 time-budget study found that the average time spent in household work for employed women with two or more children was 51 hours a week. Child care demands limit the time women can put into their jobs, and interrupt them with periodic crises, ranging from a sick child to a school's summer break. This takes its toll on both the amount and the quality of work many mothers can obtain. "There's a sad match between women's needs for a little flexibility and time, and the growth in contingent jobs, part-time jobs, jobs that don't last all year," comments Spalter-Roth. "That's the kind of jobs they're getting."

Finally, and unlike other mothers, single mothers have only one adult in the family to juggle child care and a job. Fewer adults means fewer opportunities for paid work. And while a single mother may receive child support from an absent father, she certainly cannot count on the consistent assistance — be it financial support or help with child care — that a resident father can provide.

NO ROOM AT THE BOTTOM?

Suppose Clinton and company make good on their promise to give welfare mothers a quick shove into the labor market. What kind of prospects will they face there? Two-thirds of AFDC recipients hold no more than a high school diploma. The best way to tell how work requirements will work is to look at the women who already have the jobs that welfare recipients would be compelled to seek.

The news is not good. An unforgiving labor market, in recession and recovery alike, has hammered young, less-educated women, according to economists Jared Bernstein and Lawrence Mishel of the Economic Policy Institute, a Washington, D.C. think tank. Between 1979 and 1989, hourly wages plummeted for these women, falling most rapidly for African-American women who didn't finish high school. This group's hourly wages, adjusted for inflation, fell 20% in that ten year period. Most young high-school-or-less women continued to lose during 1989-93. At the end of this losing streak, average hourly wages ranged from $5 an hour for younger high school drop-outs to $8 an hour for older women with high school diplomas.

Unemployment rates in 1993 for most of these young women are stunning: 42% for black female high school dropouts aged 16-25, and 26% for their Latina counterparts.

But young women don't have a monopoly on labor market distress: workforce-wide hourly wages fell 14% between 1973 and 1993, after controlling for inflation. Given the collapse of wage rates, work simply is not enough to lift many families out of poverty. Two-thirds of all people living in poor families with children — 15 million Americans — lived in families *with a worker* in 1991, report Isaac Shapiro and Robert Greenstein of the Center on Budget and Policy Priorities. And 5.5 million of these people in poverty had a family member who worked *year-round, full-time*.

REFORMS THAT WOULD WORK

The problems of insufficient pay and time to raise children that face single-mother families — and indeed many families — go far beyond the welfare system. So the solution must be much more comprehensive than simply reforming that system. What we need is a set of thorough changes in the relations among work, family, and income. Some of the Clinton administration's proposals actually fit into this larger package, but these positive elements are for the most part buried in get-tough posturing and wishful thinking. Here's what's needed:

• *Provide supports for low-wage workers.* The two most important supports are universal health coverage — go-

ing down in flames in Congress at the time of this writing — and a universal child care plan. Two-thirds of welfare recipients leave the rolls within two years, but lack of health insurance and child care drive many of them back: over half of women who leave welfare to work come back to AFDC. A society that expects all able-bodied adults to work — regardless of the age of their children — should also be a society that socializes the costs of going to work, by offering programs to care for children of all ages.

• *Create jobs.* This item seems to have dropped off the national policy agenda. Deficit-phobia has hogtied any attempt at fiscal stimulus, and the Federal Reserve seems bent on stamping out growth in the name of preventing inflation. And yet Clinton and Congress could call for reform at the Fed, use government spending to boost job growth, and even invest in creating public service jobs.

• *Make work pay by changing taxes and government assistance.* Make it pay not only for women working their way off welfare, but for everybody at the low end of the labor market. Clinton's preferred tool for this has been the Earned Income Tax Credit (EITC) — which gives tax credits to low-wage workers with children (this tax provision now outspends AFDC). Although they get the EITC, women on welfare who work suffer a penalty that takes away nearly a dollar of the AFDC grant for every dollar earned. Making work pay would mean reducing or eliminating this penalty.

• *Make work pay by shoring up wages and benefits.* To ensure that the private sector does its part, raise the minimum wage. A full-time, year-round minimum wage job pays less than the poverty income threshold for a family of one. Conservatives and the small business lobby will trot out the bogeyman of job destruction, but studies on the last minimum wage increase showed a zero or even positive effect on employment. Hiking the minimum wage does eliminate lousy jobs, but the greater purchasing power created by a higher wage floor generates roughly the same number of *better* jobs. In addition, mandate benefit parity for part-time, temporary, and subcontracted workers. This would close a loophole that a growing number of employers use to dodge fringe benefits.

• *Make a serious commitment to life-long education and training.* Education and training do help welfare recipients and other disadvantaged workers. But significant impacts depend on longer-term, intensive — and expensive — programs. We also need to expand training to a broader constituency, since training targeted only to the worst-off workers helps neither these workers, who get stigmatized in the eyes of employers, nor the remainder of the workforce, who get excluded. In Sweden, half the workforce takes some time off work for education in any given year.

• *Build flexibility into work.* "Increasingly," says Spalter-Roth, "all men and all women are workers *and* nurturers." Some unions have begun to bargain for the ability to move between full-time and part-time work, but in most workplaces changing hours means quitting a job and finding a new one. And though employees now have the right to unpaid family or medical leave, many can't afford to take time off. *Paid* leave would, of course, solve this problem. Failing that, temporary disability insurance (TDI) that is extended beyond disability situations to those facing a wide range of family needs could help. Five states (California, New York, New Jersey, Rhode Island, and Hawaii) currently run TDI systems funded by payroll taxes.

• *Mend the safety net, for times when earnings aren't enough.* Unemployment insurance has important gaps: low-wage earners receive even lower unemployment benefits, the long-term unemployed get cut off, new labor market entrants and re-entrants have no access to benefits, and in many states people seeking part-time work cannot collect. Closing these gaps would help welfare "packagers," as well as others at the low end of the labor market, to make ends meet. But even with all of these policies in place, there will be times when single mothers will either choose or be compelled to set aside paid work, sometimes for extended periods, to care for their families. For the foreseeable future, we still need Aid to Families with Dependent Children as a backstop. But at its current level, AFDC rarely acts as a safety net: Hartmann and Spalter-Roth found that AFDC recipients without significant earnings received incomes worth only two-thirds of the poverty line on average.

So welcome to reality. Most single mothers *cannot* work their way out of poverty — definitely not without supplemental support. There are many possible policy steps that could be taken to help them and other low-wage workers get the most out of an inhospitable labor market. But ultimately, old-fashioned welfare must remain part of the formula. ∎

Resources: Heidi Hartmann and Roberta Spalter-Roth, "The real employment opportunities of women participating in AFDC: What the market can provide" (1993) and "Welfare that works: An assessment of the administration's welfare reform proposal" (1994), Institute for Women's Policy Research; Jared Bernstein and Lawrence Mishel, "Trends in the low-wage labor market and welfare reform: The constraints on making work pay," Economic Policy Institute 1994; Isaac Shapiro and Robert Greenstein, *Making Work Pay: The Unfinished Agenda*, Center on Budget and Policy Priorities 1993; Randy Albelda and Chris Tilly, *Glass Ceilings and Bottomless Pits: Women, Income, and Poverty in Massachusetts*, Women's Statewide Legislative Network (Massachusetts) 1994.

January/February 1994

FEAR OF FOREIGNERS

DOES IMMIGRANT LABOR DRIVE DOWN WAGES?

BY GREGORY DEFREITAS

What do rising unemployment, falling wages, soaring budget deficits, and the bombing of New York's World Trade Center have in common? The answer for more and more politicians and others of late has been: immigrants. Last year's arrests of alien suspects in the twin towers bombing and the grounding nearby of a ship smuggling almost 300 Chinese refugees reignited the long-simmer- ing national debate over whether immigration is "out of control."

The debate has been most intense in recession-weary California, home to the largest number of new entrants. In July 1993, Governor Pete Wilson attacked immigrants for "eroding the quality of life for legal residents of California," and launched a campaign to refuse public services to undocumented aliens and to amend the Constitution to deny their U.S.-born children the right to citizenship. Wilson's actions were widely recognized as ploys to revive his record low popularity ratings before the 1994 election by shifting the blame for his state's problems to a federal issue over which he has little control.

But both of California's Democratic senators quickly followed with their own, if qualified, criticisms of current immigration levels, and President Clinton announced a $173 million proposal to reinforce the border patrol, tighten the asylum process, and introduce a national worker identity card. These politicians have a receptive audience: surveys by *Newsweek* and other publications show that over three-fifths of Americans believe that immigration should be curbed.

The public has three major concerns. First, that the country is "under siege" by unprecedented waves of immigrants. Second, that job-hungry newcomers aggravate U.S. unemployment by competing with the native-born for scarce openings, as well as weakening natives' ability to resist wage cuts. And finally, that many low-skilled migrants are exploiting public programs such as welfare, straining already overburdened state and local budgets.

These fears are largely unfounded. Immigration rates today are lower than at other times in U.S. history; immigrant workers do not harm the bargaining positions of native workers; and immigrants contribute more in federal, state, and local taxes than they use in social services. There are cost pressures on government budgets in localities where immigrants are concentrated, but they could be eased by progressive federal policies.

Although "open borders" would not be a feasible policy, current immigration levels are not a significant cause of U.S. economic problems. Popular anger at immigrants is a misguided response to the nation's prolonged high unemployment levels and declining real incomes.

THE NUMBERS DEBATE

While immigration is now higher than in recent decades, it is not growing as fast as some statistics suggest. Nor are the levels unprecedented compared to other periods of U.S. history.

The United States granted "green cards" (permanent resident immigrant status) to nearly 974,000 people in fiscal year 1992. This was one-third more than the annual average in the 1980s, which was itself two-thirds higher than the 1970s average (see table). And the view is commonplace that massive illegal entry adds many hundreds of thousands more. But the legal migration figures for 1989-92 were inflated by the special amnesty of 2.6 million undocumented aliens under the 1986 Immigration Reform and Control Act (backed by then-President Ronald Reagan and then-Senator Pete Wilson). Excluding them, there were 759,000 new legal immigrants in 1992 and an average of under 600,000 per year in the 1980s (see box).

Although the Immigration and Naturalization Service (INS) once claimed that the number of illegal entrants was between 8 and 12 million, research by Census Bureau and academic demographers in the 1980s put the figure closer to three million — about how many eventually sought legalization under the 1986 Immigration Reform and Control Act. Recent INS reports of over one million arrests of undocumented aliens per year are invalid, since multiple arrests of repeat border crossers inflate those numbers greatly. In contrast, the Census Bureau estimates that an average of about 200,000 have been entering annually so far in the 1990s.

The relevant measure of immigration levels is the *net* increase in population, after subtracting emigrants leaving

---

HOW MANY IMMIGRANTS ARE THERE?
(thousands of legal immigrants)

Main Categories	1971-80 average/yr	1981-90 average/yr	1991	1992
Family-sponsored	328	410	453	449
Employment-based	32	52	60	116
Refugees, Asylees	54	105	160	148
Other	26	34	31	46
SUBTOTAL	439	601	704	758
IRCA Legalization				
Legalized aliens	na	136	123	163
Dependents	na	na	na	52
TOTAL	439	737	1,827	973

Source: Statistical Yearbook, U.S. Immigration & Naturalization Service.

---

the United States. The Census Bureau projects that, adjusting for emigration of 160,000 people a year, the average annual net immigration will be 880,000 in the near future. This is fewer than the number successfully absorbed by the country's much smaller economy in the peak period 1900-1910. At the end of that decade, the foreign born were 14.6% of the U.S. population, compared with only 8% today. The nativists of those years blamed recent (mostly southern and eastern European) immigrants for everything from "racial dilution" to importing Bolshevism to inciting the 1919 steel strike.

JOB THEFT OR JOB CREATION?

Regardless of the precise number of new immigrants, many Americans are concerned about their impact on the economy. The common belief is that, given the limited number of jobs available, more immigrants mean more competition with native workers, pushing down wages and causing job losses. Some economists say this is particularly true for those occupations in which immigrant workers are concentrated. If immigrants, on average, have relatively low skill levels, then less-skilled native workers, including minorities, could be hit the hardest. Anti-immigration organizations like the Federation for American Immigration

Reform (FAIR) have widely publicized a few case studies, like that of Rice University's Donald Huddle on Houston's construction industry, in support of such claims.

But empirical research by a diverse array of economists refutes such arguments. Economists have faulted local studies for deriving misleading conclusions based on partial and static evidence. Huddle simply assumed that the presence of undocumented workers on a job site meant that natives must have been displaced. He ignored a host of other possible adjustments — such as natives moving into higher-pay and status occupations; natives' unwillingness to accept the poor wages and working conditions of certain firms; and immigrant entrepreneurs' formation of new firms in untapped market "niches."

In contrast, studies of the entire labor market of specific cities like Los Angeles and Miami have found that increased immigration had no overall effect on the unemployment of native-born workers. Several national studies covering multiple cities have produced similar results. I looked at 1980 census data on the 79 largest metropolitan areas and found no statistically significant negative effects of immigration on either the wages or employment of native low-skilled workers.

Moreover, other studies show that average skill levels have risen for immigrants from most countries, so that many of them are competing for high- rather than low-skill jobs. This has taken place at the same time that the immigrant share from less-developed countries has grown. A preliminary Census Bureau analysis of 1990 survey data shows that 24% of migrant adults arriving in the 1980s had a college degree, compared with 19% of earlier migrants and 20% of American adults in general.

As with the less-skilled, researchers have found that skilled natives have not lost their jobs or faced lower wages due to recent immigration. In fact, the only group which may experience adverse effects is the older immigrant population: Some studies suggest a degree of job competition between earlier and recent arrivals.

New immigrants have not worsened the lot of the native born because their arrival has increased not only the supply of workers, but also domestic job growth. Immigrants have above-average self-employment rates, and the new businesses they create mean new jobs, tax revenue, and often new life for marginal and declining urban areas. In addition, they spend their earnings on local consumer goods, cars, and houses, generating multiplier effects that spur more labor demand. And many fill the harshest, low-wage jobs spurned by natives, instead of competing for similar work.

TAXES AND BENEFITS

Do immigrants overuse welfare and other social programs and underpay taxes? Two recent, much-publicized reports claim that they do. A 1992 Los Angeles County study alleged that immigrants cost the county $947 million in social services in 1991, but paid county taxes of only $139 million. Another study by Donald Huddle extrapolated from the Los Angeles report to conclude that, nationally, immigrants drained the public treasury of $45 billion.

MAJOR CHANGES IN U.S. IMMIGRATION POLICY

1965 Immigration Act
- Abolished the European-biased national origins quota system in effect since the 1920s.

- Established a new system of granting permanent residence visas ("green cards") on a first-come, first-served basis within several "preference categories": 74% were reserved for certain relatives of U.S. citizens and permanent resident aliens, 20% were skill-based, and 6% were for refugees.

RESULTS: A dramatic shift in the composition of immigration away from Europeans toward Asians and Latin Americans (now over four-fifths of all entrants). The actual numbers admitted annually have far exceeded the nominal 290,000 ceiling, due mainly to large numbers of quota-exempt immediate relatives of U.S. citizens and to the Cuban and Indochinese refugee influx. By the late 1970s, nine out of ten visas were given for family immigrants and refugees.

1980 Refugee Act
- Changed the US definition of "refugee" from the Cold War version limited to anyone fleeing Communism to that approved by the UN: "persons with a well-founded fear of persecution based on race, religion, nationality, membership in a social group, or political views."

- Set the "normal flow" of refugees at 50,000 per year and reserved 5000 places annually for asylum-seekers.

RESULTS: In practice, most admitted have still been under Cold War criteria. From its first year (when President Carter admitted 125,000 in the Mariel boatlift from Cuba), far more than 50,000 have entered each year. The number seeking asylum in the law's first year was 5 times the expected number and has risen to over 100,000 per year. Applicants are routinely allowed to live and work in the country for years until a hearing is scheduled.

1986 Immigration Reform and Control Act (IRCA)

• Penalized employers knowingly hiring illegal immigrants with fines and possible imprisonment.

• Amnesty offered to most resident undocumented aliens, granting legal status to those who had been in the U.S. since January 1982 or those who had done U.S. farm work for at least 3 months in 1985-86.

RESULTS: A total of 2.65 million undocumented aliens were granted legal immigrant status through 1992. The spread of inexpensive fraudulent documents and weak INS enforcement have rendered the employer sanctions ineffective.

1990 Immigration Act

• Increased the number of immigrants admitted each year to at least 675,000. This was designed as a "flexible ceiling" which could be exceeded in years when more visas for immediate relatives of citizens are deemed necessary, while still allowing no fewer than 226,000 places for other kinds of family migrants.

• Family-based claims again allocated most visas, but the number for employment-based applicants was doubled.

• Allowed refugees and asylum-seekers to be admitted outside the "flexible ceiling" limits. Doubled the annual number of asylees eligible for green cards. Created a new "temporary protected status" for Salvadorans and certain others seeking short-term haven from wars or natural disasters.

RESULTS: Over 758,000 were admitted in 1992, of whom 62% qualified based on family relationships. An additional 216,000 slots went to aliens amnestied under the 1986 law and their dependents. Over 188,000 Salvadorans applied for the new temporary protected status.

Subsequent research by Jeffrey Passel and Rebecca Clark of the Urban Institute has shown that the Los Angeles figures overestimated immigrant social service costs by one-third and underestimated their taxes by nearly one-half. Moreover, the Los Angeles report itself estimated that the total taxes (local, state, and federal) paid by these immigrants exceed their total social service costs by $1.8 billion. The discrepancy emerged because most tax revenue flows to Washington, while many of the program costs are borne locally.

Most research has found that immigrants are overwhelmingly drawn by the hope of better jobs, not by U.S. benefits programs. When job prospects dim, many (especially Mexicans) return home.

For refugees without that option, such as the Vietnamese, program usage is more common, at least during the resettlement period. Undocumented aliens are legally barred from most such programs, and seem to largely avoid contact with government agencies out of fear of detection.

Many legal immigrants also think twice about seeking government benefits, since a record of welfare usage can increase their risk of deportation and decrease their ability to sponsor the entry of other relatives. Moreover, since immigrants tend to arrive at young ages, they have less need for many services than do natives, especially the growing number of elderly citizens.

Rapid influxes of immigrants to particular local areas do impose economic costs, since the federal government provides inadequate resettlement assistance to cities and states. About 60% of all new arrivals move to just four states — California, New York, Florida, and Texas — resulting in strains on local school systems, infrastructure, and the environment.

A NEW APPROACH

Despite the mounting evidence that immigration is not responsible for our current economic ills, it remains one of the most difficult issues for either the right or the left to reach a consensus on. While the nativist wing of the Republican Party wants sharp cuts in both legal and illegal migration, libertarians propose an "open borders" policy that would allow markets to set supposedly optimal migration and population levels. Many progressives favor reducing immigration in the hope that it will help stem the decline in union organizing and in job and wage prospects. But others on the left espouse open borders as a humanitarian gesture and/or as a means to redistribute income from rich to poor nations.

While individual immigrants and their families usually do raise their living standards by working abroad, exporting workers is a very inefficient approach to Third World economic development. Those with the motivation and resources to emigrate are seldom from the poorest segments of Third World populations, but rather are the semi-skilled and skilled. Their emigration represents a subsidy to the receiving country from the nation that trained them, as well as a loss of valuable talents to their homeland.

Migrants often do send sizeable remittances back home, but research shows that these typically increase income inequality and dependence on consumer imports among migrants' relatives, rather than helping to meet the social investment needs of their home countries. If the same amount of money was bundled in assistance packages from the West to progressive Third World governments, the long-term development benefits would be markedly greater.

Although research shows that current immigration levels do not harm native workers, an "open borders" policy, resulting in much-expanded immigration, might do so. Such a policy would also be likely to cause social and political disruption in the United States. For example, the Census Bureau estimates that even if annual immigration were only to rise to 1.4 million, by the year 2020 this would drive the U.S. population up to 340 million — nearly 90 million more than today. The foreign born would more than double their share of the country's population. History suggests that the more sudden are such large demographic shifts, the more likely they are to fuel racial frictions and a nativist backlash.

Rather than either highly liberalized or highly restrictive policies, a realistic progressive approach would combine a humanitarian admissions system with adequate protections of labor and living standards both here and abroad. This would require, first, ending the still-strong Cold War bias toward accepting largely economic migrants from Cuba, Indochina, Eastern Europe, and the former Soviet Union. Instead, the United States should give preference to genuine political refugees.

Where massive refugee displacements occur, as in the recent case of Haiti, multinational resettlement efforts should be made. The federal government, which alone controls immigration policy, must provide those states in which new arrivals are concentrated the financial aid they need to expand their services accordingly.

Next, we should oppose increased admissions of people based solely on their skills, a policy built into the 1990 law by pro-business groups. Instead of meeting supposed "skill shortages" by importing people trained elsewhere, the United States should finally commit the resources needed to provide first-class schooling and training for the rising numbers of less-skilled and underemployed Americans. As native workers are preparing to fill skilled openings, any short-term employer needs can be met by selectively granting the one- to two-year temporary visas already used under current law. These visas and the more than 300,000 student visas now granted each year will provide ample opportunity for foreigners seeking direct access to U.S. training. Occupational qualifications might still be one useful criterion for evaluating the large number of applications from relatives of U.S. residents.

So long as unlimited immigration between high- and low-income countries remains an unrealistic prospect, some form of border control will be necessary. But the Immigration and Naturalization Service (INS) is terribly inefficient and understaffed. The INS needs thorough re-

organization, as well as better screening, training, and supervision of its agents. This would help to expedite visa application and review processes, and to assure that the increasingly harsh treatment reported among detained undocumented aliens ceases.

To diminish the need of so many Third World workers to emigrate, the United States must end its historic pattern — from Vietnam to the Caribbean to Central America — of itself creating large displaced populations by giving military and economic support to repressive regimes. Recent revelations of CIA support for the opponents of Haiti's elected President, Jean Bertrand Aristide, are only the latest examples of this behavior.

The United States has also helped to aggravate unemployment in many countries, leading to greater emigration, through its influence on the International Monetary Fund's (IMF) policies. The IMF, which controls much of the lending available to Third World nations, has pushed its borrowers to engage in extreme privatization measures, causing untold economic damage. Instead, the United States should lead other rich nations in funding projects that foster sustainable development and job growth in poor countries. This could be partially financed by imposing "social tariffs" on the products of multinational companies whose labor and environmental safeguards are below acceptable levels. As capital becomes ever more mobile, the only way to reduce labor migration is through improving living and working standards in both sending and receiving countries.

The best way to curtail U.S. employers' preferences for the undocumented is to aggressively enforce health, safety, and other workplace labor standards, raise the minimum wage, and change labor laws to encourage greater unionization. This will reduce the competitive advantage of many firms relying on exploited migrants, at the same time that it betters the lot of both native- and legal foreign-born workers.

Immigration today remains essential to the basic humanitarian goals of offering a haven to refugees and reuniting families. It also offers a valuable source of cultural diversity and dynamism for this country. Since most research studies have found that, at least at recent levels, immigration is not responsible for adverse economic trends, efforts to cut immigration should be opposed, as should nativist efforts to widen racial and ethnic divisions. Rather than scapegoating immigrants for the worsening job prospects of so many Americans, we must place the blame where it belongs: on deindustrialization, deunionization, shortsighted corporate responses to global competition, and the government's economic policies of the past decade. ■

Resources: "Immigrants: How They're Helping the U.S. Economy," *Business Week*, July 13, 1992; *Inequality At Work: Hispanics in the U.S. Labor Force*, Gregory DeFreitas, 1991; Population Projections by Age, Sex, Race and Hispanic Origin: 1992-2050 U.S. Census Bureau, 1992; *The Effects of Immigration on the U.S. Economy and Labor Market*, U.S. Dept. of Labor, Bureau of International Labor Affairs, 1989.

ARTICLE 27   *September/October 1995*

IT'S BETTER IN THE UNION —
IF YOU CAN FIND ONE

Although the sad decline in union membership and bargaining power continued in 1994, for the remaining members the financial benefits of belonging to a union were dramatic. In new contracts, however, average wage increases dipped to a record low level.

Continuing a 15-year slide, 16% of all workers (16.7 million people) were represented by unions in 1994. Men had a higher rate of membership (18%) than women (13%), and blacks had a higher rate (21%) than whites (15%) or Hispanics (14%). Among population groups, black men had the highest proportion of membership (23%).

Unionization rates for men, and especially African-American men, have dropped rapidly in recent decades. Combined with the large disparity between union and nonunion wages, declining unionization has imposed severe losses on black men.

The median union pay premium (the amount by which union wages exceed nonunion wages) shows one of the great advantages of being part of organized labor. These premiums become even larger when total compensation is compared, because union members receive health insurance and pension benefits that are more than double those of nonunion workers.

Workers represented by unions earned $160 (37%) more per week on average than non-union wage workers. White, black, and Hispanic women all had union pay premiums of about 39%. Male union members earned 26% more than non-members, with Hispanic men benefitting the most, earning 60% more than non-members. Black men earned 46% more, and white men 25% more (in this Census Bureau data Hispanics are also included in both the black and white figures).

Union membership averaged 39% in the public sector, but only 11% in the private sector. Among private industries, transportation and public utilities (28%), construction (19%), and mining (16%) were well above the average. Manufacturing had the largest number of union members with 3.5 million, followed by transportation and public utilities (1.8 million), services (1.7 million), wholesale and retail trade (1.4 million), and construction (0.9 million).

The union pay premium was highest in the construction (64%), transportation (35%), and retail trade (34%) sectors. It was lowest in communications and public utilities (5%); mining (5%); and finance, insurance and real estate — the only industry in which nonunion members actually make slightly more than union members.

The pay premium is significant in nearly every occupation, exceeding 30% in all but managerial, professional, technical, and sales occupations.

These numbers represent the workers who are dues-paying members of unions. There are an additional 2.1 million workers who are represented by unions at their workplace and receive the same wages and benefits but are not union members (they pay an equivalent fee to the union instead of dues).

Although the pay premium continues to be high, contract settlements in 1994 showed little gain for workers, and probably left them falling behind inflation. Wages increased by an average of 2% in the first year of contracts — the second lowest level since records have been kept — and by an average of 2.3% per year over the life of the contract. These negotiated contracts will be in effect for an average of 38 months — the first time the average contract has exceeded three years. The duration of contracts has been increasing in recent years, despite the lack of protection against inflation for most workers. In 1994, only 35% of workers were covered by COLAs (cost of living adjustments) or a lump-sum inflation provision.

These small wage increases may indicate that union negotiators are placing a higher value on total compensation, including fringe benefits, rather than the wage alone. For settlements covering 5,000 or more workers, wage rates increased 2.2% a year over the life of the contract, while compensation rates increased 2.4%. For the third consecutive year, however, average compensation changes were lower in new contracts than in the contracts that they replaced. ■

—Joy Beggs

Resources: "Union Members in 1994," Bureau of Labor Statistics; "Collective Bargaining in Private Industry, 1994" in *Monthly Labor Review,* June 1995; *Statistical Abstract of the United States,* 1994.

UNION MEMBERS AS A PERCENT OF THE WORKFORCE

Source: "Union Members in 1994," Bureau of Labor Statistics.

September/October 1996

COMPUTER WORKERS FEEL THE BYTE

TEMP JOBS IN SILICON VALLEY

BY CHRIS BENNER

As the global center of innovation in high-technology industries, Silicon Valley has grown dramatically in recent decades, while leading the nation into the new "information economy." But more recently job insecurity has found its way to this valley just south of San Francisco.

Silicon Valley is leading the way in creating unstable jobs for many millions of workers. Permanent workers are being replaced by "contingent" work — temporary, part-time and contract workers. These trends exist throughout the U.S. economy, but are particularly pronounced in the Valley. As employers demand "flexibility" to help them adjust to increasing global competition and rapid market shifts, hundreds of thousands of Valley residents are being turned into economic shock absorbers.

Labor unions and community groups in Silicon Valley are responding to these dramatic changes by developing new models of labor organization and calling for major shifts in public-policy that will address employment insecurity. The goal of these efforts is to build organizations that can represent contingent workers and provide security for workers even as they are forced to move from job to job and employer to employer. Representation for workers at all skill levels must go beyond a single worksite and focus on building career or employment security, even if job security is impossible to achieve. These recent initiatives are beginning to provide models for labor organization in the new economy.

WHAT ARE THE SIGNS?

Current government statistics don't track contingent employment as a single category. But if all categories of contingent workers are included — temporary, part-time, self-employed and contract work — almost 40% of all employees in Silicon Valley are contingent workers. This is up from 32% ten years ago. The contingent workforce is growing two to four times as fast as overall employment, and is responsible for nearly all net job growth in the county in the last 10 years.

The most visible sign of this trend is the rapid rise of temporary agencies in the region. Here are a few facts:

• Between January 1991 and January 1995, employment in temporary agencies in Santa Clara County grew by 48%, while overall employment in the County declined by 2%. In 1995, a time of economic recovery in the area, employment in temporary agencies grew by another 40%.

• According to the California Employment Development Department, since 1984 employment in temporary help agencies has grown by 150%, more than 15 times the overall employment growth rate in the region.

• Temporary agencies now employ 32,000 people in the county, out of a workforce of some 800,000. The percentage of workers employed in temporary agencies has grown from 1.5% to 4% in the last ten years. This is nearly triple the national average.

• More than 250 offices of temporary agencies operate in Silicon Valley.

• Manpower Temporary Services (now the largest employer in the United States with over 800,000 workers) operates 15 offices in Silicon Valley, placing over 5,000 people a week.

Temporary agencies are now hiring people of all skill levels, including computer programmers, systems analysts and physicians. "The time has long passed since the clerical/light industrial sector was considered 'the center of the universe' of the temporary help industry," boasts Ray Marcy, President of Interim Personnel Services, the second largest temp agency in the Valley. "Today, virtually any skill can be, and is, provided on a temporary basis."

The use of temporary employees has become a permanent and central part of corporate personnel strategies, as companies seek shelter from unstable economic conditions, rapid technological change and shorter product life cycles. The central motivation isn't always reducing labor costs, but can also include avoiding long-term commitments to permanent employees and the costs of lay-offs. "It often costs us more to hire temporary employees," according to a human resources manager from Cisco Systems who wished to remain anonymous, "but we avoid the embarrassment and costs associated with lay-offs."

The rise in employment in temporary agencies is only one strategy among many that corporations are using to maintain "flexibility" in their hiring practices. Many corporations increasingly hire temporary employees directly. Pacific Bell, for instance, hires temporary (up to one year) and what they call "term" (up to three years) employees in their operator services division. The use of part-time workers has also increased, growing from 15.6% of the workforce in 1972 to 17.5% in 1993. Nearly all of that growth is in involuntary part-time work.

Perhaps the most significant increase in contingent employment, however, comes in the form of corporations out-sourcing and contracting-out functions that previously had been performed in-house. Much of the assembly work in the Valley is now done by a range of contract electronic assembly companies employing large numbers of immigrant Asian women. Such contracting out helps corporations ramp-up production of new products, but leaves employees vulnerable to shifts in the market. Corporations avoid the negative publicity and costs associated with "downsizing" their operations, by simply not renewing contracts with their suppliers.

Corporate strategies for labor "flexibility" translate into employment insecurity, declining wages and no access to health care and benefits for large sectors of the workforce. "Even if you have a job, you are constantly worried about when it will end and where your next job will come from," says Keith Copeland of Compression Labs Inc. Contingent workers can lose their job at any moment, without any recourse.

Contingent employment drives down wages and economic security for even highly skilled workers. For instance, between 1989 and 1994 wages in professional specialty occupations (a category that includes systems analysts) within temporary help agencies have declined 9% in real terms, according to data from the Bureau of Labor Statistics. Temporary workers employed in technical occupations (including computer programming) saw their wages decline by 28% in real terms during those years.

NEW MODELS OF LABOR ORGANIZATIONS

The dramatic rise in contingent employment is sparking new thinking within labor organizations in Silicon Valley. "Labor in Silicon Valley needs to be at the forefront of confronting these new ways of organizing work," says Amy Dean, head of the South Bay Labor Council (AFL-CIO) and founder of Working Partnerships USA, a labor/community alliance formed to help develop new directions for the labor movement. "We need to be developing new models of labor organizations, at the same time that we continue to fight the elimination of permanent positions."

Organizations representing contingent workers must aim to provide security for workers even as they are forced to move from employer to employer, say community and labor leaders in the area. These organizations must recognize that although workers will typically have multiple employers, many will stay within the same occupation and the same geographical region.

These facts indicate the need to develop a model of unionism with members organized around broad occupational areas within a region. Membership would not be based on workers' place of employment, but rather on the sense of solidarity developed through their occupation and position in regional labor markets. In addition, the primary goal of such organizations would be career or employment security, rather than job security. Their functions should include:

• *Coordinate Training Programs:* These would be geared towards improving workers' career paths, providing training that can allow them to move into better jobs. This requires identifying opportunities for job mobility, while having the organizational flexibility for workers to maintain membership in the union as they move from job to job.

ORGANIZATIONS REPRESENTING CONTINGENT WORKERS MUST AIM TO PROVIDE SECURITY EVEN AS WORKERS ARE FORCED TO MOVE FROM EMPLOYER TO EMPLOYER.

• *Defend Employee Rights:* Employee rights (such as anti-discrimination and occupational safety and health legislation) have actually expanded over the last 25 years, at the same time as union membership has been declining. But in environments without collective organization, many workers don't know their rights, or don't have the organizational strength to pursue grievances. Occupational/geographic unions could provide education and representation for members based on their legal rights, even without collective bargaining agreements.

• *Develop Multi-Employer Regional Collective Bargaining:* The goal is to prevent companies that are competing within the same industry from taking the low-road by cutting labor costs, and instead force them to take the high-road toward competing through improved productivity.

New organizations, however, must also represent workers prior to achieving collective bargaining. Such pre-collective bargaining representation can be achieved through an expanded associate membership program, or through representation in guild-type associations. In addition, while collective bargaining needs to build wage floors and minimum standards for employment conditions, it should also allow individual flexibility in conditions and compensation, depending on workers' skills.

• *Provide Portable Benefits:* These new organizations should provide workers with benefits, particularly health care and pension programs, that they can maintain as they move from employer to employer and even during periods of unemployment. Collective bargaining programs need to be geared toward employer contributions to these portable benefit plans.

PRECEDENTS

Precedents exist for many of the ideas presented here. The building trades have long developed aspects of this model, representing workers with temporary attachments to particular firms, while developing multi-employer bargaining units. In these industries, the unions themselves provide stability in wages, health benefits, and pensions, and in many cases actually control the hiring process. Arts and entertainment unions which represent workers with short-term, project-based jobs provide services to ease job transitions, and have developed multi-employer bargaining that sets compensation procedures across the industry.

CONTINGENT EMPLOYMENT DRIVES DOWN WAGES AND ECONOMIC SECURITY FOR EVEN HIGHLY SKILLED WORKERS.

Aspects of this model also have been developed in organizing campaigns in low-wage service sectors. The Justice for Janitors campaign in San Jose, for example, built on strong social ties within the Latino community to develop unionization across the industry, and it recently won a regional multi-employer master contract in the area.

Within high technology industries, employee associations are emerging that embody aspects of this model. The Graphic Artists Guild assists free-lancers working in high-technology media. They provide suggestions for negotiating individual contracts (the free-lancers' equivalent of a collective bargaining agreement), and provide guidelines for pricing and ethical standards that help workers to coordinate the prices they charge even without collective bargaining.

The National Writer's Union (already affiliated with theUnited Auto Workers) performs a similar function for many technical writers. The Association of Technical Communicators, the Systems Administrators Guild, Computer Professionals for Social Responsibility, the Association of Mexican Engineers and dozens of other associations all represent members' interests across the industry. Their weaknesses lie in their fragmentation and isolation. But just as affiliation with staff associations helped expand unionism in the public sector during the 1960s and 1970s, affiliating with these associations in high-technology industries could provide the basis for expanding unionism to the center of the information economy.

PUBLIC-POLICY REFORMS

Adequately protecting contingent workers will also require regulation. The temp industry in the United States is largely unregulated. In Europe, by contrast, hiring temporary help is highly regulated, with legislation to ensure that temporary work complements stable employment rather than undermining it. Many of these regulations could be adapted to suit U.S. conditions. Temporary employment remains essentially banned in Greece, Italy, and Sweden. In other countries, regulations:

• Manage conditions for establishing a temporary help agency, including requiring licenses to operate and conducting regular reviews of operations. In some cases temp firms are prohibited from operating in particular sectors of the economy. This helps prevent abuses and provides channels for hearing grievances against corporations.

• Govern conditions for the use of temporary workers, ensuring that such workers are not used to replace permanent employees, limiting the maximum number of jobs in an enterprise that can be filled by temps, or limiting the duration of temporary assignments.

• Provide adequate social protection for workers in temp agencies, ensuring adequate wages and benefits. In France, for instance, temporary workers must be paid the same wage as permanent workers, and upon conclusion of their assignment, temporary workers also benefit from a "precarious employment allowance" which is increased by 50% if the temp agency does not offer them a new assignment within a period of three days.

These regulations, while not sufficient in themselves, would provide important legal protection for workers in the temporary industry, and help highlight problems of contingent employment. They would help ensure that the fly-by-night temporary agencies would disappear, and temp agencies would be forced to provide more support for their employees.

LABOR AND WORK IN SILICON VALLEY

As the home to the most dynamic sectors of the U.S. economy, Silicon Valley in many ways represents the future of industrial America. Some analysts argue that unions have no place in this new information age. Yet a second look at labor in the region provides an entirely different story. Out of over 600 labor councils in the country, the South Bay Central Labor Council represents the 15th highest per capita level of unionization in the country. It is true that unions have not achieved significant presence in high-tech industries, but they are strong in the more traditional sectors — including the public sector, building trades, retail sale and transportation — and have grown in low-wage service sectors. Organized labor has developed a strong presence within the community and in regional politics.

Amy Dean and other community and labor leaders believe that Silicon Valley can help lead labor's renaissance in the country. To get there, they believe labor needs to develop the next generation of unions in response to the changing organization of capital and to meet the needs of today's workforce. But to succeed they must draw significant resources to the area (from the national AFL-CIO and one or more international unions who share their vision), and they will need to attract talented organizers who are willing to develop new models of organizing and labor organizations.

As Dean says, "Capital doesn't have a monopoly on entrepreneurialism and innovation. We intend to show that labor has that potential also." ■

Resources: Shock Absorbers in the Flexible Economy: The Rise of Contingent Employment in Silicon Valley, Chris Benner, 1996, available from Working Partnerships USA, 2102 Almaden Road, Room 100, San Jose, CA 95125, (408) 269-7872, Fax: (408) 266-2653, Email: wpusa501c3@aol.com; *Contingent Work: A Chart Book on Part-Time and Temporary Employment,* Polly Callagan and Heidi Hartmann, 1991, Economic Policy Institute, Washington, D.C.; "Piecing Together the Fragmented Workplace: Unions and Public Policy on Flexible Employment," Francoise Carre, *et al.,* in *Unions and Public Policy: The New Economy, Law and Democratic Politics,* Lawrence Flood, editor, 1995.

September/October 1997

HITTING BOTTOM

WELFARE 'REFORM' AND LABOR MARKETS

BY ELAINE MCCRATE

Last April, President Clinton announced that the federal government would do its share to move welfare mothers into jobs by hiring 10,000 recipients in the next four years — including six at the White House. The president promised that his administration would create 10,000 new jobs and not replace other workers. But a quick look at government hiring trends shows just how shaky this promise is. Since 1989, federal civilian employment has fallen 6%. The new balanced budget deal with Congress promises more of the same.

Clinton's dubious promise is typical of the determined refusal of welfare "reformers" to admit that public assistance for low income families critically affects the labor market prospects of all low-wage workers. From its start, welfare was a safety net that enabled many job seekers to refuse some of the worst jobs offered. They could hold out for jobs with higher wages and benefits because they had an alternative source of income. Since millions of recipients did not compete for jobs at whatever rock-bottom terms employers were offering, the labor market was not flooded with every single, desperate parent of a young child, displacing workers and driving down the earnings of the working poor and near-poor.

Southern Congressmen knew this when the Aid to Dependent Children program was being debated in 1935. Because they feared that welfare would reduce the inclination of laborers to toil long hours for low pay in cotton fields, they successfully fought for individual states to determine benefit levels. The higher standards of the north would not interfere with the low-wage labor markets of the south. For the same reason, 35 years later, a clique of Dixiecrats opposed President Nixon's proposal to establish a national guaranteed minimum welfare level well in excess of southern benefits. They voiced sentiments similar to Phil Landrum of Georgia, who declared, "There's not going to be anybody left to roll those wheelbarrows and press those shirts."

To this day, the lowest welfare benefits are concentrated in the south. In 1989, even before welfare reform really swept the nation, Louisiana's total monthly package of welfare, food stamps and Medicaid for a single-parent family of three with no other income was $506. In New York, it was $1052.

The new federal and many state welfare laws greatly weaken the wage protecting features of welfare. States can no longer use federal welfare funds to help families for more than five years (although they have the option of exempting 20% of the families on their rolls from this cutoff if they face special hardships). They can set time limits shorter than that — in fact, as short as they like. Parents who otherwise would be out of the labor force will now be competing for entry-level jobs. Moreover, they are competing, in most cases, without the protection of minimum wage and occupational health and safety laws, or the right to organize into unions because they are not seen as "real" workers (see article by Bader). The Department of Labor's May ruling that workfare workers must be covered by the minimum wage has been met with fierce resistance by some governors and is now being fought out in Congress as well as on a state-by-state basis.

My research shows that even before welfare reform hit, women working in high-benefit states got higher pay than those in low-benefit states because of reduced competition for jobs. There is also a "feedback" effect, so that higher wages also tend to lead to higher benefits. Politicians went along with higher benefit levels in those states because the benefits did not compete with paychecks from the higher-waged jobs. Conversely, employers and politicians in low-wage states probably work the hardest to keep benefits low, forcing people into the labor force. Statistically, an additional $100 in benefits was associated with women's wages that were 2.5% higher. This was true even after taking into account that high-benefit states also tend to have higher minimum wages, lower unemployment, more unions, different industries and higher costs of living — which all tend to raise wages as well.

Now with welfare reform, researchers at the Economic Policy Institute estimate that the bottom 30% of earners will fall on average by 11.9% to absorb the nearly one million new low-wage workers it will produce. The wage drop will be even worse in states with large numbers of people on welfare. Local studies bear this out. In New York City alone, Chris Tilly found in a study for the Russell Sage Founda-tion that 30,000 workfare placements would displace 20,000 other workers and reduce wages for the bottom third of the labor force by 9%. In Minnesota, 31 workers would compete for every job that required little training and paid a livable wage (set at $10.96 after taxes).

Maryland shows the perils of states now being allowed to offer employers various types of subsidies to hire welfare workers. Two years ago, Baltimore passed a "living wage" law that over time raised the wage of 4,000 workers employed by city contractors to $7.70 an hour. The wage increase began to spill over to other workers, and employers found themselves needing to pay more to attract labor. Some Baltimore employers responded by taking advantage of Maryland's tax subsidies and hired workfare workers (paid as little as $30 a week) instead of giving their current workers raises. Progress on one front, then, is in danger of being wiped out on another.

There are many reasons why wages have dropped so dramatically for people at the bottom of the labor market in the last 20 years. Most economists, rightly or wrongly, emphasize international competition, the "reskilling" of jobs, the fall in the purchasing power of the minimum wage and competition from immigrants. The studies discussed here suggest another important reason: the tremendous fall in the inflation-adjusted value of welfare benefits since the 1970s, forcing more women and some men to compete for jobs. Now the government is making the problem worse by becoming an enforcer of labor discipline for the private sector and forcing all low-income people to take jobs, regardless of the pay, needs of their families or working conditions. ■

January/February 1997

HIGHER MINIMUM WAGES

GOOD FOR MOST, BUT NOT ALL, WORKERS

BY MARC BRESLOW

The federal government raised the minimum wage from $4.25 to $4.75 per hour on October 1, 1996, with another 40 cent increase scheduled for September 1, 1997. Opponents argued that the boost would cause disastrous job losses, particularly among those groups who already had the highest unemployment rates, such as blacks and teenagers. "Raising the minimum wage destroys job opportunities for unskilled workers," says Mark Wilson of the Heritage Foundation. And the conservative Employment Policies Institute projected that the eventual hike to $5.15 would cost 621,000 jobs.

In contrast, the Economic Policy Institute (EPI) reports that the first six months of the minimum wage jump were good for the vast majority of employees affected. However, EPI's data also show that a significant number of young black workers may have lost their jobs.

EPI economists Jared Bernstein and John Schmitt compared the October 1996 through March 1997 period (immediately after the wage hike) to the prior six months. They found that the number of people earning less than $4.75 per hour fell from 5.7% to 3.4% of all employees, a drop of 2.3 percentage points. Meanwhile, the number earning $4.75 or more rose an equal amount, based on a sample survey of 76,000 people by the U.S. Census Bureau.

Applying these percentages to the entire U.S. population yields an increase of about three million workers making $4.75 or more. At the same time, the wage increase "had no significant effect on the employment of teens or young adults," say Bernstein and Schmitt.

Simply comparing these six months to the prior half a year leaves the potential for inaccuracy, for three reasons: employment and wages vary seasonally, there was economic growth between the two time periods, and growth varied among the states. But even after controlling for these factors, EPI's analysis produced similar results. Adjusted employment for both teenagers (16-19) and young adults (20-24) actually rose slightly (although due to the limited sample size, the increase was not statistically significant).

The story is more mixed when one examines specific racial and ethnic groups. On the plus side, people of color who kept their jobs benefited disproportionately from the wage hikes caused by the new law, because they are over-represented in low-wage positions. For blacks, 19% of teenagers and 5.1% of young adults saw their wages rise from below $4.75 an hour to this level or higher. For Hispanics (the Census Bureau's term), the gains went to 19.6% of teenagers and 8.5% of young adults.

On the other hand, there was one danger sign: Adjusting the data for seasonal variation and economic growth, black employment fell by 1.8 percentage points for teenagers and 2.5 points for young adults, while employment rates for Hispanics rose significantly and those for whites were unchanged. If the survey is accurate this is a serious concern, since among young blacks 44,000 men and 8,000 women would have lost their jobs. But EPI argues that because the sample size was small (about 1,000 blacks between ages 16 and 24) and because "employment data for these subgroups are volatile," they advise against drawing strong conclusions from the results for minority subgroups.

Jared Bernstein acknowledges that "there is some truth" in the statistics showing a drop in employment for young blacks, and believes "it is indicative of blacks being the most disadvantaged group in the labor force, both due to their skill levels and to discrimination." But Bernstein argues that rather than respond by slashing the minimum wage, the United States should "raise the employability of the most disadvantaged workers and combat the forces of discrimination." ■

ARTICLE 31

January/February 1997

A BUSINESS SHOWCASES ITS SEGREGATED STAFF

BY BARBARA R. BERGMANN

Would we have a meritocracy if we got rid of affirmative action in employment and its "unfair preferences"? The Texaco case suggests the answer is no. An even more graphic demonstration that segregation by race and sex remains a problem — not only among the top ranks, but in the less exalted jobs as well — ran recently as a full-page advertisement in *The New York Times*. It showed pictures of 36 of the people who wait on tables at Smith and Wollensky, a leading New York City steak house. A few were Hispanic, and a few were Asian, but the largest group consisted of white men of European extraction. Not a single one of those people was African-American, and not a single one was female.

The S&W ad was celebrating their corps of experienced waiters, and all of those pictured had between seven and 18 years of service with the restaurant. A call to the company confirmed, however, that none of the waiters S&W currently has who were hired in the last seven years is female or black either. The likelihood of that occurring by chance in New York City is smaller than one in a billion, so something systematic is going on; some process has created and continues to perpetuate total exclusion of these kinds of people. S&W is, of course, far from unique. Many fancy restaurants in the United States hire no women and no blacks.

The explanation the company gave me when I called was that they employ waitresses in their other restaurants, but that for some reason or other they don't get many applications from women for jobs waiting on tables at S&W, even though the tips there are the very best. Blacks don't want those jobs, the manager conjectured, because they would be reminded of the bad old days when nothing else was open to them.

Is it likely that no blacks, no white women would ever want to take a waiter's job in this kind of restaurant, and that none ever apply? Why wouldn't they want such a job? These jobs pay more than jobs that most blacks and women with modest educational credentials hold. Is it really likely that blacks and women would turn up their noses at a job for which white men, with all their access to other good jobs, can be recruited? If we are looking for innocent reasons for the segregation the ad reveals, we have to conclude that the voluntary shunning of such jobs by blacks and women is not a plausible candidate.

Maybe some blacks and white women would like a job in S&W, but their experience is exclusively in less pricey restaurants. They might not be as qualified as the men who were actually hired. The restaurant understandably favors those who have had experience in fancy restaurants like this one. After all, such work requires some expertise. The need for that expertise might well preclude the hiring of blacks and women inexperienced in this kind of a restaurant, strictly on a merit basis. Isn't that the answer?

While the "experience" and "qualifications" argument sounds plausible, there is a big hole in it. If the only people ever hired for jobs waiting tables in fancy restaurants were people who had experience in such restaurants, the corps of waiters in them would inevitably shrink down to zero, as deaths, retirements, firings, and moves by waiters to other kinds of jobs depleted their numbers. That doesn't happen, so we know that the corps of such waiters, like the corps of workers in any other type of job, is maintained by the recruitment of inexperienced people. Neophytes have to acquire the expertise required in such restaurants on the job. In fact, the number of fancy restaurants is growing, so the number of people entering as inexperienced recruits must be growing too.

When S&H hires neophytes, why are women and African-American men invariably and without exception excluded, as must happen for the restaurant to maintain a corps of waiters free of them? Is it their lack of merit? That is difficult to believe, unless one believes that there is something in blackness or femaleness that is always disqualifying.

The truth is that the problem is not a lack of ability on the part of blacks and women to learn the necessary skills on the job. The reason blacks or women won't do is that S&W wants to project an ambiance like that of a male club. (In downtown Washington there used to be a large restaurant that projected an "old South" ambiance, and used only black male waiters. That would no longer be politically correct. In any case, it moved out to the suburbs and now employs as waiters only white females.) Blacks and females don't have the ability to project an image that a proper waiter in a men's club traditionally should have. At least they can't project that image to the person doing the hiring at S&W.

Shouldn't S&W be able to project whatever ambiance it wants, and hire waiters who will fit in with that? If the laws against discrimination in employment were interpreted to allow such behavior, there are very few jobs that blacks and women could get, aside from the ones they have traditionally held. Law firms and accounting firms would say that the ambiance they want to project would preclude their hiring anybody but white men. Department stores would say that the ambiance they want to project means they have to hire whites as sales people and blacks to clean up. The courts have not allowed employers to get away with that; if they had, the laws against discrimination would be totally ineffective.

What method could S&W use to desegregate, if it were moved to do so? Just telling the person who hires waiters not to discriminate would not do the trick. That person probably thinks he or she has been doing nothing but sizing up the applicants and hiring "the best." No woman or African-American has been able to fill that bill for 18 years, though. So perhaps being of the right race and sex is, consciously or not, part of the qualifications looked for. If S&W wanted to hire waiters who are white women and waiters who are African-Americans, it would have to stop filling its vacancies with the male friends and relatives of the people who already work there. It would probably have to use the method that President Clinton used to hire women cabinet officers — earmark a fraction of the vacancies for people like that and go out and look for highly suitable candidates to fill them.

Lets face it: that's not only a "preference," it's a "quota." Putting in an affirmative action plan at S&W would indeed create preferences for women and blacks in a fraction of the jobs that would be filled in the next few years. Is that unfair? Shouldn't we worry about the injustice to the man pushed aside to make room for the woman, and the white person pushed aside for the black person?

It's not unfair and we shouldn't worry. If it doesn't adopt affirmative action methods, S&W will continue to have a one-hundred percent quota for the non-black, non-female part of the population. That quota will continue to be implemented by relatively low-level employees who think they are doing what their bosses want.

Those opposed to affirmative action say that we should just enforce the laws against discrimination. In the case of S&W, that would mean that somebody would have to file a lawsuit against them. With the publication of S&W's ad in *The Times*, that might happen. The final decision in that lawsuit, if it is filed, will not be rendered until a decade or more has passed, and thousands of dollars in expenses and legal fees have accrued. Had the ad not appeared, the people who had no chance to get hired as waiters at S&W, but might have been hired under another policy, were unlikely to sue. So was the Equal Employment Opportunity Commission. The ad that S&W published testifies to the company's lack of fear in that regard. The Urban League, the NAACP, and NOW also appear to pose no threat.

Those who composed and authorized S&W's ad, of course, were not conscious that its content might be displaying anything unfortunate or illegal, and apparently they expected little or no adverse reaction to it on the part of the public. The customers obviously haven't complained in large numbers. This universal complaisance in the face of openly exhibited segregation is the most disturbing aspect of the incident. ■

(The ad referred to appeared in *The New York Times*, 4/5/96, p.A21.)

January/February 1997

LAST IN, FIRST OUT: BLACK MEN TAKE THE HEAT

BY MARC BRESLOW

The widely-syndicated economics columnist Robert Samuelson recently wrote, "Most men, whatever their race, shouldn't regularly be without work. If they are, the main reason is that they lack the skills, discipline or desire to find and keep jobs." Samuelson went on to argue that since most blacks have jobs, for those who don't the problem must be within themselves rather than resulting from racism or the structure of the U.S. economy.

Contrary to Samuelson's moralizing, the truth is that African Americans are victims of an economy that has been failing most workers for more than two decades, of employment trends that increasingly confer benefits only on those with advanced degrees, and of continued racism. Equally destructive, the current political climate blames them for their own suffering.

Since the early 1970s real wages for American workers have been falling, while unemployment rates have risen. For African Americans, and particularly young male workers, the trend has been worse. Average wages have fallen more than 15%, while unemployment, even during the current economic "boom," remains above 11% for all black men, and around 25% for those under the age of 25.

Racists, such as Charles Murray and his *Bell Curve* supporters, claim that this trend can be explained by genetics, or by the moral failure of black families. Conservatives blame the government for interfering with free markets, arguing that the minimum wage, welfare and other federal policies have reduced the available jobs and destroyed work incentives. Yet another explanation, favored by moderate economists, says that whites have more "human capital" — education and experience — than blacks, so they are worth more on the job market.

The racist arguments are so offensive that I would rather ignore them. But, briefly, consider — is it reasonable to suppose that either the genetic endowments, or the cultural backgrounds, of African Americans deteriorated so quickly as to explain a rise in unemployment from 8% during 1970 to 15% during the recession of the mid-1980s?

The answer is no — blacks have always been the last hired and the first fired in the United States. When the U.S. economy provided close to full employment, white employers hired African Americans even when they might have preferred not to. But when there are many applicants for every available job, it is far easier for employers to discriminate — and to indulge the racist preferences of their white employees and customers.

Job opportunities for all Americans have been on a long downward trend, and they are far lower today than the official five point something percent unemployment rate indicates. Because federal statistics ignore all potential workers who are too discouraged to have looked for work in the past month, and all those who want full-time jobs but can only find part-time ones, the real "underemployment" rate is actually about 12% at present.

And while the classified ads may show many jobs available for skilled workers in the largely-white suburbs, there are few openings for people in poor inner-city neighborhoods — who often cannot get to suburban jobs due to lack of public transportation. For example, 14 people applied for every job opening at fast food restaurants in the predominantly black central Harlem neighborhood of New York City during one five-month period in 1993, according to a study by Katherine Newman for the Russell Sage Foundation. Among those people who applied for such jobs but were rejected, 73% still lacked jobs a year later.

Blaming the existence of welfare or other low-income government policies for blacks' worsening plight also makes little sense, since the real value of such programs has been steadily decreasing. How can the minimum wage, for example, be a main cause of job losses when it had (until the rise in October 1996 from $4.25 to $4.70) lost 30% of its value since 1970? Similarly, how can welfare benefits cause joblessness when the value of welfare grants fell by 45% since 1970, even before the new legislation radically downsized the welfare system?

The real causes of the severe drop in black mens' earnings versus white mens' lies in the restructuring of the U.S. labor market. Economists John Bound of the University of Michigan and Richard Freeman of Harvard University attribute this drop first to the rapid disappearance of factory jobs in the United States, where black men had been highly concentrated. In 1973 42% of black men in the Midwest held manufacturing jobs, compared to 33% of white men. But by 1989 there was a dramatic turnaround — only 12% of blacks held such relatively-well paying jobs, compared to 21% of whites.

This incredible shift occurred because workers who had the most seniority got to keep the much-reduced number of union jobs. African American men, who had less seniority because discriminatory barriers had only recently come down and because they were on average younger, were the first to be laid off.

Second, the one-third fall in the inflation-adjusted value of the minimum wage harmed blacks more than whites since more black Americans held jobs paying the minimum. And third, the decline of unions in America has particularly hurt African Americans, 32% of whom held unionized jobs in 1983, compared to 22% of whites.

For black women, average wages have fallen only slightly, in contrast to the severe 15% drop for men. But their situation relative to white women has gotten worse, since white women's wages have risen significantly over the past two decades.

The declining minimum wage has hurt African-American women, as has reduced funding for education and government. Racial and gender discrimination has been less severe in the public than the private sector, so that many black women found jobs there during the 1960s and 1970s. But as government spending has dropped, these jobs have dried up. In 1973, for example, 70% of young college-educated black women, and 57% of white women, found jobs in education. But by 1989 only 20% of young female college graduates, both black and white, were employed in education.

Although genetics, culture, and welfare policies do not explain the worsened circumstances of African Americans, the "human capital" argument does have some truth. Even though African American educational levels have been catching up to whites (68% of blacks had high school degrees in 1992 versus 31% in 1970), whites still have twice as high a proportion of college graduates as blacks (thanks in part to falling funding for public education). Whereas in years past a high school degree was enough to

provide access to reasonably-paying jobs, it no longer does so. In today's restructured labor market only people with college and graduate degrees (and not all of them) have seen their wages rise over time.

Moreover, Bound and Freeman's data shows that even among college graduates the gap between white and black earnings has widened in recent years. One reason for this is the continued prevalence of racist attitudes among employers. In 1991 the Urban Institute conducted a study in which they sent out pairs of "testers," one black and one white, to apply for the same jobs. The pairs were carefully matched to have equal qualifications for the jobs, including not only paper qualifications, but also personal qualities such as openness and articulateness. One striking finding of the study was that in 15% of cases only the white tester received a job offer, while only the black tester received an offer in a mere 5% of cases.

Such evidence tends to undermine the validity of the "human capital" argument, since the paired testers had the same education and experience. And the implied discrimination is enough to explain much of the difference between black and white unemployment rates.

The U.S. economy is badly serving the needs both of those who have jobs and those who want them, and people of color are particularly hard hit. There are no easy answers to our long-term economic decline. But it is high time to stop blaming the victims. ■

Resources: This article draws heavily on "The Racial Divide Widens," *Dollars & Sense*, Jan/Feb 1995, and "To Be Young, Black, and Female," *Dollars & Sense*, May/June 1995. Also see "What Went Wrong? The Erosion of Relative Earnings and Employment Among Young Black Men in the 1980s," John Bound and Richard B. Freeman, *Quarterly Journal of Economics*, 1992; "Finding Work in the Inner City: How Hard is it Now? How Hard will it be for AFDC Recipients?," Katherine Newman and Chauncy Lennon, NY: Russell Sage Foundation Working Paper #76, October 1995.

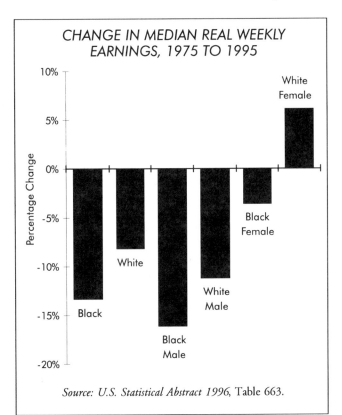

CHANGE IN MEDIAN REAL WEEKLY EARNINGS, 1975 TO 1995

Source: U.S. Statistical Abstract 1996, Table 663.

WELFARE MYTHS AND REALITIES

BY TERESA AMOTT

MYTHS	REALITIES
1. The average family on welfare has more children than the average family that does not collect welfare benefits.	The average welfare family has two children — the same as the national average. Seven out of 10 AFDC (Aid to Families with Dependent Children) families have two or fewer children.
2. A growing share of poor children receive AFDC.	In 1992, only 63% of poor children received AFDC, compared to 81% in 1973. The combination of rising poverty but roughly constant AFDC rolls has meant that the program serves a falling share of poor children.
3. The more generous a state's welfare benefits, the more female-headed families you are likely to find in that state.	Studies show no correlation between the level of benefits and the prevalence of female-headed families. During the 1980s, when the share of poor children receiving AFDC fell, the share living in female-headed families rose.
4. If families leave the AFDC rolls and find a job, chances are good that they can move out of poverty.	Millions of jobs pay less than poverty-level wages. In 1993, 42% of single mothers working full time year round earned poverty-level wages. Fewer than 55% of AFDC recipients had high school degrees. Fewer than 1 in 100 was a college graduate.
5. Welfare creates an inherited dependency, with generation after generation on welfare.	Studies suggest that AFDC is rarely received by successive generations of dependent families. One study found that three of four daughters from families that received welfare did not go on to receive AFDC as adults. And, studies suggest that welfare-dependent children are no more likely than other poor children to receive AFDC later in life.
6. Since most mothers work outside the home, it is only fair to expect welfare mothers to support themselves.	While the majority of married mothers with children do work for pay, they work only part time or part year. Is it reasonable to require AFDC mothers, who are solely responsible for childrearing and whose children are significantly less healthy than more affluent children, to work full time or full year?
7. Spending on welfare programs to aid needy families is a major part of the federal budget.	Federal spending for poor families with children, including paying for medical care, amounts to about 6% of the budget. In 1992, the federal government spent $464 billion on Social Security, veterans' benefits, unemployment and other such programs that don't test the income of the recipient. That was ten times more than it spent on AFDC and Food Stamps, two programs recently cut back further by welfare reform.

Sources: U.S. House Ways and Means Committee, *The Green Book 1994*; David Ellwood, *Poor Support: Poverty in the American Family*; Child Trends, *The Life Circumstances and Development of Children in Welfare Families.*

November/December 1996

FAREWELL TO WELFARE

BUT NOT TO POVERTY

BY RANDY ALBELDA

Welfare as we knew it is gone.

What is in its place? A federal mandate to states to force poor mothers into the low-wage labor market any way they see fit. What is not in place, however, is the funding, or even incentives needed to create the jobs or work supports that would make this a poverty-fighting strategy. There are no federal requirements to increase the supply or funding of child care. Little is being done to create jobs for women that pay living wages. There are no plans to expand health care to low wage workers. And there is no talk of boosting the educational and training opportunities for single mothers.

Welfare as we knew it — AFDC (Aid to Families with Dependent Children) — was no one's dream program, but it did guarantee cash assistance to very poor families, mainly single women and their children. Welfare as we have it — TANF (Temporary Assistance to Needy Families) — does more than remove the guarantee that needy families will receive assistance. It provides incentives for the states to spend less than they did under AFDC, includes a 60-month lifetime limit for assistance, and requires states to put a substantial percentage of all adult recipients into paid or unpaid jobs almost immediately.

Besides further eroding the safety net and fracturing an already ill-funded program, TANF makes it more difficult for states to help low-income mothers support their families through their own earnings. TANF's financial incentives are to place recipients directly into jobs — any jobs — making states less likely to provide education or meaningful job training. And while the new legislation will reduce welfare rolls, unless there are creative state initiatives and some federal changes to the law, poverty as we know it will increase.

EVERY MOTHER A WORKING MOTHER

Jobs have always been promoted as this country's best solution to poverty, but this has never worked well for women, since women's wages alone are too low to support families. Yet work has never before been so explicitly forced on mothers, especially those with young children. The 1988 Family Support Act required states to turn AFDC into a jobs and training program for single parents. But more than half of them fulfilled the requirement by going to school. The 1980s emphasis on making recipients work-ready has turned into a 1990s mandate that mothers work.

What happened?

Close to 70% of mothers are in the paid labor force. Public sentiment appears to say that if other mothers must work, why not single mothers? This rationale has been used to push poor women into an unrelenting labor market, but it won't work — and not just for poor single mothers. Our economy depends on women for free care of children and for doing low-wage jobs, yet there is an increasing expectation that every adult earn wages sufficient to support a family. For mothers, this is virtually impossible — you can't both provide free care and work enough hours to earn a family wage.

While many families fare poorly under society's new work expectations for women, single-mother families fare the worst for three simple reasons. First, like all women, single-mothers earn less, on average, than men do when they work. Second, raising children is time-consuming work, and children increase the cost of family life (they need food, clothing, shelter and care). Finally, in single mother families, there is only one adult to both earn income and take care of children.

The difficulties single mothers face are borne out in the poverty statistics. In 1994, half of single-mother families were poor, compared to one out of every 20 married couples with no children. While only 8% of all people in the United States live in single mother families, they make up 28% of all poor persons.

ENDING WELFARE

In August 1996, President Clinton signed the Personal Responsibility and Work Opportunity Act. Along with 22% cuts to Food Stamps and Supplemental Security Income (SSI) over the next six years, the bill eliminates AFDC. In its place is the Temporary Assistance for Needy Families (TANF) block grant.

The Republican Congress takes credit for this bill, but it is a scaled-down version of previous efforts to reform welfare. The Republicans also hoped to eliminate the Medicaid entitlement and severely reduce Food Stamps for all, but were repeatedly stymied because the political stakes were too high. State medical establishments receive too much Medicaid money to let it be discarded. Agribusiness made it clear they didn't intend to lose their best customer — the federal government — by dismantling Food Stamps.

AFDC, on the other hand, didn't have strong enough "interest groups" protecting it. Two-thirds of the 13 million people receiving AFDC in 1996 were children. The Catholic church and women's groups — the two most active groups lobbying against passage of this bill — clearly did not hold much sway among the current crop of Republicans. Once the Republicans were able to isolate AFDC from Medicaid and drastic Food Stamps cuts, the President (running as an un-Democrat for re-election), couldn't resist signing a bill that assured him of much coveted suburban votes.

THE TERMS OF TANF

There are four main components to TANF:
• ending the guarantee of cash assistance to poor families.

• establishing a new fiscal relationship, under which the federal government will provide fixed block grants to states, while no longer providing them with a financial incentive to spend additional money on low-income families.

• establishing a lifetime time limit of 60 months (not necessarily consecutive) on receiving assistance from federal TANF funds.

• penalizing states which do not force a substantial portion of their adult recipients into narrowly defined work programs.

While the first change has received the most attention, all four drastically change the nature of poverty programs. Relying on the rhetoric that states know best and dependency is bad, the Republican Congress eliminated the federal promise of cash assistance to needy families. The hard-earned struggles of the welfare rights movements of the 1960s and 1970s to assure that those eligible to receive AFDC (particularly African Americans) know their rights and receive their assistance, were erased with a stroke of the pen. With federal eligibility requirements eliminated, states may now define "needy" any way they want. They don't even have to use the same definition of needy across their state: needy in the city can be defined differently than needy in the suburbs.

States no longer have to provide cash assistance if they don't want to and can completely privatize their welfare system. The lack of uniform eligibility provisions opens the door to the systematic disentitlement of groups of people that was prevalent before the welfare rights movement. Anyone convicted of a drug-related felony cannot receive TANF funds, and immigrants who come to the United States are denied benefits until they have been here for five years (unless a state changes its own law).

FIXED FEDERAL FUNDING

TANF also profoundly alters the fiscal relationship between states and the feds. The new law requires the feds to provide each state with the highest of their 1995, 1994 or average of 1992-94 federal allocation of AFDC during every year from 1997 through 2002. There are no automatic adjustments for inflation or for need. This represents a dramatic change from AFDC, which was a matching grant: for every dollar a state spent on the program, it received a dollar (or more than a dollar for poor states). Although many states did not take full advantage of the match, this funding mechanism intentionally provided a strong incentive to increase spending.

Under the new block grant structure, states can spend as much as they please, but will not receive an extra penny from the feds. And once the money is gone, there is no more. With a recession and an increase in poor families, states will not necessarily have more resources to help out than they did in the past. There are several pools of money that states may tap into in case of deep recession, or if they reduce their TANF rolls, or if they reduce the number of out-of-wedlock births. But these are small bundles of cash and are set at fixed amounts to be split by all qualifying states.

Further, TANF actually permits states to spend less money. As long as states meet federal work participation requirements, they can cut up to a quarter of their 1994 spending levels without penalty (although to qualify for additional assistance in a recession, states must maintain full funding). One aspect of the bill that helped assure its passage was that most states will actually see a windfall for the first year or so of TANF, provided there is no recession. Because national AFDC rolls have fallen since 1994, federal and state spending levels in 1994 were higher than in 1996. But, as inflation erodes the grant and as the business cycle turns, states will find themselves with less money from the feds and permission to spend less of their own money.

A particularly cruel aspect of the new law is the time limit. States are not allowed to allocate TANF money to any adult who has received TANF money for 60 months — regardless of how much assistance was received in any month or how long it took to accrue 60 months of aid. At present, the average length of time any AFDC recipient receives aid over her lifetime is seven years. Sixty months is an arbitrary number and it will not serve the needs of many poor families. If fully enforced, this provision will throw many families into the street.

The time limit also works against the most positive reform already implemented by many states: allowing employed AFDC recipients to keep more of their cash assistance, even though it may be a small amount. Given the difficulties that single mothers face juggling jobs and kids, and given their relatively low average wages, most will need some form of support until their children are old enough to take care of themselves. That usually is more than 60 months.

The 60-month time limit pushes states concerned about families hitting the limit to avoid giving aid in small monthly amounts, even though this is precisely what some families need in order to make holding a job possible. While states can use their own funds to extend the limit or boost other programs that supplement work, the current political climate makes that unlikely. The only good thing about the time limit provision is that the feds did not set up or fund a national registry for TANF recipients, so implementing time limits will be difficult.

WORK, WORK, WORK

The final major piece of TANF is the federal requirement that states put recipients to work. The new law requires recipients whose youngest child is more than one year old to do some form of paid or unpaid work after 24 months of receiving benefits. Most schooling and job training will not count as "work." Further, unless states specifically opt out, adult recipients with children older than one must perform community service (meaning workfare) after only two months of obtaining benefits.

Although previous federal provisions also had work requirements, the 1988 law exempted women with a disabled child or whose youngest child was less than three, and most education qualified as being part of a work program. Plus, it paid mothers' day care and transportation costs, neither of which is required under the new law.

In addition to the work requirements, states must meet work participation rates or risk losing some of their federal grant. Every year a certain percentage of all adult recipients (whose youngest child is older than one) must be in a work program for a certain number of hours a week. In 1997, 20% of single-mother families must be at "work" for at least 20 hours a week, gradually increasing to 50% of mothers working for at least 30 hours during the year 2002.

The work requirements are structured in such a way to discourage states from providing education and training that would allow at least some women to move into decent paying jobs. States can provide education and training if they want, but most of the programs cannot count toward the federal work participation requirement. For states to hit their "quotas" they will want to place women into the labor market immediately.

The bottom line? The new law is designed to encourage states to reduce funding and welfare rolls by pushing women into an unrelenting low-wage labor market without the vital supports that make employment possible.

The Urban Institute has carefully documented the damage this law is likely to do. It estimated that the cuts in Food Stamps and SSI to legal immigrants, coupled with the changes to AFDC, will push 2.6 million more people into poverty by 2002 — a 9% increase in poverty. Because single-mother families are 22% of all families with children, the range of the bill's impact is far-reaching. Over 20% of all families with children will see their incomes fall by an average of $1,300 a year. And despite all the rhetoric about reducing "dependency," the Urban Institute found that half of the families affected by the new law already have at least one family member in the labor market. The new welfare system will increase poverty — not reduce it.

WHAT IS TO BE DONE?

If there is a silver lining to this new law it is that most states will get more federal money in 1997 than they did in 1995 or 1996. States can spend that money in any way they like. As everyone knows, welfare needs drastic reform. If some of the federal provisions can be amended and states can be persuaded to implement programs that support work, there may be some possibilities for a saner support system for poor families.

For example, creative states can fund more expansive unemployment insurance systems, allowing part-time

SCAPEGOATING IMMIGRANTS

The welfare mythology which has long stigmatized poverty and fomented racial prejudice now has a new scapegoat: immigrants. While undocumented immigrants were already excluded from most entitlement programs, the August 1996 welfare law denies most benefits to documented immigrants, supposedly to eliminate welfare as a "pull" factor for immigration.

Most documented immigrants who are not citizens are banned from receiving Supplemental Security Insurance and Food Stamps. States may deny them Temporary Assistance for Needy Families (TANF) — AFDC's replacement — and non-emergency Medicaid. The law also bans most future documented immigrants from receiving TANF or other "means tested" benefits during their first five years in the United States. Listen to Senator Phil Gramm's (R-TX) reason why: "[I]mmigrants should come to Texas with their sleeves rolled up, ready to go to work, not with their hands out, ready to go on welfare."

Let's lob a few facts at the anti-immigrant fable. According to the 1990 Census, immigrants work and use public assistance at rates similar to the U.S.-born. The employment rate (for those 16 or over) was 60% for the U.S.-born, 59% for the foreign-born, and 60% for foreign-born non-citizens. Meanwhile, few households received public assistance, no matter what their immigration status. Those receiving no assistance included 93% of the U.S.-born, 91% of the foreign-born, and 89% of foreign-born non-citizens. The small differences are due to immigrants' higher poverty rates. The family poverty rate is about 1 and 1/2 times as high for the foreign-born as for the U.S.-born, and it is twice as high for foreign-born non-citizens as for the U.S.-born.

Anti-immigrant types claim they are concerned about the work ethic of immigrants receiving public benefits. But they also rail against immigrants who "take American jobs." If the anti-immigrant crowd doesn't like immigrants who don't work, and doesn't like immigrants who do, that means they just plain don't like immigrants. Unless, of course, immigrants work in jobs no one else wants, without benefitting from social programs. Then the anti-immigrant crowd may find a way to tolerate them.

— *Alejandro Reuss*

workers or workers with sporadic work histories (like many welfare mothers) to collect. In doing so, they would provide needed cash assistance and not run down TANF's 60 month clock. States could beef up current housing and child care programs to funnel resources to where families need it. Finally, states could create public sector jobs at decent wages with health benefits for welfare recipients.

In addition to working to construct state programs, we need to change the current law. Federal changes that reduce the work participation requirement, that allow for more of the population to be exempt from work requirements (such as adult recipients with children under age six), and that broaden the definition of work to include participation in education and training would give states more leeway to fashion programs that assist the poor. As bad as this bill is, the mourning time should be limited. The law went into effect on October 1, 1996 and states must meet the work participation rate requirements by July 1, 1997 to receive full funding. Since few actually thought this bill would pass, the law's provisions for the transition from AFDC to TANF are vague. States with approved waivers may continue to operate under those rules (including using the federal definition of eligibility under AFDC) and will not have to comply with the provisions of TANF if they are inconsistent with the waiver. Many of the 42 states with waivers are likely to do that.

The clear message of this bill is "work your way out of poverty." And states are saddled with the responsibility of making mothers work. But they will find that for women, especially those with low educational attainment and little job experience, this is not possible without the supports necessary for mothers to work. The struggle now is to make painfully apparent that the only viable methods of putting poor mothers to work are ones that will make work better for all workers: child care, affordable housing, health care and livable wages. ∎

Resources: "Potential Effects of Congressional Welfare Reform Legislation on Family Income," Urban Institute, July 1996; "A Brief Summary of Key Provisions of the Temporary Assistance for Needy Families Block Grant of H.R. 3734," Mark Greenberg and Steve Savner, Center for Law and Social Policy, Washington, D.C. August, 1996; also see the World Wide Web site: http://EPN.ORG.

ARTICLE 35

January/February 1994

LENDING INSIGHTS

HARD PROOF THAT BANKS DISCRIMINATE

BY JIM CAMPEN

"These really are horrifying numbers."
— *Comptroller of the Currency Eugene A. Ludwig on banks' 1992 record denying mortgages to minorities, Nov. 4, 1993.*

As appalling as it was, the latest annual report on mortgage lending shocked few observers when the Clinton Administration's top regulators unveiled it before the Senate Banking Committee in November 1993. In keeping with past patterns, black mortgage applicants were turned down more than twice as often as whites in 1992. Indeed, the most closely watched single number indicated that things were getting worse rather than better: the ratio of the black denial rate to the white denial rate rose from 2.16 in 1991 to 2.26 in 1992.

But instead of denying the obvious as they have in the past, in 1993 government officials acknowledged that discrimination is "alive and well in America," as Housing Secretary Henry Cisneros put it. Bank regulators, along with Attorney General Janet Reno, testified that they were intensifying efforts to identify and punish lenders who discriminate. And bankers, rather than disputing charges that they had discriminated, emphasized their efforts to do better.

Ever since researchers found what one Massachusetts banker referred to as a "smoking gun" in October 1992, bankers recognized that they could no longer offer credible denials. The crucial evidence, from a study by the Federal Reserve Bank of Boston, finally established beyond a reasonable doubt that banks discriminate along racial lines when making mortgage loans.

THE "SMOKING GUN"

The Federal Reserve Bank of Boston has been a somewhat liberal outpost in the overwhelmingly conservative Federal Reserve System. Taking advantage of the Fed's status as a banking regulator, researchers there conducted the first study to take into account virtually all of the factors used in mortgage lending decisions. They asked the 131 banks in the Boston area that had received 25 or more mortgage applications in 1990 to review their loan files and gather 38 additional pieces of information for each application from a black or Hispanic (about 1,200 applications) and for a randomly selected set of 3,300 applications by whites.

Using a special variant of the standard statistical technique known as multiple regression analysis, the Boston Fed's analysts then sought to explain why minorities in the Boston area were denied mortgages 2.7 times as often as whites. To what extent, the researchers asked, did legitimate factors account for the disparity?

Banks, hoping to be exonerated by the Boston Fed's study, were dismayed at the results. The additional information showed that, as the banks claimed, blacks and Hispanics were on average poorer, had worse credit histories, and requested mortgage loans that were larger relative to their incomes. But it also showed that these and similar factors only told part of the story. Even if black and Hispanic borrowers had been just as creditworthy as the average white applicant with respect to all 38 of the factors considered, they still would have been 56% more likely to be denied a mortgage. Only the applicants' minority status could account for the difference. As Alicia Munnell, who was then the Boston Fed's Research Director, put it, "The study eliminates all the other possible factors that could be influencing decisions." The long-sought "smoking gun" had been found.

The Boston Fed offered a plausible account of the way that discrimination took place. As most of those who have sought home mortgages know from personal experience, the application process can be complex and intimidating. The Boston Fed's data showed that only 20% of all applicants had flawless credit records. Within that group virtually all applicants were approved, regardless of race. But the great majority of applicants — including most of those ultimately receiving loans — had one or more imperfections in their loan files. These problems could have legitimately justified denying them mortgage loans.

To be successful, applicants generally need help and counseling, and often benefit from a willingness on the part of bank personnel to "stretch" or overlook one or two of the requirements. Whites appeared to have received this assistance more frequently than blacks or Hispanics — perhaps because the loan officers, who were overwhelmingly white, were simply more comfortable with other whites. Even though there may have been a valid technical reason for every denial of a minority application, banks were still guilty of treating white

THE BOSTON FED STUDY

The Boston Fed's researchers examined data on 38 variables that bear on loan applications, in addition to data on the race, income, and sex of applicants. Ranked by how much they increased the probability that an application would be denied, here are the factors that the Fed found mattered most:

Denied private mortgage insurance	596%
Public record of debt problem (e.g., bankruptcy)	114%
Race (black or Hispanic applicant)	56%
Purchasing 2-4 family home	42%
Poor consumer credit history*	37%
Self-employed	35%
Housing-costs-to-income ratio over 30%	34%
High total-debt-payment-to-income ratio*	33%
High loan-value-to-appraised-home-value ratio*	12%
Employed in industry with high unemployment rate*	11%
Late payments on previous mortgage loan*	11%

To estimate the impact of an individual factor, the analysts calculated the percentage increase in the probability of denial that would result from the variation of that factor alone, assuming that all other variables held constant at their average values. For example, they figured out that when nothing else varies, the probability of denial increases from 11% to 17% if an applicant's race is black or Hispanic rather than white. Alternatively, if a mortgage applicant is refused private mortgage insurance, the probability of being denied the mortgage loan increases from about 17% to over 99%. For most factors, including these two, the stated condition was either present or absent; for the other five factors — those marked by an asterisk (*) — the estimation process was more complicated. The percentage shows the estimated effect of that variable's increase of one "standard deviation" from its average value.

Source: See *Resources* at end of article.

and minority applicants unequally. As activist Bruce Marks of the Boston-based Union Neighborhood Assistance Corporation explained, "it's a mortgage minefield," and banks are much more likely to guide white applicants through it.

AFTER THE SMOKESCREEN CLEARS

Pushed beyond the stage of denial — in spite of the inevitable, and quickly discredited, objections published by *Forbes, Business Week,* and *The Wall Street Journal* — bankers and federal regulators have begun to recognize the value of measures that had been urged on them for years by community advocates. Bank responses have included taking a systematic "second look" at minority loan applications recommended for denial; training bank employees to increase understanding of fair lending issues and sensitivity to cultural differences; hiring more minority loan officers; revising certain traditional credit standards that are biased toward white cultural practices; forging working relationships with realtors and appraisal firms that have positive records in minority communities; developing new mortgage lending products adapted to the special circumstances and needs of minority borrowers; and using internal "testing" programs to identify whether or not bank employees are in fact offering equal treatment to minority applicants.

At the same time, the four federal bank regulatory agencies have begun taking steps to ensure that banks are complying with fair lending laws. One agency, the Office of the Comptroller of the Currency (OCC), estimated in November that it will complete 20 in-depth fair-lending examinations by the end of 1993. The OCC also announced that in early 1994 it will begin the use of undercover testers to detect racial discrimination at the pre-application stage of the mortgage lending process. For the first time, regulators are actually referring cases to the Justice Department when their own investigations suggest that discrimination is occuring. And, most dramatically, the Federal Reserve Board denied a routine application by Connecticut-based Shawmut Bank to acquire a smaller bank in New Hampshire, citing the ongoing Justice Department investigation of Shawmut's alleged lending discrimination.

These things happened only after Congressional hearings had brought to light what Deepak Bhargava of the Association of Community Organizations for Reform Now (ACORN) characterized as "a long and sorry record" of regulatory failure. Even New York's Republican Senator Alphonse D'Amato was moved to ask whether the "regulatory agencies [were] asleep at the switch, or worse, turning a blind eye?"

THE POWER OF DISCLOSURE

The Boston Fed study established the *fact* of discrimination in mortgage lending. But with its narrow focus on data from completed loan applications, the study did not attempt to measure the full *extent* of discrimination. For example, many potential minority borrowers encounter responses to their initial contacts with banks that discourage them from ever applying, and the property values recorded in loan files may have been furnished by appraisers who systematically undervalue homes in minority neighborhoods.

The community reinvestment movement is right to insist that the 1977 Community Reinvestment Act obliges banks to do more than simply deal fairly with the loan applicants who come through their doors. A whole range of aggressive, affirmative initiatives will be necessary to extend credit and financial services to currently underserved communities. Moreover, without constant pressure from community groups, regulators will likely bow to pressure from banks and fail to enforce community-oriented laws and regulations. ■

Resources: "Expanded HMDA Data on Residential Lending: One Year Later," *Federal Reserve Bulletin,* November 1992; Alicia Munnell and others, "Mortgage Lending in Boston: Interpreting HMDA Data," Federal Reserve Bank of Boston, October 1992; "Discrimination in the Housing and Mortgage Markets," a special issue of *Housing Policy Debate,* Vol. 3, No. 2, 1992; "Your Loan Is Denied," a one-hour documentary broadcast on PBS's *Frontline* June 23, 1992; videotape available from the Center for Investigative Reporting, 530 Howard St., 2nd Floor, San Francisco CA 94105 (415-543-1200).

MORTGAGE DENIAL RATES BY RACE, 1990-92

1990 / 1991 / 1992

Percent of Applications Denied

White: 14.2% (1990), 17.3% (1991), 15.9% (1992)
Hispanic: 21.4% (1990), 26.5% (1991), 27.3% (1992)
Black: 33.6% (1990), 37.4% (1991), 35.9% (1992)

Source: Federal Reserve Board; *American Banker,* 11/5/93.

CHAPTER 8
The Environment

ARTICLE 36   *May/June 1997*

DOES PRESERVING THE EARTH THREATEN JOBS?

BY EBAN GOODSTEIN

Back in 1990, the U.S. Business Roundtable published a study predicting that the Clean Air Act amendments, which were passed later that year, would lead to massive job loss: There is "little doubt," they claimed, "that a minimum of two hundred thousand (plus) jobs will quickly be lost, with plants closing in dozens of states. This number could easily exceed one million jobs — and even two million jobs — at the more extreme assumption about residual risk." Because of these concerns, the amendments budgeted retraining funds of $50 million per year for displaced workers.

Six years later, a front page *New York Times* article seemed to confirm this prediction. Titled, "Eastern Coal Towns Wither in the Name of Cleaner Air," it detailed the five-year impact of the amendments on Appalachian communities, as electric companies switched to low sulfur western coal to meet tougher air pollution standards. Curiously, though, the article never gave a number for job losses — perhaps because a number would have undercut the headline. By reading carefully, and doing some math, one could calculate that at most 1,000 job losses per year, over a multistate region, could be attributed to regulation. From another source, we know that by 1995 fewer than 3,000 workers nationwide had applied for Clean Air Act retraining funds.

I do not mean to downplay the devastating impact that layoffs have in communities — especially small communities that depend on natural resource industries. But the facts suggest that perceptions and reality are way out of line concerning jobs and the environment. The job losses in the coal industry have been as bad as they get from environmental regulation, but nevertheless were of little significance in a nation with more than 100 million people working. The same week that the *Times* ran the coal story on the front page, buried in the business section was the news that "trade and technology" had eliminated a whopping 100,000 textile jobs in the previous year *alone*.

BLAME THE FEDERAL RESERVE, NOT THE EPA

When a sentence begins with "all economists agree," it is a good idea to head for the door. But stay seated for these three facts: (virtually) all economists agree that, for the economy as a whole there is no trade-off between jobs and the environment. Moreover, as the coal case suggests, actual layoffs from regulation have been, relatively speaking, quite small. Finally, regulation has not damaged the international competitiveness of U.S. manufacturing.

The first fact — no economy-wide trade-off — is an easy one to check, simply by looking at U.S. economic growth in recent years. In 1995, in spite of spending $160 billion per year on environmental protection, the U.S. economy was growing too fast from the Federal Reserve Bank's point of view. Too many people were employed in the United States, according to the Bank, raising the specter of inflation. As a result, the Federal Reserve hiked interest rates several times, in an effort to cool the economy down and *raise* unemployment rates towards the 6% level. Put another way, in 1995 the brake on job growth was clearly not excessive environmental regulation, but rather the (excessively) firm hand of the Fed.

Regulation is indeed expensive. Spending on a cleaner environment raises the costs of other goods and services, and reduces their consumption. This is the cost that we, as consumers, pay for regulation. In exchange, of course, we get the truly valuable benefit of a cleaner environment.

But it is a mistake to confuse costs of environmental protection with job losses from environmental protection. At a nationwide level, unemployment rates ultimately depend on the health of the macroeconomy, which has not been impaired by environmental regulation.

Indeed, environmental costs translate into environmental spending, which also provides jobs. As I document in a recent report, most studies find that jobs created in environmental and related sectors outweigh jobs lost due to higher regulatory costs, leading to small overall "net" employment *gains*.

Net increases in employment can happen in several ways. First, environmental spending pumps demand into the economy during recessions, dampening business cycles. Second, some environmental production, (recycling, for example), is more labor intensive than the alternative (incineration), leading to more jobs per dollar of Gross Domestic Product.

THE OVERALL COMPETITIVENESS OF U.S. FIRMS HAS NOT BEEN DAMAGED BY REGULATION.

Third, environmentally preferable means of meeting our energy needs (a sector that currently causes much of the nation's air pollution) would yield more jobs than our current reliance on burning fossil fuels and uranium. This is because energy conservation, wind energy and solar energy substitute for capital-intensive electricity generation plants and for imports of oil and natural gas. Such spending contributes little to employment in the United States.

But what about the quality of jobs? More labor intensive jobs are generally lower paid, whether in the service or manufacturing sector. On the other hand, much environmental spending, like defense spending, is heavily concentrated in the manufacturing sector. Spending on pollution control equipment, sewage treatment facilities or plastic liners for landfills promotes both direct and indirect job growth in traditional blue collar industries.

In fact, one study found that environmental protection provides employment heavily weighted to the transportation, communication and utility sectors, and away from services, both private and governmental (see the figure). While only 22% of all non-farm jobs were in the manufacturing, transportation, communication and utility sectors in 1991, 57% of jobs generated by environmental spending fell in one of these categories. By contrast, only 22% of environmentally-related jobs were in wholesale and retail trade, finance, insurance, real estate or services, compared to 55% for the economy as a whole. And in spite of criticisms that environmental regulation only creates jobs for pencil-pushing regula-

tors, only 11% of environmental employment was governmental, compared to an overall 17% share for government employment.

BLAME DOWNSIZING, NOT THE EPA

If there is no job trade-off nationally, what about at the local level? Again, in contrast to the conventional wisdom, the number of workers laid off due primarily to environmental regulations has been quite small. A series of studies found that manufacturing layoffs due to environmental regulation were on the order of 1,000 to 3,000 jobs per year nationwide in the late 1970s and 1980s.

More recently a U.S. Department of Labor survey, covering 57% of the manufacturing workforce, identified an average of four plant closings and 648 workers laid off due to environmental and safety regulation each year during the late 1980s. This was *less than one-tenth of one percent* of all major layoffs in manufacturing. The major source of job loss has been "corporate restructuring" — the 4,400 layoffs that Aetna Insurance Company announced last October, for example, were double the total number of jobs lost nationwide due to environmental regulation over the four-year period of the Labor Department survey.

A paper released by the Economic Policy Institute this spring looks carefully at manufacturing job losses in heavily regulated southern California. Boston University economist Eli Berman finds no reduction in businesses' demand for workers — indeed, perhaps because of large investments in pollution abatement equipment in the oil industry, employment actually rose slightly after the introduction of stricter air quality regulations.

Local trade-offs between jobs and the environment are most severe in the timber and mining industries — but even in the eastern coal-fields and the logging communities of the Pacific Northwest, total job losses from regulation have been in the low thousands — well below the total from a single corporate downsizing. These cases take on a high media profile because the jobs pay well, because reemployment opportunities are limited for many (but not all) laid off rural workers, and because the industries in question are facing larger scale layoffs due to automation, import competition and/or declining natural resources. In the coal case for example, even the *Times* attributed less than half of the job loss in the first half of the 90s to the Clean Air Act.

Again, this is not to minimize the impact that any plant closing has on a community. Clearly, in a world of increasing job instability, we need good legislation to protect workers who are faced with plant closings, expanded educational opportunities for laid-off workers, and affordable health care coverage that stays with workers when they lose their jobs. But the reasons for this have very little to do with environmental regulation, and much, much more to do with international trade, technology, and corporate downsizing.

REGULATION AND COMPETITIVENESS

OK, so maybe there is no national job trade-off, and lay-offs due to regulation have been small. But aren't we losing manufacturing jobs to countries overseas that have lax environmental standards? Again, the answer is no. The overall competitiveness of U.S. firms has not been damaged by regulation. Moreover, few firms are relocating to take advantage of lightly regulated "pollution havens" in poor countries. For decades economists have been looking quite hard for exactly these effects. But in their recent survey article on this topic, Harvard economist Adam Jaffe and his co-authors report, "studies attempting to measure the effect of environmental regulation on net exports, overall trade-flows, and plant location decisions have produced estimates that are either small, statistically insignificant, or not robust to tests of model specification." In other words — no observable impact.

Why? One answer is that most trade flows and foreign investment in manufacturing occur between developed countries, all of whom have comparable environmental regulations. A second answer is that, for most industries, environmental costs remain low — on the order of 1% of total business costs.

A third, intriguing answer comes from Harvard Business School professor Michael Porter. Porter argues that regulation, while imposing short run costs on firms, actually enhances their competitiveness in the long run. This can happen if regulation favors companies that are forward-looking, meaning, for example those that anticipate trends, invest in modern production processes, and stress research and development.

There is some evidence for the Porter view. In a forthcoming EPI report I show that heavily regulated industries actually faced less growth in import competition during the 1980s than the average for all industries.

PERCEPTION AND REALITY

In a poll taken in the early 90s, one-third of working adults in America felt that *their own job* was somewhat or very threatened by environmental regulation. It is not, unfortunately, hard to see how beliefs like this get shaped and reinforced. In 1990 the Business Roundtable offered up their take on environmental regulation: Job losses from the Clean Air Act alone are on the order of two million. The media widely reported their prediction. The reality, six years later, has been closer to 3,000 total layoffs, yet you wouldn't know it from reading *The New York Times*.

These skewed perceptions take a heavy political toll. On the table this year are proposals by the EPA to tighten air quality regulations, and expand the chemical emission reporting requirements for manufacturing industries. Congress is also considering weakening the Superfund legislation, which provides for the clean-up of hazardous waste sites. In all cases, the anti-environment argument boils down to one word: jobs.

In spite of the conventional wisdom, however, the underlying economic realities are clear:

• national employment levels are determined largely by federal fiscal and monetary policies, not environmental regulation;

• regulation causes small local job losses in manufacturing;

• regulation has no negative impact on the international competitiveness of U.S. industry; and

• there is little capital flight to pollution havens.

These points run so counter to the popular perception — manufactured by corporate lobbyists and repeated daily in the press — that I suspect that having read this article, many readers probably still don't believe them. ■

Resources: "Environmental Regulation and Labor Demand: Evidence From the South Coast Air Basin," Eli Berman and Linda T. Bui, forthcoming from Economic Policy Institute, Washington, DC; "Why No Pollution Havens? Environmental Regulation and U.S. Net Export Performance," *EPI Working Paper*, Eban Goodstein, 1996, Economic Policy Institute; "Jobs and the Environment: An Overview," *Environmental Management*, Eban Goodstein, 1996; "Environmental Regulation and the Competitiveness of U.S. Manufacturing: What Does the Evidence Tell Us?", Adam B. Jaffe, Steven R. Peterson, Paul R. Portney and Robert N. Stavins, *Journal of Economic Literature* 33-1, 1995.

PRAWN FEVER

RESOURCE DEPLETION THREATENS THAILAND'S SHRIMP FARMERS

BY ALFREDO QUARTO AND BETSY REED

For centuries, small villages clustered around Thailand's mangrove swamps, surviving off the myriad varieties of sea life that flourished in their dense, brackish waters.

But in the 1980s, a subtle invasion began that would bring ruin to the villages and pollution into their surroundings. The prawn industry, which produces jumbo shrimp for a luxury market, offered a get-rich-quick scheme that had few rivals in rural Thailand. It would provide plenty of capital and a ready market, if the villagers simply agreed to clear their mangrove forests and harvest prawns.

The honeymoon was lucrative, indeed: during the first one to three years, the villagers' investments sometimes yielded a 1000% profit. Then, polluted by toxic prawn excrement, the shallow pits that harbored the prawns would become worse than useless. In many areas, the hazardous substances produced by the prawns spread to the sea and killed off coastal sea life. Sea water, imported into the ponds to nourish the prawns, in turn salinated ground water and ruined farm land.

Prawn farmers have scrambled to save themselves, sinking deeper and deeper into debt in a vain quest to rid their property of pollutants. When the pollution begins to eat away at its profits, the industry turns to a new village, leaving in its wake a trail of filthy ponds, dry pits, and polluted soils. Bankrupt and faced with an exhausted environment, villagers have moved in droves to cities, where they live in shantytowns and work for scant wages in the burgeoning service sector.

The prawn industry is one of Thailand's ten biggest foreign exchange earners, generating nearly 22 billion bhat (almost one billion U.S. dollars) with the sale of 160,000 tons of prawns in 1991 alone. About 90% of production typically goes to exports, mainly to Japan, the United States, Hong Kong, Singapore, Europe and Canada.

Before 1986, small fishermen caught most of Thailand's prawns in the open sea. Today, small farmers indebted to large corporations grow prawns through the artificially maintained system of aquaculture based in mangrove forests. The Charoen Pokphand Group (CP), the country's largest aquaculture firm, pushes the farmers to produce as much — and as quickly — as possible, because over half of its profits come from selling them prawn feed and other essentials. Such pressure from CP has meant destruction for the mangroves. In 1961, there were an estimated 2 million rai (around 1 million acres) of mangrove forests along Thailand's 2600 kilometers of coastline. By 1989, only a few years after the introduction of the jumbo prawn industry, only 1.2 million rai of mangrove remained. Although nearly half the farms are in so-called "protected" areas, the government has done little to dissuade violators.

This insidious cycle of unbridled production followed by ecological devastation is appearing in a growing number of tropical and sub-tropical regions around the world. Largely because of the irreparable environmental damage it has caused, the prawn industry in Thailand is already past its peak. CP is now courting the governments of other mangrove-rich countries, including India, Mexico, Burma, Vietnam, Cambodia, Malaysia, and Indonesia.

CP recently gestured its willingness to accept limits on the growth of the industry in Thailand by proposing to require all farms over 50 rai (23 acres) to register with the government and be regulated. Like CP, the Thai government has publicized its interest in preservation, but its actions have been softer than its words. When a number of illegal farms were discovered this spring near the Cambodian border, the Thai central government forbade their expansion but allowed the existing farms to remain. And, say local environmentalists, the government's promise to ban prawn farming altogether by 1997 is not unrelated to the fact that most of the country's mangroves will be gone by then anyway.

VILLAGES ON THE VERGE

Some friends of mine and I recently visited Trang Province, on the southwest coast of Thailand. We met with villagers from three small fishing communities bordering the Andaman Sea. The people of Bahn Laemmakkan, Bahn Laemsai, and Bahn Toong are in a constant state of anxiety about the encroaching prawn industry. We arrived in Bahn Laemmakkan by small motor boat, moving past the mangroves that line the neighboring channel. Our guide, Dot Chatril Reutreemontree, works with the Yad Fon (Rain Drop) Association and has lived in these villages for three years, building the relationships necessary for effective grassroots organizing against the industry.

Though immature, the mangroves along the channel were impressive. At high tide, the sea floods the trees, allowing small boats to wander among the spreading branches. Soon we approached a prawn farm: shallow pits back to back across an expanse of muddy land, cleared of forest in blatant violation of Thai law.

About 70 families live in Bahn Laemmakkan. The village has an elementary school, but students travel to the nearby mainland for higher education. Though they are mainly fishing people, the villagers also farm, tending vegetable gardens, a small amount of rice, and banana, mango, jack-fruit, and papaya trees.

For diet as well as income, the villagers raise grouper fish in offshore pens. They described recent problems, mainly due to pollution from prawn farms and a nearby rubber-processing factory. Since the arrival of the prawn farms, many fish have died.

"No one in this village likes the prawn farms," said a villager named Ma Sanee Nunsii. As yet no farms had come to the peninsula where she lives, but prawn farmers had illegally cleared and occupied over 200 acres of mangrove forest nearby. The owners, she explained, are "influential people."

Her husband, Pa Sanee Nunsii, had nearly succumbed to "prawn fever" when his younger brother, who lived in another village, asked for financial help to set up a farm. The brother mortgaged his home and land to initiate the venture, but needed more capital. But Pa Sanee Nunsii couldn't mortgage their land, and the brother went bankrupt shortly thereafter.

He couldn't sell his own land because in many areas in Thailand, even centuries of occupation do not guarantee ownership. Although Bahn Laemakkan has been at its present site for over 50 years, villagers never knew to file claims for land titles. Technically, the occupants are leasing it from the government, even if money hasn't ever changed hands. As a result of this state of affairs, the prawn industry has been unable to buy up villagers' land from under them, and instead has had to cajole them into cooperation. Land rights reform, many activists argue, should return ownership of the land to the original occupants, but should include a serious commitment, on the part of the government, to its protection through law.

Prawn farms, according to Pa Sanee Nunsii, came to the district a year ago, and already the pollutants have had a noticable effect. The villagers have asked those who run the prawn farms to control their waste effluents, but to no avail. "We can deal with small business people, and we can deal with middle-sized ones. But we

SWAMP LIFE

Dense mangrove forests — sometimes called the rainforests of the sea — line swamps and shores along many tropical and sub-tropical coasts throughout Asia, Africa and North and Latin America. The specially-adapted roots and unique wood of mangrove trees create diverse habitats for rare and endangered coastal species, such as dolphins, sea turtles and other wild plants and animals that feed off the fish, mollusks and crustaceans in the swamps.

The mangroves play a vital role in protecting the coastlines from soil erosion, storm damage and excessive siltation, in addition to providing great quantities of decaying biomass from fallen leaves and branches — an essential source of rich nutrients for many coastal marine creatures. Indigenous communities of farmers and fisherpeople not only depend on the forests for food. The mangroves also offer a wealth of wood products, including charcoal, paper, building materials and firewood.

Close to the sea and on level ground, mangrove forests are easy to clear to create shallow prawn ponds. Yet the favored "intensive production" method cannot sustain itself for long. It depends on hatchery-bred larvae, manufactured feed, and chemical and medical water treatments, all maintained in controlled artificial ponds. To ensure a stable environment, the ponds must be regularly refreshed with sea water, while fouled waters containing the toxic excrement and additives from the feed and water treatments are pumped out.

Early on, a system of aquaculture called extensive production raised prawns in pens set up off the coast, usually within a protective bay or estuary. Though this method was less costly to establish and maintain than intensive production because it caused less ecological wear-and-tear, it also yielded less profit in the short run. Semi-intensive production, which utilizes both sea-bred and hatchery-bred prawns and relies on manufactured prawn feed and artificial barriers more than the extensive method, has proved fairly profitable but environmentally risky. A 1992 study of prawn production in the Philippines found the semi-intensive method to cause similar, though less serious, environmental damage to that associated with the intensive method (primarily polluted water and salinated land). So far, the natural growth of prawns at sea is the only method known to be completely harmless.

can't deal with the big investors. At that level, there's nothing we can do."

The people of Bae Laemakkan fear the repercussions of speaking out. "We can't even look at abandoned prawn farms for fear of reprisals from the owner's private security guards," a fisherman says. Many villagers believe that high-ranking government officials exploit their power over both forestry and fishery decisions to further their personal financial interests in the rapid expansion of the prawn industry. And for its part, the industry is notorious for using both bribery and coercion to influence political decisions.

It has even come to murder. On April 5, 1993, Pererasak Adisonprasert, a forestry official for the Ranong province, was shot to death. Adisonprasert had been the principal architect of a crusade to enforce previously dormant forest protection laws. He was responsible for 54 arrests and the confiscation of vast quantities of prawn farming equipment. Two weeks after his body was found, several people were arrested in connection with the crime. Among them was a policeman with close ties to a family that operates illegal prawn farms in the same area Adisonprasert had devoted himself to protecting.

AVERTING DISASTER

On Thailand's east coast lies a nightmare vision of Bae Laemakkan's future. The provinces of Songkhla and Nakhon Sri Tammanat are a wasteland of prawn farms that saw their heyday come — and go — in the late 1980s. "Some are beginning to see that prawn farming is not a good thing," said one prawn farmer in Songkhla Province.

CORPORATIONS GO TO GREAT LENGTHS TO CURRY FAVOR WITH THE GOVERNMENTS OF MANGROVE-RICH COUNTRIES.

"One to two years of profit, after that losses. If I had it to do over again, I'd stay in mixed agriculture. But the incentives were greater than the warnings, and so people took chances."

Over 70 percent of the territory of the three Trang Province villages is mangrove forest. For years, the villagers harvested mangroves for charcoal. The business was profitable when trees were full grown, but when the forests were cut without giving trees time to mature, it became less so. Eventually, people returned to fishing, although two charcoal facilities remain. Outside workers — about 20 for each factory — come in to maintain operations, and mangrove stands continue to shrink.

Thai law reserves about 80% of this mangrove forest for charcoal production, even though it lies within a national forest. The 15% of the forest with "full protection status" is often violated. About 260 acres of mangrove forest comprise "community forest" — land the provincial govern-ment presented to the three villages for community use. The community forest acts as a buffer against hard times and a way to ensure a future for a village dependent on its resources. Each village lets its members in need of extra earnings use some of the community forest, with certain restrictions.

Over the past three years, the villages have established strict rules for sustainable forest management. Recently, they replanted 23 acres of degraded forest, starting young mangroves from hanging shoots and pods harvested from mature trees.

To help villagers attain more autonomy and resist the expansion of the prawn industry, Yad Fon has worked with community leaders to establish grassroots structures to deal with local problems. Village cooperatives help people with interest-free loans, and a central warehouse provides spare boat-engine parts and fishing equipment. These collective efforts help co-op members stay out of debt and avoid high interest loans, and strengthen the villagers' resolve to hold their own against intruding interests.

THE GLOBAL DIMENSION

Despite the devastation it has wreaked in places like Thailand, the prawn industry is expanding and decimating the mangrove forests of the Philippines, Bangladesh, India, Mexico, and Panama, among other countries. Existing corporations are vying for overseas investment opportunities, and realizing great profits in their new overseas joint ventures and exports. In addition, they capitalize on the expanding markets for their own brands of prawn feed, water treatment additives, and specialized pond equipment needed in aquaculture enterprises. Even when a corporation's own prawn production is declining, sales of supplies to other prawn farms locally and abroad bolster profit margins.

Characteristically, governments encourage the expansion of the industry as a way of increasing export potential and the industrial exploitation of natural resources. The prime minister of Malaysia recently ordered the reclamation of the entire west coast of the Malaysian Peninsula, to conduct a massive landfill operation along more than 600 kilometers (about 360 miles) of mangrove-rich coastline. The plan is to dredge landfill materials from nearby hill-sides and mountains and extend the coastline over three kilometers (around 1.8 miles) seaward to offer the industry more room for development.

Moreover, the government is pushing plans to develop over 100,000 hectares (around 250,000 acres) of man-grove-forested coast into prawn farms. Industry representatives there have expressed an ambition to become the 5th largest exporter of jumbo prawns in the world. According to Nora Ibrahim of the Consumers' Association of Penang (CAP), there is a lack of public awareness in Malaysia of the issues at stake. "Too many city people think of smelly mud and useless swamp, which is inaccessible to them anyway. They fail to see the vital role mangroves play in fish production and coastline protection."

CAP is mainly concerned with consumer protection, but lately the magnitude of the threat to Malaysia's environment has taken precedence for the organization. Even if the government's grandiose reclamation plan falls short of its goals, the aquaculture industry is poised to consume acres and acres of forest.

Corporations go to great lengths to curry favor with the governments of mangrove-rich countries. CP is now making a bid for friendly relations with the Cambodian government, and the World Bank has tentatively agreed to offer the company a $100 million loan to finance the development of prawn farms in the Kampot, Kampongsom, and Koh Kong provinces.

A CP memorandum to the Cambodian government painted a rosy picture of prawn production, claiming that "sound shrimp culture techniques for sustainable production," coupled with the "resettlement of poor people living in the coastal area," will render the industry a great thing for all involved. The proposal requires the government to provide necessary infrastructure, including a maindrain canal and a pumping system to dispose of effluents. But the memo omits mention of the destruction that the prawn industry has left in its wake elsewhere, and assumes that substantial profit for major corporations is compatible with environmental health. The memo is explicit on this point: "The development objective of this project is to improve an unproductive agricultural land along the coastline into high profit shrimp farms while ensuring long term sustainability..." After environmentalists brought the prawn industry's sordid past to the attention of government officials, the Cambodian government decided to ban both intensive and semi-intensive prawn farming, but upcoming elections may jeopardize that resolution.

The very possibility of sustainable prawn production that is not *au naturel* is still in question. Only the big players in the industry can afford the technology necessary to solve the problems inherent in even the least harmful farming methods. Insuring environmental sustainability could therefore require the exclusion of indigenous people from the business. Aquastar, a Seattle subsidiary of British Petroleum, offers technical assistance that is far beyond the reach of small farmers. The pipelines that Aquastar builds to dispose of pond effluents extend 500 kilometers into the ocean and cost millions to construct. And even such elaborate maneuvers to sustain the ponds have not yet stood the test of time. It remains to be seen whether problems internal to the soil of the ponds can be completely avoided, and whether dumping pollutants out at sea has unforeseen environmental costs.

Local opposition to the prawn industry has been growing. Environmental and consumer protection groups have been working to limit industrial growth and warn developing nations about the impact of uncontrolled prawn farming on their as yet intact mangrove forests. As many governments persist in their unwillingness to regulate the industry adequately — and as limiting its profit potential by slowing down world demand seems the logical alternative — some environmentalists have been advocating an international boycott of prawn products. But the Mangrove Action Project (MAP), an international coalition of environmental, human rights, and community-based groups, warns that a boycott could be premature. By working with governments, industry, consumers, and indigenous people, MAP seeks to find locally acceptable solutions to the problems posed by prawn aquaculture, and its constituency of Third World farmers fears the impact of a sharp drop in demand. Until alternative enterprises can be developed, MAP is supporting a worldwide "slowdown" in prawn consumption, which would discourage the more intensive methods of production.

A public relations war is raging between prawn companies and environmentalists in many countries that are contemplating prawn production. The industry has responded to threats of a boycott by slashing prices, and arguing that it should receive government indulgence because soon, the shrimp will actually be available for domestic consumption in the Third World countries that produce them. MAP has countered these arguments with examples of past destruction. Apocalyptic rhetoric has begun to serve its purpose in India, where a joint sector project between the local Orissa government and the private Tatas corporation was being planned for the Chilka lake. MAP sounded an alarm in the press about the dangers of such a venture, and the government balked.

ENVIRONMENTAL AND CONSUMER PROTECTION GROUPS HAVE BEEN WORKING TO LIMIT INDUSTRIAL GROWTH AND WARN DEVELOPING NATIONS ABOUT THE IMPACT OF UNCONTROLLED PRAWN FARMING.

No final decision, however, has yet been made in India. The ecological fates of many other countries are similarly undecided. Much depends on the success of efforts to pressure governments to protect the mangroves. As we've seen in Thailand, there is a world of difference between good public relations and good policy, and governments can be much more forthcoming with the former. ■

A version of this article appeared in *Cultural Survival Quarterly*.

November/December 1996

TRASHING RECYCLING

THE NEW FACE OF ANTI-ENVIRONMENTALISM

BY FRANK ACKERMAN

The crisis is over. You can relax, stop recycling, and throw it all in the trash. In fact, you'll save money and help the environment if you do.

Or so you learned, if you read (and believed) the *New York Times* magazine on June 30, 1996. Staff writer John Tierney launched a full-scale assault on everyone's favorite environmental activity, recycling of household waste. Tierney's article, headlined "Recycling is Garbage," challenges all the major beliefs of contemporary recycling advocates. In the end, he recommends everyone's favorite economic panacea: reliance on the free market.

Tierney is just the latest voice to join the anti-recycling chorus. A lengthy article by Jeff Bailey in the *Wall Street Journal*, reprinted in the *Reader's Digest*, raised similar charges last year. A number of business-oriented economists, consultants and industry executives have also criticized the popular and ever-expanding commitment to recycling. Environmental advocacy of all varieties has faced right-wing, free-market critics, and recycling is no exception.

The anti-recyclers have a more plaintive, defensive tone than other anti-green crusaders. In the 1990s, at a time when many environmentalists have been struggling to protect past gains, recycling has been spreading rapidly across the country. By 1994, more than 7,200 recycling programs provided regular curbside collection to more than 40% of all U.S. households, according to *Biocycle* magazine. Almost all of these programs were new since 1988, when the first comprehensive survey appeared. One study by Franklin Associates estimated that 21% of all municipal solid waste was recycled or composted in 1992, up from 10% just seven years earlier.

Opinion polls confirm that virtually everyone believes in recycling. A clear majority of households say that they participate in recycling; no other environmental activity approaches this level of involvement. According to Jerry Powell of *Resource Recycling* magazine, in the first week of November 1992 more adults participated in recycling than voted. "Recycling," says Powell, "is more popular than democracy."

Regardless of its popularity, is recycling a mistake? Tierney is correct that recycling advocates have spread some myths and exaggerations, for example claiming that the United States was literally running out of landfill space. But more importantly, there are a number of critical long-run problems concerning the use of natural resources which recycling can mitigate. These problems include depletion of nonrenewable resources, overuse of potentially renewable ones (as in current forestry practices), and pollution created by extraction and processing of materials.

In addition, many crucial environmental values are not reflected in market prices, so the success of recycling should not be measured by whether it is cheaper than old-fashioned trash disposal in the short run. When people participate in recycling, they are in part affirming the importance of nonmarket environmental values. This affirmation should be supported and broadened, not attacked for its lack of validation in the marketplace.

THE DISAPPEARING LANDFILL CRISIS

Anti-recyclers generally begin by attacking the myth of the landfill crisis. Ominous projections of impending landfill scarcity were common in the late 1980s, as the current wave of recycling programs emerged. Many people still believe it is urgent to recycle because there will soon be nowhere to put their garbage.

Yet a funny thing happened on the way to the landfill crisis. As the anti-recyclers observe, most places never ran out of disposal capacity. In part this is due to a simple error, now widely recognized. Data on landfills are sparse, and many early accounts merely compared the numbers of landfills closing and opening each year, without considering their size. Since many small landfills are closing, while a few huge ones are opening, disposal capacity has increased recently in some states. The nationwide average cost of landfilling waste has remained around $31 to $34 per ton for several years, hardly evidence of a crisis.

The anti-recyclers also debunk the legend of the Mobro 4000, the garbage barge from Long Island that was turned away from one port after another in 1987. Bailey's 1995 *Wall Street Journal* article focused on this incident. At the time, the voyage of the Mobro was widely interpreted as evidence that there would soon be no place left to put our garbage, thus emphasizing the need for recycling.

The revisionist history, supported by other sources as well as anti-recyclers, presents the Mobro as an isolated incident, not a symptom of widespread landfill shortages. This history attributes the Mobro's troubles to an unsuccessful deal between a Long Island Mafia boss (now in jail for conspiring to murder other trash haulers) and an inexperienced barge owner. The Mobro arrived in several southern states, and later in Caribbean ports, before signing firm agreements with any landfills — leading to suspicion that it carried hazardous waste. Meanwhile, other shippers, who had obtained signed disposal agreements before they departed, continued to unload garbage at the same destinations.

Oddly enough, Tierney's *New York Times* article fails to mention that the New York City area is the part of the country where local landfill shortages may soon be the most severe. Some of the suburbs already ship waste long distances, and the city itself will have to close its huge landfill at Fresh Kills on Staten Island, perhaps in 10 to 15 years (Staten Island residents want to close it even sooner). Fresh Kills, said to be the world's largest landfill, receives up to 18,000 tons of waste per day, a quantity that other nearby facilities would find almost impossible to absorb.

But, says Tierney, "Why assume that New Yorkers have a moral obligation to dispose of their garbage near home?" He offers a glowing description of a small, rural Virgina county where a landfill accepts New York-area waste; the landfill operator's $3 million annual payment to the county has helped upgrade the local schools. This Virginia landfill has about one-fifth the capacity of Fresh Kills, so New York City may be in the market for several more like it.

LEARNING TO LOVE PACKAGING

Tierney's list of recycling myths include "We're a wicked throwaway society" and "Our garbage will poison us." Throwing things away is not wicked, in his view, because packaging can reduce food waste: a 1980 survey found that Mexico City households generate more pounds of waste per capita than U.S. households, since packaging-deprived city residents buy so much more fresh food, and discard so much more food waste. (While food waste may sound pleasantly organic, it is almost certain to end up on a garbage truck headed for a landfill, like any other household waste.) The survey result was something of a surprise, since other research has routinely awarded the American team the gold medal for per capita waste generation.

The point made by the Mexican survey is a valid, but limited, one. Some forms of packaging do indeed save many times their own weight in reduced spoilage and food waste. A world of zero packaging is neither plausible nor desirable. But at the same time that some packaging plays a useful role, a large and growing portion of all packaging could still be wasteful. The purpose of packaging is to make money for the producer; one way to make money is to reduce waste in packages or products, while another way is to make bigger, flashier packages that will attract more attention in the store.

Tierney observes that the worst environmental fears of landfills are based on stories like Love Canal, which involve toxic industrial waste rather than household trash. Federal and state laws require modern landfills to be far cleaner and safer than their predecessors; this is one of the little-noticed success stories of contemporary environmental regulation. It is true that the household, commercial and construction wastes found in a typical non-industrial landfill today are unlikely to poison you.

While true, this fact misses a larger point about pollution and the things we throw away. Pollution due to waste disposal is not the whole story. The products we buy and discard are made by industry. Manufacturing ordinary products causes far greater environmental damage — for example, much greater toxic emissions — than disposal of the same products. Using less stuff, and reusing the products we have, is good for the environment because it reduces the need for manufacturing, and hence reduces the associated emissions.

Recycling is environmentally beneficial because making almost anything out of recycled material causes lower industrial emissions than making the same thing out of virgin material. (For a few low-grade paper products, emissions from recycled and virgin production are roughly comparable; Tierney exaggerates the confusion surrounding these products to suggest, utterly inaccurately, that there are many cases where recycled production is environmentally comparable to or worse than virgin production.)

Tierney's recital of myths about recycling goes on to encompass "We're cursing future generations with our waste" and "We're squandering irreplaceable natural resources." Future generations won't mind our waste, he thinks, because there is so little of it, and because "Eventually, like previous landfills, the mounds of trash will be covered with grass and become a minuscule addition to the nation's 150,000 square miles of parkland."

More significant is the issue of squandering irreplaceable natural resources. Paper, as Tierney suggests, can be made from trees grown on sustainable, carefully managed tree plantations. So far, this possibility has escaped the attention of much of the forest products industry. Metals cannot be grown; bury them in landfills

TIERNEY'S *NEW YORK TIMES* ARTICLE FAILS TO MENTION THAT THE NEW YORK CITY AREA IS THE PART OF THE COUNTRY WHERE LOCAL LANDFILL SHORTAGES MAY SOON BE THE MOST SEVERE.

and they will be lost under the future parklands forever, reducing the useable supply of metals for posterity.

Plastics, interestingly enough, could be made on a sustainable basis from renewable biomass (plant) materials, but so far only a few scientists have noticed this possibility. Today's plastics, of course, are made from fossil fuels. Production of lightweight snack packs may not be the highest-value use of the world's limited supply of petroleum.

BEYOND THE BOTTOM LINE

From the anti-recyclers' point of view, all would doubtless be forgiven if recycling reliably made a profit — that is, if it reduced total waste management costs compared to the alternative of throwing everything in the trash. The introduction of a curbside recycling program reduces a community's costs for garbage collection and garbage disposal, but imposes new costs for recycling collection and processing of the collected materials. It also receives revenues from the sale of the recovered materials. The net cost naturally varies widely from one community to another, and from one year to another due to changing material prices.

Unfortunately, only the very best recycling programs reduce municipal waste management costs every year. Average programs are profitable only in years like 1995, when they receive high prices for the materials they sell. In my forthcoming book I estimate that a curbside recycling program with nationwide average costs and efficiency might have reduced total municipal costs by $5 per household in 1995 when material prices were unusually high. This compares to a cost increase of $21 per household in 1993 when prices were low. So if prices remain between the 1993 and 1995 levels, and recycling program efficiencies remain unchanged, the average program will fluctuate from year to year between a small municipal cost increase and an even smaller cost savings.

Even at 1993 prices, the average cost increase due to recycling is an entirely affordable expenditure for a wealthy country to incur. In exchange for that small monetary cost, we gain reductions in manufacturing emissions, conservation of nonrenewable natural resources, and promotion of an ethic of environmental concern and public participation. There is no sensible way of placing a dollar value on these benefits — to me, they seem well worth the price. Implicitly, millions of people seem to agree, as they continue participating in their community recycling programs.

For anti-recyclers such as Tierney, even modest monetary costs are outrageous — and are described in a manner that makes them sound as big as possible. New York City's recycling program, we are told, costs $50 mil-

MANY CRUCIAL VALUES ARE NOT REFLECTED IN MARKET PRICES, SO THE SUCCESS OF RECYCLING SHOULD NOT BE MEASURED BY WHETHER IT IS CHEAPER THAN TRASH DISPOSAL IN THE SHORT RUN.

lion to $100 million annually, which amounts to $7 to $14 per capita for the seven million city residents. Rather than investigating hidden benefits of the recycling program (such as the savings on future disposal costs by prolonging the life of the Fresh Kills landfill), Tierney embarks on a financial fantasy designed to show that the expense of recycling is absurdly large.

First, he asks a college student to record the time required to handle one week's recycling, and calculates the cost of paying everyone $12 per hour for time spent in recycling. Then he estimates the cost of renting a square foot of floor space ($4 a week, in New York) in everyone's kitchen to store the recycling containers. These fictitious costs of recycling are 14 times as large as the real costs, allowing him to claim that recycling a ton of material "really" costs as much as buying a one-ton used car.

If this is a good idea for recycling, surely it should be applied in other areas of life. We all could bill the IRS for time spent keeping records and filling out forms, and for rental of file drawers used in these activities. But that way lies madness, or at least the dissolution of civil society advocated by the militia movement. Life is not a business, and participation in society is not a reimbursable business expense. Trying hard to reduce the question of waste to a matter of dollars and cents, Tierney suggests that recycling rules and regulations could be replaced by a system of charging by the bag for garbage collection — giving everyone a financial incentive to reduce waste.

Such systems have been implemented in many communities, with modest results. Their popularity reflects the ideological certainty that market incentives are the answer, not their overwhelming performance in practice. Small changes in garbage collection charges have little effect on the quantity of waste, while a large increase in rates would provide a strong incentive for illegal dumping. Moreover, the most successful programs have used pay-per-bag garbage collection in combination with free curbside recycling collection, not, as Tierney suggests, as an alternative to it.

Tierney mocks the commitment to recycling with a misused image from John Bunyan's classic tale, *The Pilgrim's Progress*. In the course of his travels Bunyan's pilgrim encounters a "muckraker" in the original sense of the term, a man raking through muck, or compost piles, searching for discarded items of value. The muckraker is so intent on recovering waste materials that he does not notice an angel offering him a celestial crown in exchange for his rake. The moral, the pilgrim learns, is that "Earthly things, when they are with power upon men's minds, quite carry their hearts away from God."

Yet the pilgrim's progress is not along a road paved with market incentives. Bunyan's vision of salvation does not involve pay-per-bag muck charges, nor celebration of capitalism in general. Indeed, the pilgrim turns away from the marketplace, allegorically named Vanity Fair, and the likes of Lord Luxurious and Sir Greedy. What, then, does salvation consist of? Might it include a sharp reduction in consumption of luxuries and waste of scarce materials, or a decision to spread the muck to fertilize next year's crops? Might it include the search for a more ethical allocation of wealth and resources than the pilgrim found?

Alas, no. Recycling is the only earthly pursuit that Tierney feels the pilgrim should reject. Tierney closes, under the heading "The Celestial City Glimpsed at Long Last," only with a vision of the rural Virginia county that is profiting from its huge landfill — which sounds remarkably like raking a much bigger pile of muck. ∎

Resources: Why Do We Recycle? Markets, Values, and Public Policy, Frank Ackerman, December 1996, Island Press; "The State of Garbage in America," Robert Steuteville, *BioCycle*, April and May 1996; *Rubbish! The Archaeology of Garbage*, William Rathje and Cullen Murphy, 1992; "Recycling is Garbage," John Tierney, *New York Times Magazine*, June 30, 1996.

ARTICLE 39

March/April 1996

ENVIRONMENTAL JUSTICE

THE BIRTH OF A MOVEMENT

BY DORCETA E. TAYLOR

Hazel Johnson lives in Altgeld Gardens, a predominantly black housing project on Chicago's Far South Side. She refers to the neighborhood of 10,000 residents as a "Toxic Doughnut" because the homes are encircled by landfills, factories and other industrial sites that emit toxic and/or noxious fumes. West of the Doughnut, the coke ovens of Acme Steel discharge benzene into the air, to the south is Dolton's municipal landfill, to the east is Waste Management's landfill, and to the north lie beds of city sewage sludge. There are 50 abandoned hazardous dump sites within a six-mile radius of the neighborhood. The toxic stew around the Doughnut is so potent that Illinois inspectors aborted an expedition in one of the dumping lagoons when their boat began to disintegrate.

Illness was common in the area, but it wasn't until her husband died of lung cancer and other family and friends became ill that Hazel wondered if the death and illnesses were linked to the environment. She surveyed 1,000 of her neighbors and was astounded at the number of cancers, birth deformities, premature deaths, skin rashes, eye irritation, and respiratory illnesses that they reported. Hazel and the group she founded, People for Community Recovery (PCR), contacted the City of Chicago about the findings and urged them to investigate the illnesses. The City conducted a controversial study that found high rates of cancer among African Americans on Chicago's South Side, but did not investigate whether the rate was higher than that for African Americans elsewhere, or whether the health effects were related to the toxins in the area.

Dissatisfied with the findings, PCR commissioned its own study, and persuaded the federal Agency for Toxic Disease Registry to do a health study. Meanwhile, because the neighborhood was not connected to Chicago's water supply system, residents suspected that some of the health problems were caused by contamination of their well water. PCR lobbied for and obtained a hookup to municipal water pipes. Then, after discovering that Waste Management wanted to expand its landfill, PCR staged a series of protests (with the help of Greenpeace) that blocked the expansion.

The Toxic Doughnut is but one of many environmentally hazardous areas where poor and working-class people make their homes. Community activists in the burgeoning "environmental justice" movement have given names like "Street of Death," "Cancer Alley," and "Death Valley" to similar areas.

Organizations such as the Sierra Club, Audubon Society, Wilderness Society, and Nature Conservancy focus much of their attention on wildlife and wilderness preservation, and attract a mostly white, upper-middle class following. In contrast, environmental justice groups recruit a broad coalition of working- and middle-class activists from various racial backgrounds. Such organizations focus on toxic contamination, occupational safety, and the siting of noxious and hazardous facilities.

Groups whose members are people of color, on which this article focuses, are a vital component of the environmental justice movement. They have brought national attention to environmental racism (when people of color

THE REAL COSTS OF PENTIUM CHIPS

"Intel Inside" is the mantra sung by computer manufacturers whose machines use chips made by Intel Corporation. But while America may run on Intel, the corporation endangers its workers and the communities around its plants, while gobbling up huge tax subsidies.

In New Mexico, the SouthWest Organizing Project (SWOP), a social and environmental justice group, has been battling Intel for years. In 1993 Intel announced plans to build a "flagship" plant in Rio Rancho, near Albuquerque — but only if the state provided sufficient subsidies, and assured Intel that the necessary environmental permits would come quickly.

New Mexico gave Intel $114 million of incentives to expand at Rio Rancho, including property tax abatements, waivers of sales taxes, and manufacturing tax credits. The state also provided $1 billion in industrial revenue bonds (IRBs), shielding Intel from paying local property taxes. It is not a coincidence that Rio Rancho now generates 50% of Intel's total revenues, and 70% of its profits.

"This is a highly stratified industry," points out Jeanne Gauna of SWOP, "with women at the bottom producing the product, and being exposed to chemicals that may hurt them forever, while white males are at the top, earning huge wages." One analysis of high-tech employment in Albuquerque found that factory laborers were 57% ethnic minorities and 63% women, but white males held 72% of managerial positions. Studies of California's Silicon Valley — of which Rio Rancho is an outgrowth — have found that semiconductor workers suffer from high rates of miscarriages, genetic and brain damage, skin lesions, and cancers due to chemical exposure.

Outside the plant, Intel has been allowed to pollute the air at 35 times the rate permitted at its California plants. And despite New Mexico's arid climate, Intel is consuming huge volumes of water: two to three million gallons a day at present, all at bargain rates, with plans to raise its use to between nine and fifteen million gallons.

— *Marc Breslow and Matthew O'Malley*

Resources: Intel Inside New Mexico: A Case Study of Environmental and Economic Injustice, 1995, SouthWest Organizing Project, 211 10th St. SW, Albuquerque, NM 87102.

suffer disproportionately from health hazards) and environmental blackmail (when communities are forced to choose between protecting their health or losing their jobs). Until people of color made these terms commonplace in environmental circles, more traditional environmental activists paid little attention to policies that led to grave impacts on minority communities.

ENVIRONMENTAL RACISM

There is ample evidence that the operations of the Environmental Protection Agency (EPA) and other federal and state agencies have had discriminatory impacts on communities of color. A 1992 *National Law Journal* study, for example, found that fines for hazardous waste violations under the Resource Conservation and Recovery Act varied greatly between white and minority areas. On average, companies were charged $336,000 for violations in white neighborhoods, but only $55,000 in minority neighborhoods. Similar imbalances held for violations of other environmental laws.

The study also showed that the EPA waited longer to evaluate whether dangers in minority areas should be placed on the National Priorities List of "Superfund" sites, and once evaluated, the agency was less likely to place such sites on the list. One reason is that EPA's "Hazard Ranking System" scores sites individually, so that it fails to take into account the cumulative effects of having several hazardous sites near a poor community. And even for those designated, it took less than 10 years to clean up sites in white neighborhoods, but between 12 and 14 years for sites in minority areas.

The courts have also responded badly to environmental justice cases. Even when communities have shown that there is a discriminatory pattern of siting facilities, the courts contend that simply proving discriminatory impact is not enough. To win a suit, communities must prove that the offending corporation or agency *intended* to discriminate when they made siting decisions.

Examples abound. In Houston, six out of eight municipal incinerators were placed in predominantly African American communities. During a 20-year period in King and Queen County, Virginia, all the landfills were placed within one mile of communities that were at least 95% African American. But in both cases, the courts ruled against the communities which brought lawsuits over these issues.

A VIABLE MOVEMENT

This failure of government to protect people of color in the face of increasing environmental threats, along with the dismissive attitude of corporate decision-makers, led to the growth of the environmental justice movement. Also important has been dissatisfaction by grassroots activists with the agenda of mainstream environmental organizations. Some of these are direct-action-oriented groups like Greenpeace and Earth First! that focused their attention primarily on whales, nuclear disarmament and forest preservation. Others are legal, technocratic, and lobbyist-oriented associations like the Natural Resources Defense Council and the Environmental Defense Fund.

Although many organizations formed during the 1960s and 1970s began as grassroots groups critical of the reform agenda of the pre-1960s environmental organizations, most eventually adopted similar agendas and lost their close ties to the grassroots. Like their predecessors, these associations lacked racial and social class diversity and failed to adopt an environmental justice agenda.

Filling the vacuum, people of color environmental justice organizations have grown rapidly in recent years — despite the failure of the mainstream to recognize them. As late as 1994 only five people of color groups were listed in the Conservation Directory, and none were listed in the Gale Environmental Sourcebook. Yet in the same year, the People of Color Environmental Groups Directory contained over 300 such organizations.

ROOTS OF STRUGGLE

Organizations devoted to combatting environmental racism emerged out of struggles for social, political, and economic justice. Native American groups, for example, contending with the erosion of cultural values and treaty rights, have used these issues to call attention to the environmental hazards on their reservations. In one case, the Navajos living near Rio Puerco, New Mexico face increased health risks from the numerous uranium mines around them, which contaminate their drinking water and animals. As a result, the Navajos have developed a strong environmental justice agenda.

Many African American associations and leaders have their roots in the Civil Rights movement. Some, like the Gulf Coast Tenants Association (GCTA), which was founded to improve housing conditions for Blacks, have taken on environmental justice agendas. Working in and around "Cancer Alley," the 90-mile stretch running along the Mississippi River from Baton Rouge to New Orleans, and home to about one-fourth of the chemical manufacturing plants in the United States, the GCTA constantly communicates with communities in which chemical spills and "accidental" releases of toxins are routine. These communities have high rates of cancers, birth defects, spontaneous abortions, infant mortality, and respiratory illnesses.

Latinos in the farmworker movement have made the link between labor and environmental justice struggles into a key organizing tool. Farmworkers in California and other parts of the South and West, through their participation in the United Farm Workers union, have launched successful grape boycotts and focused the nation's attention on the harmful effects of pesticides. They have documented illnesses from pesticide poisoning, including death, infertility, birth defects and miscarriages, and respiratory infections.

ON AVERAGE, COMPANIES WERE CHARGED $336,000 FOR VIOLATIONS IN WHITE NEIGHBORHOODS, BUT ONLY $55,000 IN MINORITY NEIGHBORHOODS.

Similarly, Asian Americans concerned about immigrant rights and hazardous working conditions in the computer and garment industries have formed environmental justice groups. These include the Asian Women's Advocates and the Santa Clara Center for Occupational Safety and Health, both in California.

Throughout the United States, environmental justice groups are now able to mobilize many people and to raise questions about environmental racism in corporate decision making, government policies, and within the environmental movement itself. They are increasingly effective at disrupting the status quo on the siting of dangerous facilities. As a result, many are taking notice of these organizations and are either incorporating them into the environmental dialogue, or attempting to discredit their claims and destroy their credibility. We can expect continued struggle in the years ahead. ∎

Resources: Race and the Incidence of Environmental Hazards: A Time for Discourse, Bunyan Bryant and Paul Mohai, 1992; *Confronting Environmental Racism: Voices From the Grassroots*, Robert Bullard, 1993; "Unequal Protection," Marianne Lavelle and Marcia Coyle, *National Law Journal* supplement, 9/21/92.

CHAPTER 9
The Global Economy

ARTICLE 40

September/October 1994

MARKETS UNBOUND

THE HEAVY PRICE OF GLOBALIZATION

BY ARTHUR MacEWAN

My morning coffee came from Brazil. A GM subsidiary in Mexico produced the wiring system for my car. Three items in my medicine cabinet were produced in a German-owned plant in the United States. My son's new tape recorder is from Japan. My clothes arrive from ten or more different countries, produced mostly through sub-contracting arrangements with large U.S. retailers.

What difference does it make where my coffee came from or where the wiring system for my car was assembled? Does it matter to me whether my clothes come from Brazil, Bangladesh, or from a local factory? What about the Brazilian, Bangladeshi, and local workers? How are they affected by the international movement of goods? And does the nationality of the factory owners matter? Should I care whether a U.S., Japanese, German, or Brazilian owner profits from my purchases?

These sorts of questions are at the center of discussion about the "globalization" of the economy, and they are given fresh urgency by recent changes in the rules of international commerce. In mid-April, representatives of 109 countries signed a new trade agreement that will greatly reduce national barriers to the movement of goods

and services. This signing marked the conclusion of several years of negotiations under the General Agreement on Tariffs and Trade (GATT) — called the "Uruguay Round" of negotiations because they began in Punta del Este, Uruguay, in 1986. The agreement will lower import tariffs by an average of 40%, and it establishes new rules that will make it more difficult for national governments to restrict their countries' foreign commerce.

Certainly the new agreement will lead to greater international trade and investment. Advocates of this "free trade" regime claim that the result will be higher incomes around the world, and higher incomes are supposed to be good for everyone. But greater economic integration among countries is not likely to produce the promised benefits.

In fact, the current wave of globalization is bringing severe problems: greater inequality; restriction of social programs; new threats to our physical environment; ever-greater concentration of power in the hands of a few very large corporations.

Moreover, the deregulation that currently characterizes globalization and that is embodied in the new GATT agreement makes it even harder for people to exercise political control over their economic lives. Globalization, then, is an issue of power. People concerned with progressive social change — and, indeed, anyone who wonders about the significance of where their coffee comes from — will do well to understand it in that light. What is globalization?

Globalization in its broadest sense is nothing new: we have long relied on international commerce to meet our economic needs. The events of 1492 set in motion one era — though not the first — of globalization, and the Industrial Revolution in the 19th century both drove and was driven by another. The current surge in world economic integration appears so great largely because the disruption of the Great Depression and World War II reduced international economic ties. It was only in the 1970s that U.S. commerce with the rest of the world leapt up in a way that elicited popular attention.

Between 1965 and 1990, U.S. exports of goods and services rose from 5% of gross domestic product (GDP) to 10%. Most of our GDP is "non-tradables" (public and private services, construction, and transportation). Of goods produced in the United States (agricultural products, manufactured items, and minerals), only 8% was exported in 1965; the figure rose to 18% by 1990.

Furthermore, U.S. firms are increasingly involved in foreign commerce both through lending money abroad (financial investment) and by owning firms in other countries (direct investment). Foreign inflows of interest payments to the United States increased (in real terms) some thirteen-fold between 1965 and 1990, more than twice as rapidly as total net interest payments. Profits from direct foreign investment accounted for 13% of after-tax corporate profits in the 1960s, rising to 26% in the 1970s and 1980s, and to more than 30% in the early 1990s as domestic profits slumped.

Beyond the numbers, modern globalization also involves a grand surge in the spread of capitalism; production virtually everywhere is now based on wage labor and organized for profit. Not only have the former socialist countries entered the orbit of capitalism, but in the underdeveloped regions of Latin America, Asia and Africa, family farms, semifeudal agriculture, small shops, and home production are also giving way to capitalist enterprise. More and more, in all parts of the world, the same things are done in the same way for the same sorts of markets. This homogeneity is a distinguishing feature of modern globalization.

Another distinguishing feature of the current phase of globalization is reduced regulation of the international movement of goods and capital. Deregulation, as epitomized by the new GATT agreement, facilitates both quantitative integration and qualitative homogeneity. It also generates problems.

THE LOGIC OF FREE TRADE?

Benefits from cutting tariffs are supposed to come from increased specialization among countries, yielding improved efficiency, and so greater economic growth. Accompanying announcements of the new GATT accord were estimates that its changes would raise global income by $235 billion a year, about 1% of the total.

But when reduced import restrictions lead consumers to purchase foreign goods instead of domestic ones, resources are saved only if the displaced workers find new jobs. Yet in the United States and around the world there is considerable unemployment. Thus, for example, when U.S. auto workers lose their jobs because less expensive imported cars are available, they do not automatically become computer programmers, chemical engineers, or, for that matter, anything else. As long as they remain underemployed, their labor is wasted.

Another problem with free international commerce is its impact on technological development. When firms can profit from using low-wage foreign labor, they are less likely to develop new, more efficient technologies for production

at home. Moreover, when the government commits itself to free trade — and is dominated by corporations that benefit from free trade — it will not take the steps that nurture general technological development. In particular, the government is less likely to spend heavily on education, or to support those industries and activities that promise long-run technological gains. What we do today determines what we can do tomorrow, and there is no reason to believe that by doing what is most profitable today we will obtain what is economically or socially best for tomorrow.

Free trade can harm long-run growth even further by hampering a government's ability to provide economic stability. For example, a government's effort to stimulate growth by lowering interest rates may cause owners of capital to move their funds out of the country. Or an effort to stimulate growth through government spending may be dissipated in rising imports. Put simply: When the economy is thoroughly international, it cannot be regulated by a national government. Yet there is no international government.

Recent experience suggests that modern globalization is not good for economic growth: While the last two decades mark an era of increasing globalization, they also mark an era of relatively slow growth. The longer historical record also does not support the argument that deregulation of international commerce is the route to more rapid economic growth. Virtually all countries that have attained what we call "economic development" have done so with substantial state intervention in their country's foreign commerce. The Industrial Revolution in Great Britain took place behind substantial tariff walls. In the 19th century, the United States accomplished its industrial expansion with a high degree of tariff protection, as did Germany. In Japan, the great success story of the second half of the 20th century, the government tightly controlled both foreign trade and foreign investment.

In the 25 years following World War II, one important foundation of economic growth in the United States was the major role of government. High levels of state spending, income security programs, and the stability of financial regulation all provided a framework for growth. Sustained economic expansion, it seems, must be supported and nurtured by government. Whenever such expansion has taken place, part of that support has been regulation of international commerce.

POWER SHIFT

Yet even if the new GATT agreement were to usher in an era of economic growth, there would still be problems in the free trade formula for international commerce. These are problems of power.

Consider what happens to U.S. automobile workers who can no longer compete when restrictions on automobile imports are removed. They may end up without any jobs at all, and even when they do find other jobs, they often will suffer pay losses. Simply the fact that these workers are forced to switch jobs weakens their power in relation to their employers. Workers build their power, their ability to gain better pay and more control over their working conditions, through long periods of struggle. Workers who are continually forced to switch jobs in response to each new wave of imports or technological change cannot build strong unions.

The United Automobile Workers (UAW) has been one of the United States' most powerful and important unions. It has set a standard, making it possible for industrial workers to have well-paying jobs with considerable job security. Today, however, change in the international economy is weakening the UAW and eroding that standard.

Not only will particular groups of workers suffer severe losses when the rules of international trade are altered. More broadly, wage and benefit standards are undermined, power shifts, and workers in general lose.

In the United States, for example, employers have used international competition to keep wages down and to control the work force. When workers demand higher wages, the company may move to another location where wages are lower and workers are poorly organized. Even when the company does not move, it may sub-contract some of the work and buy parts from foreign sources; or it may simply threaten to move. The result is lower wages and a more unequal distribution of income.

In 1992, average individual weekly earnings in the private non-agricultural part of the U.S. economy were 19% below their peak of the early 1970s, lower than in every year since 1958. Income disparity has also widened. In the mid-1970s, the after-tax income of the richest 20% of families was about eight times that of the poorest 20%. By 1990, it was almost 12 times as much.

Globalization has not been the only cause of this deteriorating situation. Higher unemployment rates have weakened workers' bargaining strength; government policies have moved in favor of business; and technological change seems to have worked against less skilled workers. Yet the greater power that U.S. firms have gained from international expansion has been a major contributing factor.

This business power also affects many social programs. For example, in an open international economy, it is difficult for a national government to effectively tax businesses. An effort to raise taxes is met by firms threatening to move abroad where taxes are lower. In fact, once a firm has established extensive international operations, it can adjust its accounting procedures to assure that profits appear in those locations where taxes are minimal. Without an adequate tax base, a government must curtail social programs.

Likewise, without the ability to control its country's foreign commerce, a government is in a weak position to limit environmental destruction. If the government moves to impose stricter pollution controls on industries, for example, many of those industries will threaten to cease operations and supply the market from another country where pollution standards are less stringent. Then the government will be faced with a choice: either accept the pollution or lose industry and jobs. The movement of "pollution-intensive"

firms across the Rio Grande in recent years has both illustrated this problem and transformed northern Mexico into a vast hazardous waste dump.

NEW TERRAIN FOR STRUGGLE

Inequality, attacks on social programs, and environmental destruction did not begin with the new GATT trade agreement. Nor did the new accord create a world economy in which large and mobile businesses have great power. Unfortunately, all this existed before 1994.

People engaged in labor struggles and other social movements are confronted with the same paradox that has limited our success for years. On the one hand, our political struggles are most effectively organized on a local or, at most, a national level. On the other hand, we face an economy that operates on a global level. In making the economy even more global, the new trade agreement confronts popular movements with even graver difficulties.

Yet this new terrain of struggle may force popular movements to alter their strategies, leading to some positive results. Popular movements — environmental movements, labor movements, and others — cannot succeed unless they find ways to operate internationally. A successful local wage struggle may simply result in a firm moving to a country with low wages. A successful environmental struggle may simply relocate a polluting plant across the boarder. The greater homogeneity of the world economy means that firms can relocate much more readily than in an earlier era. So any lasting success must be attained on a wider geographic basis.

Moreover, greater homogeneity is likely to facilitate cooperation across national boundaries by popular movements. Workers in rich and poor countries are increasingly doing the same things in the same ways for the same markets. This sameness creates a basis for solidarity. Just as auto workers, electronics workers, teachers, and teamsters in different parts of the United States have formed themselves into national unions because of their common positions, workers in different countries are now more likely than before to join together. The potential for such international solidarity is all the greater because workers in Sao Paulo and Chicago, in Frankfort and Singapore, in Tokyo and Tijuana are often working for the same company.

Environmentalists are in a similar situation. In struggles over the destruction of the forests or the generation of air pollution, they face the same international corporations. Also, the environmental problems themselves have become increasingly global. Destruction of the rain forests in either the Amazon basin or the U.S. Pacific Northwest will devastate the climate and atmosphere of the entire world, harming people regardless of nationality.

So, as it turns out, it matters very much where my coffee comes from. And my shoes, my car, and my clothes. It also matters who owns the companies where these goods are made. All these factors are important in defining the terrain on which struggles for social progress take place, now and in the future. ∎

November/December 1995

MACHO ECONOMICS

CANADIAN WOMEN CONFRONT FREE TRADE

BY MARJORIE GRIFFIN COHEN

When the United States and Canada proposed a free trade agreement in 1985, Canada's major feminist organization, the National Action Committee on the Status of Women (NAC), was among the leaders in opposition. NAC helped initiate a coalition of farmers, unions, the poor and unemployed, seniors, religious groups, aboriginal peoples, immigrants, and artists. Together these groups made trade the focus of the 1988 national election.

A pre-election poll found 53% of men supported free trade, while only 33% of women did. In the United States, trade did not seem like a feminist issue. But in Canada, women perceived that they stood to lose a great deal: jobs, public services, and political clout.

The United States already had a huge edge over Canada in international trade. With barriers lifted, NAC believed, Canada would be at an even greater disadvantage, especially in low-wage industries where women were concentrated, such as clothing, textiles, food processing, and electronics. In addition, the Free Trade Agreement (FTA) would be the first international trade pact to include the whole service sector, the area of the economy in which most women work.

As details of the trade pact took shape, and the North American Free Trade Agreement (NAFTA) followed a few years later to include Mexico, women saw a threat to the workings of the entire national government. Facing heightened competition, corporations would argue for tax cuts to help them survive, leading to cuts in social spending. The agreements also included provisions that were explicitly hostile to the public sector. Among them was a rule that if the government wanted to create a new program to replace private enterprise, it would have to compensate any cross-border firms that stood to lose. If Canada wanted to establish a national day care program or provide national dental or disability insurance, for instance, it would have to pay off U.S. businesses that already sell these services in Canada.

If anything, NAC's predictions have turned out to be too mild. Women along with men have suffered massive job losses under the FTA, which took effect in 1989, and under NAFTA. For the first time in the 20th century, female participation in the labor force has declined. The government is scaling back social programs, often in ways that are a direct affront to women. Canada has eliminated its family allowance, a monthly stipend to all mothers of about $40 per child. And the government is gradually restricting eligibility for unemployment insurance, moving toward coverage only for full-time, year-round workers. Fewer than half of Canadian women meet that standard.

As an economically disadvantaged group, women have relied on the public sector to redistribute income and rectify inequities. Twenty-five years of feminist activism brought more women-centered policies, and however elusive equality remained, women gained power. Now the free trade laws are carried out and enforced outside the domain of Parliament, beyond the democratic legislative process. Multinational business has the upper hand.

DEPENDENCE ON TRADE

Free trade accentuates problems that the Canadian economy has faced for a long time. The country is a huge land mass, the second largest in the world, but its population is small, about one-tenth that of the United States. Holding the country together and moving people and things around has required considerable cooperation and ingenuity by government. Most of the nation is cold most of the time, which makes agricultural production precarious and requires special measures to ensure food production.

As a result, from the beginning Canada has needed a strong public sector and heavy public investment to build its infrastructure. Government accounts for about half of the economy, compared to 38% in the United States. Canada is also distinct from the United States in its reliance on trade. In a manner typical of colonial relationships, Canada has developed largely on the basis of exporting natural resources, first to England, then to the United States. Because of this, for a country that is considered modern, wealthy, and developed, Canada is unusually vulnerable to swings in the international economy.

The country consistently faces higher rates of unemployment, even in good times, than the United States.

Regional disparities are greater than in any other western industrial country. Canada's dependence on trade increased in the decades preceding free trade. Exports accounted for about 30% of national income in the 1980s, up from 20% in the 1960s. The United States, by comparison, export only 10% of goods and services. Most of Canada's trade, about 75%, is with the United States. When things go wrong on the international market, Canada tends to feel the impact first, experience it harder, and take longer to recover than most industrialized countries.

FREE TRADE

With tariffs lifted under the FTA and NAFTA, Canada now has little power to protect domestic production, which was already largely run by foreign firms. U.S. firms often find it cheaper to sell to the Canadian market from home. They frequently save on labor costs, since Canada's strong trade unions have meant higher wages in some industries than in the United States. About 38% of the labor force belongs to a union in Canada, compared to 16% in the States. Lower-paying industries are especially subject to competition from plants in low-wage regions of the States.

FOR THE FIRST TIME IN THE 20TH CENTURY, FEMALE PARTICIPATION IN THE LABOR FORCE HAS DECLINED.

During negotiations over the FTA, free-trade advocates in business and government insisted that bad jobs in sunset industries would be replaced by new, high-technology employment. They promised retraining for workers. But women knew such training was unlikely: In the most vulnerable industries, women tend to be among the marginal workers. They are older and have less formal education than the average female worker. And they are more likely to be immigrants, unable to speak English or French.

In the first three years after the FTA took effect, employment plummeted by 500,000, in an economy that normally adds 300,000 jobs each year. Unlike previous downturns, most of these losses are permanent, due to plant closures. Unemployment rates are now chronically above 10%, up from a norm of 7.5% before the FTA.

As expected, the biggest losses have been in industries that employ large numbers of females. Closures have put downward pressure on wages and working conditions. In clothing, female employment dropped 23% between 1989 and 1992; wages fell from a high of 65% of the average manufacturing wage in the early 1980s to 58% in the early 1990s.

Canada's standard of living has fallen in each of the past five years. After-tax incomes dropped an average of .9% a year from 1989 to 1994, after increasing 1.9% a year during the previous 12 years.

Some free-trade advocates claim these losses result not from free trade but rather from other economic forces, such as an under- or over-valued currency, restrictive monetary policy, or the U.S. recession at the turn of the decade, which reverberated across the border. To be sure, many variables affect employment. Nonetheless, free trade shapes these variables, and so is ultimately a critical factor. Even the chief economist of the Royal Bank has stated that falling incomes are a result of industrial restructuring in response to globalization and free trade, along with monetary policy and U.S. recession.

SERVICES AND TRADE

As in most countries, women in Canada fill the majority of service jobs, in this case over 80%. Canada has in the past protected domestic services through a variety of measures, such as professional licensing, government procurement policies that favor local firms, and limits on financial, transportation and communication firms. Such laws have safeguarded national autonomy as well as jobs. Canada's Bank Act, for instance, until recently barred processing of confidential banking data outside the country, in the interest of individual as well as commercial privacy. Now nearly all services are open to foreign competition. As in manufacturing, the United States starts far in the lead, accounting for about a quarter of world trade in services as the FTA was being negotiated. By contrast, Canada has consistently run a trade deficit in services, with imports ranging from data processing and television programming to insurance and crop-dusting.

The FTA gives firms the right to establish themselves in either the United States or Canada and to be treated as national firms even if they are located across the border. As in manufacturing, women must now compete for jobs with service workers in lower-wage countries. Since the bank act relinquished privacy protection, data processing jobs have shifted out of the country.

One of the most startling effects of free trade on women has been the decline in female participation in the labor force. While male participation has decreased throughout the century, until recently women have been joining at ever higher rates, even during periods of high unemployment, like the Depression of the 1930s.

In the four years after the FTA took effect, the share of women in the labor force dropped from 58.6% to 57.5%. It is not yet clear why, but the most likely reason is the absence of any alternative employment in single-industry towns once that industry leaves. Women would feel this effect, for example, in fishing communities when fish processing plants close.

PUBLIC SERVICES

By opening services to trade, the FTA and NAFTA challenge the biggest single service provider — the public sector — as a vehicle for meeting the needs of citizens.

During negotiations over the FTA, women's groups warned of potential harm to public day care, for example.

They were ridiculed before a parliamentary committee by a supporter of free trade who asked, "Are we going to have to bus our children to Cleveland to go to school?" The idea of transporting children across borders seems ridiculous. But now that Canada gives U.S. day care firms domestic status, free trade adds a whole new dimension. For-profit firms might claim access to public funds on an equal basis with non-profit services.

The FTA allows trade in post-secondary and non-university education as well as various health care services, including ambulances, rehabilitation clinics, and public health clinics. Trade is permitted in management of health services across the board, including hospitals, and in management of most social services, such as homes for children.

Both NAFTA and the FTA encourage privatization of public institutions and virtually prohibit new public services from replacing private enterprise. A series of clauses require permission from trading partners for initiating any new public program, and compensation for any losses that the private sector might incur. Considering the extent of U.S. corporate involvement in the Canadian economy, the cost of any new program would be prohibitive to taxpayers. The compensation requirement hinders Canada far more than the United States, since Canadian service-providers barely exist in the United States, while U.S. service-providers occupy considerable space in Canada.

Already the compensation requirement has stopped the Ontario government from carrying through on an election promise by the New Democratic Party to provide public auto insurance, as some provinces already do. U.S. auto insurers threatened to take action, demanding either compensation or a withdrawal of the plan. Before the proposal could come before a trade panel for adjudication, the Ontario government withdrew it, under considerable pressure from the U.S. government. No doubt the trade pacts will be enforced over time by government self-censorship; programs will be presented as too costly, without proper explanation of the reason.

The compensation requirement applies not only to broad programs, but also to any specific services provided by private firms under government contract. Once a service has been contracted out, a move to bring it in-house is subject to the same challenge as a new program. The entire character of social services in Canada is likely to change, particularly since the government is privatizing many services as a way to control its debt. If privatization turns out to be less advantageous than expected, there will be no turning back. The trade pact produces a ratchet effect, a mechanism that allows government to privatize but never to reverse itself.

Along with the explicit restraints they place on government, the FTA and NAFTA have attacked Canada's public sector through increased competition and the resulting pressure for lower business taxes. Decreased government revenue has led to cuts in social spending and a further impetus for privatization. Even programs with strong public support, like the universal, comprehensive funding of medical care, are being abandoned. The federal government aims to eliminate its financial contribution to health insurance by the end of the century, leaving the provinces to cope on their own.

The federal government has already eliminated its contribution to unemployment insurance, leading to a major cut in benefits and stricter eligibility requirements. With the elimination of the family allowance, Canada has ended its oldest universal social program, initiated in 1944. This is a signal that universal social service will no longer be a guiding principle of the public sector.

The full implications of free trade have yet to surface, as NAFTA contains extremely broad anti-government language. The pact is distinct in challenging public services as a means to redistribute wealth, and it explicitly treats the public sector as an obstacle to the principles of free trade. It states that state-run programs must be "consistent with the normal business practices of privately-held enterprises in the relevant business or industry." This provision constrains any public agency from acting in a way other than to maximize profit, a requirement which ultimately undermines the logic of public institutions themselves. The whole point of the public sector is to provide goods and services in ways that the private sector could not or would not.

DEMOCRACY SUFFERS

Until free trade, Canada made economic and social policy through a democratic process, however imperfect. A change in policy usually required public debate, and Parliament had to deal with a range of interested groups. Free trade circumvents the legislative process. National economic and social policy is now subject to challenge through international trade law.

For example, Canada considered eliminating all brand-name cigarette packaging, replacing it with black and white wrapping and strong language about smoking's lethal nature. U.S. cigarette manufacturers argued before the House of Commons Standing Committee on Health that such a measure would violate international trade agreements. The industry said the requirement would qualify it for hundreds of millions of dollars in compensation. Parliament backed down, stating that expert testimony convinced them that the packaging and warning would not be effective, anyway.

Though cigarette packing is not exclusively a women's issue, the example shows how free trade has weakened national autonomy and thus the ability of any group, including women, to assert political influence. Trade pacts are enforced and interpreted by a plethora of supranational panels who are not elected and have no responsibility toward the people. The shift in relationship between state and economic system is changing the very concept of citizenship. Individual citizenship has been restricted to nations while world citizenship, with full rights of representation, has been awarded exclusively to corporations. Canadian women will probably continue to increase their formal representation in the federal government, as they did in the last election, but real decision-making power will continue to elude them.

INTERNATIONAL BONDS

Free trade has expanded the scope of political action among feminists. Women have realized that public policies which serve their own needs, or the needs of any disadvantaged group, are inseparable from policies that shape the entire economy.

The future for women in Canada under free trade looks bleak, but political options do exist. The positive news is that women throughout this hemisphere are beginning to work together to explore ways of challenging international corporations. The FTA debate failed to promote international links in the women's movement because feminists in the States, while sympathetic to Canadian women, did not see free trade as a personal threat. But with NAFTA, U.S. women became concerned about capital shifts and the loss of American jobs to Mexico. Mexican women have joined feminists in Canada and the States in focusing on capital mobility through such organizations as *Mujer a Mujer* (Woman to Woman) and *Mujeres en Acción Sindical* (Women in Union Action). So have women in other poorer countries of the world, such as India and Brazil. Perhaps through women's international alliances, the vision of a fair deal can become the basis for new principles of trade. ■

Resources: Marjorie Griffin Cohen, *Free Trade and the Future of Women's Work* (Toronto: Garamond, 1988); Isabella Bakker, ed., *The Strategic Silence: Gender and Economic Policy* (London, Zed Books, 1994); D. Drache and M. Gertler, eds., *The New Era of Global Competition* (Montreal: McGill-Queen's Press, 1991); Jim Sinclair, ed., *Crossing the Line: Canada and Free Trade with Mexico* (Vancouver: New Star, 1992); Isabella Bakker, ed., *Rethinking Restructuring* (Toronto: University of Toronto, 1995).

CRIMES OF FASHION

THOSE WHO SUFFER TO BRING YOU GAP T-SHIRTS

BY MARC BRESLOW

At a maquiladora plant owned by Mandarin International in El Salvador, Judith Viera earned $43 for working an 88-hour week. Conditions were horrific: the young, female workers are allowed only two bathroom breaks a day, the drinking water is contaminated, and beatings and sexual abuse are commonplace. When Viera and her co-workers tried to improve conditions by organizing a union, the company responded with violence and mass firings.

Mandarin sells to the Gap and Eddie Bauer, among other U.S. firms. Its plant can produce 1,500 Gap t-shirts a day, which sell for $20 each in the United States — while the maquiladora workers are paid 16 cents per shirt. By not owning Mandarin and similar factories, the Gap and other retailers avoid direct responsibility for pitiful wages and abusive conditions.

Meanwhile, in 1994 the Gap made $311 million in profits from its 1,300 stores throughout the United States and Canada. And Gap CEO Donald Fisher paid himself $2 million, not including stock options.

The Gap is not alone. Other popular U.S. retailers also buy from maquila firms in El Salvador, Honduras, Guatamela, and elsewhere. Gabo, for example, a Korean-owned plant also in El Salvador, sells to Marshall's, Sears, Wal-Mart, and Nordstrom's. Not only are the wages meager, but the company often cheats the women workers on their paychecks. In addition, while collecting social security taxes from its employees, Gabo regularly fails to give the money to the government, preventing the women from receiving free health care.

In July 1995 the National Labor Committee, a union-backed group in New York City that seeks to improve conditions at "maquila" plants in Central America, brought Judith Viera and Claudia Molina (from Honduras), to various U.S. cities to share their stories. The Committee pointed out that the conditions at Mandarin and other plants violate the Gap's own "code of conduct" for the factories it buys from.

This code sounds impressive, requiring, for example, that employers "must never force employees to work extra hours" and "may neither threaten nor penalize employees for their efforts to organize or bargain collectively." But the code of conduct is largely a public relations exercise, as the maquila owners violate it with impunity.

Responding to publicity from Viera and Molina's tour, the Gap issued a statement asserting that "we conduct thorough investigations of all new and potential vendors, and we strive hard to ensure that all business partners meet our sourcing guidelines — which set strict standards for working conditions and human rights." But the Gap claims not to have found any violations of its guidelines at Mandarin.

Charles Kernaghan, director of the Labor Committee, visited El Salvador's free trade zone in September. "We reached fifty of the workers who were fired, and interviewed them in groups. They confirmed what Judith Viera said," reports Kernaghan. Meanwhile, the maquila owners are trying to ensure that no other such stories reach the outside world. "There are armed guards everywhere, with sawed-off shotguns," Kernaghan says. And the women employees have been warned not to talk with any *gringos* who come around asking questions, or they will lose their jobs.

Viera and Molina can speak best for themselves. On July 14, 1995 they were interviewed in Boston by Karen Kampworth of the Committee in Solidarity with the People of El Salvador (CISPES). Below we provide excerpts from that interview, which was translated by Holly Grant, also of CISPES.

SURVIVING THE *MAQUILAS*

Judith Viera (JV) and Claudia Molina (CM)

JV: I am eighteen years old and am from El Salvador. In San Salvador my family lives in San Miguel. I have no father and my mother couldn't manage with all of us, so I only studied up until fifth grade. I worked one year in the maquila, where I learned a lot but suffered a lot of mistreatment.

CM: I am seventeen years old and from Honduras. I worked in the maquila. My family is from Comayagua and Copan. I also only studied up to fifth grade. I also don't have a father and my mother couldn't handle schooling and the food and all.

JV: We decided to work in the maquilas because it seemed like a nice job. Also we are minors, and I was only seventeen years old and only in a place like that was I able to work because I was underaged. In the maquilas there are girls who are fourteen, fifteen, and sixteen years old and only in a maquila can a fourteen-year old get a job.

CM: I decided to work in a maquila because my mother earned very little money, and it wasn't enough for the food. I thought the job would be nice and easy, but it wasn't. I was only fifteen years old when I began working in the maquila.

JV: I worked as "Secretary of the Line." I was in charge of everything that came in and left the factory line, all the completed shirts. I was in charge of controlling all the permissions, etc. of the people who worked in my line. I was in total charge of production of the line.

CM: When I started I was a cutter and then I started working at the machines closing shirts. Then I worked making buttonholes and then cuffs. And then as punishment they moved me to packaging and made me work standing up. I did not like this work. But even though I didn't like the work, I had to do it because I needed the salary.

How many hours a day do you work?

CM: I work thirteen hours a day and on Saturdays it is twenty-three hours of work.

JV: My work schedule Monday to Thursday was from 7 am to 9 pm. On Fridays it was from 7 am to 5 pm, and then 7 pm to 3 am, and we stayed in the factory and slept on the floor to begin work again on Saturday from 7 am to 5 pm. For all that work the most I earned was 750 colones for two weeks, which is $43 a week.

Does the $43 per week cover your costs?

JV: No. With that all you can buy is a little food and bus fare. I take two buses — one from my house to downtown, and then another one to the free trade zone. Our budget is a lot bigger than what we earn, than what our salaries are.

JV: We brought some shirts that we make — from the Gap, and we also work with Eddie Bauer and other brands.

CM: This is the shirt that we make for Orion, Gitano, Manhattan and other brands, but the brand that we work with the most is Manhattan.

Who had the idea of forming a union?

JV: The idea came from a woman who worked in quality control because there was a lot of mistreatment... when there was a meeting in the morning to announce that a union had been formed, at lunchtime the company closed its doors and wouldn't open them for us. That is when the work stoppage began so that they would accept the union. We are paid very little; they yell at us; they hit us with the shirts; we get a ticket to go to the bathroom — we only get two tickets a day and can only go for five minutes; they put us out in the sun and make us sweep all day under the sun. There are other punishments as well. They do not give us purified water but contaminated water to drink. So we decided to form a union and there was lots of support. We were able to get the company to open again on Monday, but they have continued to mistreat us since that day, firing people, many threats.

CM: In the maquila where I worked, there was also lots of mistreatment. They also didn't give us permission. One compañera on March 20 had to miscarry in the factory because they didn't give her permission to go to the doctor. She had asked for permission beginning at 9 am until 4 pm, when they [finally] gave her permission, but it was too late.

Were you afraid of joining a union?

JV: No, because there are so many mistreatments that occur in the factory. I wasn't able to support many of the work stoppages because I was Secretary... Many times I was in meetings at which they said they were going to close the factory for two months so they could get rid of the union. They have fired many pregnant women and minors. They have fired more than 350 people solely for the reason that they were members of the union. I was fired together with my two sisters because we were members of the union.

Why did you come on tour?

JV: It is important to be here on tour representing all the working Salvadoran women in the factory, so many people. I know this tour is important and that they will accept the union, and that all the women will get their jobs back. Our idea is that the people in the United States help us and support our campaign. I don't completely know how they can help us, but I know they can and they will.

JV: In the factory there is also sexual abuse. There is an ex-colonel that is director of personnel. Many times he asked me out, he followed me in his car. He told me that if I went out with him I wouldn't be fired. Also, this man hired men who were ex-combatants in the army; these men are only there to control our union. If you try to present them something or if they fire someone and you don't like it, these men will beat or hit you. Last week, there was a work stoppage at the factory because they had fired several pregnant women and union leaders. The National Civilian Police showed up to forcibly move them by hitting them and they forced us to stop the strike. They also captured our secretary general of the union; and they hit them and threatened them. The situation now is that the factory does not want to re-instate the pregnant women and the union leaders. There are many people who've been fired. The union leadership continues to fight about this, and the factory continues to threaten to close. ■

September/October 1997

NAFTA: HERO OR VILLAIN?

BY MARC BRESLOW

The North American Free Trade Agreement (NAFTA) among Canada, Mexico, and the United States has now been in effect for three years. Globalization advocates, including Bill Clinton, have heralded it as a major step forward for all involved, while the conservative Heritage Foundation says that under NAFTA "trade has increased, U.S. exports and employment levels have risen significantly, and the average living standards of American workers have improved."

Yet the evidence shows the opposite. First, recent research by Kate Bronfenbrenner of Cornell University confirms that globalization shifts bargaining power toward employers and against U.S. workers. Bronfenbrenner found that since the signing of NAFTA more than half of employers faced with union organizing and contract drives have threatened to close their plants in response. And 15% of firms involved in union bargaining have actually closed part or all of their plants — three times the rate during the late 1980s.

Second, NAFTA has caused large U.S. job losses, despite claims by the White House that the United States has gained 90,000 to 160,000 jobs due to trade with Mexico, and by the U.S. Trade Representative that U.S. jobs have risen by 311,000 due to greater trade with Mexico and Canada. The liberal Economic Policy Institute (EPI) points out that the Clinton administration looks only at the effects of exports by the United States, while ignoring increased imports coming from our neighbors. EPI estimates that the U.S. economy has lost 420,000 jobs since 1993 due to worsening trade balances with Mexico and Canada.

Research on individual companies yields similar evidence of large job losses. In 1993 the National Association of Manufacturers released anecdotes from more than 250 companies who claimed that they would create jobs in the United States if NAFTA passed. Public Citizen's Global Trade Watch surveyed 83 of these same companies this year. Trade Watch found that 60 had broken their earlier promises to create jobs or expand U.S. exports, while seven had kept them and 16 were unable or unwilling to provide data.

Among the promise-breakers were Allied Signal, General Electric, Mattel, Proctor and Gamble, Whirlpool, and Xerox, all of whom have laid off workers due to NAFTA (as certified by the Department of Labor's NAFTA Trade Adjustment Assistance program). GE, for example, testified in 1993 that sales to Mexico "could support 10,000 [U.S.] jobs for General Electric and its suppliers," but in 1997 could demonstrate no job gains due to NAFTA. ■

CONTRIBUTORS

Frank Ackerman is an economist with the Global Development and Environmental Institute at Tufts University and a founding editor of *Dollars & Sense*.

Randy Albelda, a *Dollars & Sense* collective member, teaches economics at the University of Massachusetts-Boston.

Liberty Aldrich, a former researcher at the Advocacy Insitute, a Washington, D.C.-based health and consumer advocacy organization, is a legal services attorney in New York City.

Teresa Amott, a *Dollars & Sense* Associate, teaches economics at Bucknell University.

Rebecca Bauen, a *Dollars & Sense* Associate, works for the Insitute for Washington's Future, in Seattle.

Joy Beggs was an intern at *Dollars & Sense* during 1995.

Mike Belzer teaches in the School of Industrial and Labor Relations at Cornell University.

Chris Benner is a research associate at Working Partnerships USA, a labor-community partnership affiliated with the South Bay AFL-CIO in San Jose, CA.

Barbara Brandt is a community activist and author of *Whole Life Economics.*

Chris Bohner is research director at the Neighborhood Economic Development Advocacy Project in New York.

Marc Breslow is an economist and editor at *Dollars & Sense*.

Jim Campen teaches economics at the University of Massachusett-Boston and is a *D&S* Associate.

Nancy Carlsson-Paige teaches education at Lesley College Graduate School.

Roger Colton is an economist with Fisher, Sheehan and Colton, of Belmont, Massachusetts. FSC provides consulting on utility, housing and natural resource issues.

Gregory DeFrietas teaches economics at Hofstra University.

Laurie Dougherty, a *Dollars & Sense* collective member, is a doctoral student in public policy at the University of Massachusetts-Boston.

Robert Drago teaches industrial relations at the University of Wisconsin at Milwaukee.

Alan Durning is a senior researcher with the Worldwatch Institute.

Barbara Ehrenreich is a *Dollars & Sense* Fellow. Her latest book is *The Snarling Citizen: A Collection of Essays.*

Eban Goodstein teaches economics at Lewis and Clark College and is a research associate with the Economic Policy Institute

Barbara Goldoftas is a freelance writer based in Cambridge, MA.

Marjorie Griffin teaches political science and women's studies at Simon Fraser University in Vancouver, B.C.

Edward S. Herman, a *Dollars & Sense* Fellow, is an economist and co-author of *The Global Media: The New Missionaries of Corporate Capitalism.*

Michael Hudson is the editor and co-author of *Merchants of Misery: How Corporate America Profits from Poverty.*

David Kiron co-author of *The Consumer Society.*

Mehrene Larudee teaches economics at the University of Kansas.

David I. Levine teaches industrial relations at the University of California-Berkeley.

David Levy, a *Dollars & Sense* collective member, teaches management at the University of Massachusetts-Boston.

Arthur MacEwan, a *Dollars & Sense* Associate, teaches economics at the University of Massachusetts-Boston.

Elaine McCrate teaches economics at the University of Vermont.

John McDermott is an editor of the journal *Socialism and Democracy* and author of *Corporate Society.*

Alfredo Quarto is the director of the Mangrove Action Project.

Edie Rasell is an economist with the Economic Policy Institute.

Betsy Reed, formerly a *Dollars and Sense* editor, is an editor at *The American Benefactor.*

Alejandro Reuss was an intern at *Dollars & Sense* in 1997.

Abby Scher is a sociologist and editor at *Dollars & Sense.*

John Stamm is a senior research analyst with the Hotel Employees and Restaurant Employees International Union in New York.

Dorceta Taylor teaches environmental sociology at Washington State University.

Chris Tilly, a *Dollars & Sense* collective member, teaches public policy at the University of Massachusetts-Lowell.

Rosemary Vardell is director of the Worthy Wage Campaign.

Marcy Whitebook was the founding executive director, and is a senior policy advisor, of the Worthy Wage Campaign.